Kitchen Classics
from the
Philharmonic

Kitchen Classics from the Philharmonic

A CULINARY AND MUSICAL CELEBRATION
OF THE 150TH ANNIVERSARY
OF THE NEW YORK PHILHARMONIC

JUNE LEBELL

WITH ILLUSTRATIONS BY AL HIRSCHFELD

A JENIFER LANG BOOK
Doubleday

New York   London   Toronto   Sydney   Auckland

PUBLISHED BY DOUBLEDAY
a division of Bantam Doubleday Dell Publishing Group, Inc.
666 Fifth Avenue, New York, New York, 10103

DOUBLEDAY and the portrayal of an anchor
with a dolphin are trademarks of Doubleday,
a division of Bantam Doubleday Dell
Publishing Group, Inc.

Obituary of conductor Anton Seidl, March 28, 1898.
Recipe for Breaded Shrimps in Green Paste from "When It's Time To Eat, Chilies Replace the Baton," May 15, 1991.
Recipe for Poule au Pot from "Recipes with Carotene-Rich Vegetables," September 1, 1982.
Copyright © 1991/82 by The New York Times Company. Reprinted by permission.
Recipe for Chocolate Domingo Cake from *The Cake Bible* by Rose Levy Beranbaum, William Morrow & Co., Inc, copyright © 1988. Reprinted by permission.
Steak au Poivre reprinted by permission of Grosset & Dunlap from *The Treasury of Great Recipes*. Copyright © 1965 by Mary and Vincent Price.
Recipe for Paradise Kraut from the American Cancer Society's New York City Division *Gourmet Guide for Busy People by Famous People*. Reprinted by permission.
Words and Music for "La Bonne Cuisine" copyright © 1949 by Amberson Inc.; copyright renewed. Reprinted with permission of Jalni Publications, Inc., Publisher, and Boosey & Hawkes, Inc., Sole Agent.
Recipe for Stew in a Pumpkin from *Ruth & Skitch Henderson's Seasons in the Country,* by Ruth & Skitch Henderson. Copyright © 1990 by Ruth Henderson and Skitch Henderson. Photographs © 1990 by Lans Christensen. Used by permission of Viking Penguin, a division of Penguin Books USA Inc.
Recipe for Chicken Breasts in Phyllo from *The Complete Book of Greek Cooking* by the Recipe Club of St. Paul's Church, Hempstead, N.Y., HarperCollins, Publishers. Reprinted by permission.
Recipe for Carrot Soup from *The Moosewood Cookbook,* copyright © 1977 by Mollie Katzen. Reprinted by permission of Ten Speed Press, Berkeley, California.
Recipe for Gratin de Framboise courtesy of M. Jacques Loupiac of La Panetiere restaurant in Rye, New York.
Recipe for Adlai's Dish reprinted by permission of Tower School Associates, 61 West Shore Drive, Marblehead, MA 01945.
Recipe for 62nd Street Lemon Cake from *Maida Heatter's Book of Great Desserts* by Maida Heatter, Random House © 1992. Reprinted by permission.
Recipe for Ozawa's Yosenabe from *The WCRB Horn of Plenty Cookbook* (1990), Laura Cralo, editor. Reprinted by permission.

Library of Congress Cataloging-in-Publication Data

Kitchen classics from the Philharmonic : a culinary and musical
    celebration of the 150th anniversary of the New York Philharmonic /
[compiled] by June LeBell; with illustrations by Al Hirschfeld.
        p.   cm.
    1. Cookery.   2. New York Philharmonic.   I. LeBell, June.   II. New
York Philharmonic.
TX714.K567   1992
641.5—dc20   91-48345
                                                                     CIP

ISBN 0-385-42337-3

BOOK DESIGN AND ORNAMENTATION BY SIGNET M DESIGN, INC.

*To my parents, Harriet and Irving LeBell,
who brought me up to love music and food,
and to gobble them with gusto and passion*

Acknowledgments

Every recipe in this book was tested either by me or by Jean Galton, a musician turned professional chef, with help from Claudia Gallo and Carol Prager. I have to admit that I worked with only one or two "real" recipes, along with all the alcoholic concoctions. Both Jean and I tasted the results of our efforts, and the remainder of the food was then turned over to City Harvest, a nonprofit organization that helps to feed the homeless in New York.

Jean was amazing. She came highly recommended by some of the top food professionals in this country and she certainly lived up to her reputation. Astonishingly enough, she worked out of her New York City kitchen, which is to say that it is indeed possible to create masterpieces in a space smaller than a Hirschfeld postage stamp and remain calm, sane, and cheerful. Interestingly enough, even with all the tasting, Jean maintained her already trim figure and I managed to lose about thirty pounds in the process, proving that the better food is, the less one needs of it to be satisfied.

There are others whose help was invaluable in the making of this cookbook, starting with Judy Kern, my editor at Doubleday. Jenifer Lang and her husband, George, of Café des Artistes in New York City, helped us to choose the recipes from the hundreds that were contributed by the New York Philharmonic family. Special thanks also to Naomi Graffman for her editing skills in music and food.

When it comes to copy editing, I was really blessed with Natalie Bowen, a musicologist from Columbia University, avid food person, and spectacular wit, who allowed me to be myself while catching esoteric errors and bringing out the best in us all.

The New York Philharmonic itself was extremely helpful, especially Barbara Hawes and her staff in the Philharmonic's Archives, and several members of the Volunteer Council, particularly Karen LeFrak.

While I was personally in touch with most of the contributors to this book, I did have the help of some publicists who worked diligently to get recipes to me before my deadline from their clients performing in far-flung realms. Among them are Connie Schuman, Audrey Michaels, and Herbert Breslin.

I also want to thank David Arens, the legal department of the New York Philharmonic, and the staffs of the Museum of the City of New York and the New-York Historical Society for their help, instruction, and patient diligence. Thanks, too, to George Jellinek of WQXR for some of the worst (and most wonderful) musical puns in these pages. George has a well-earned reputation as a great scholar, musicologist, and broadcaster. I may have just ruined it!

Perhaps most important, I'm grateful to my close friends who put up with me while I read them countless lines from this book to see if they'd understand the puns and laugh.

Contents

Foreword by
Rose Levy Beranbaum

I was born with music in my ears, in my heart, and in my soul. I am sure this is because my mother, who as a young girl studied with Nadia Reisenberg, played womb concerts (the ultimate chamber music) on the piano when she was pregnant with me. She was convinced that even though I had not yet been born, I would still hear something, if only vibrations, and would grow up familiar with and open to music—one of life's greatest joys. Her theory apparently worked, because as soon as I could walk I approached the piano and picked out tunes by ear.

If I had been offered the choice of any talent in the world (if I couldn't be Mozart), it would have been to have a glorious voice and be an opera singer. But since I did not have even a passable singing voice, my instrument became the violin.

One summer, when I was at music camp near Tanglewood, studying with a violinist in the Boston Symphony Orchestra, my great-uncle, who had engineered this arrangement, came to visit me and posed the dreaded question: "Exactly what kind of talent do you possess—concert or drawing room?" The only possible answer was the disappointing truth: *neither*. As it turned out, despite the fact that I graduated from Carnegie Hall (the High School of Music and Art held its graduation there), I was an extremely mediocre violin player who preferred listening to performing; but then, the music world does need some appreciative listeners. Our family had its share of them. Legend has it that my great-aunt Beck was so moved by a concert at Lewisohn Stadium that she got up in the middle and started to dance, explaining afterward that she couldn't help herself. My mother's theory was that since she had grown up in Russia she had the passionate Russian soul. We also had two bona fide performers: Aunt Beck's husband, appropriately named Fiddler, and Uncle Tibor (Kozma), who conducted at the Met under Rudolf Bing and then went on to become head of the music department at the University of Indiana. It is thanks to him that my first "grown-up" birthday party, when I was twelve, was at a Met production of *Die Fledermaus*. The kids were all very bored (including me—*Fledermaus* has never been one of my favorites), but their parents were quite impressed. And it was never really a surprise to run into one of the great-aunts during intermission at the opera.

This generation had my cousin Andrew Schenck (pronounced Skenk), also a gifted conductor, who died too young, but left a legacy, and perhaps the next generation will have my little nephew Alexander, who, when he first started to sing had that surprised look, bordering on awe, which clearly said: Can these bell-like sounds be coming from me?

Ravi Shankar once said that for him music is the bridge between the personal and the infinite. It is my feeling that all acts of creativity, approached with the same reverence of total devotion, offer that possibility. Somehow, though, music soars above all others. My soul has been transported by a bite of still-warm-from-the-oven Chocolate Domingo Cake, but no food has given me the total corporeal and spiritual orgasm music is capable of inspiring.

My mother, whose profession was dentistry, held dear a theory that senses located in the region of the head are the most exquisite and also the ones most intimately interconnected. As a "food person," I see more and more how true this is. Taste, smell, vision, and hearing have a profound effect on each other's perception. As a very young child, I would not let my mother play the song "Ramona," because it reminded me of chocolate pudding (which I detested). I suppose I must have experienced it as equally thick and sodden with sentimentality.

The connection between food and music is found even in the words used to describe them. In the food industry, the most common word used to analyze flavor is "note." "Texture" is another word food and music have in common. One of my favorite musical memories is of the time I met Isaac Stern at a party celebrating the birth of Jenifer Lang's book *Tastings*.

I had provided the Chocolate Oblivion Truffle Torte that was featured in the book. When George Lang introduced me to Isaac Stern, he rose up, took my hand, and bowed deeply from the waist, saying, "Your cake was like velvet." My response: "That is the very word I used to describe your playing the first time I heard you play the Tchaikovsky Violin Concerto when I was sixteen!"

When June LeBell and I were classmates at Music and Art—what seems like only a few years ago—it seemed inevitable that her future would be in music. My fate was far less certain. When we met again, it was when I came to WQXR to advertise my cooking school on the radio. I brought with me my then-favorite cake, Gâteau Grand Marnier et Chocolat. I must admit, I felt that I was entering into a musical temple with something perhaps not quite worthy, though quite delicious. But June did not seem at all surprised or condescending regarding my transition from violin to cake. In fact, to my relief, it seemed that as far as she was concerned, I was still in "the arts." Several years later, when she started "Kitchen Classics," featuring recipes accompanied by "appropriate" music, I became a frequent guest on the show, which gave us a chance to renew our friendship—often on the air. In fact, we had so much fun catching up and reminiscing, we often forgot where we were! The best part was that we share a similar sense of humor, which is most likely to happen between people whose frame of reference is so similar. We often felt we would make a great vaudeville team. I would read my favorite buttermilk cake recipe, to which June would play a recording of what she referred to (with a gleam in her eye) as "Madama Buttermilk"! We laughed almost the whole show through and got lots of delightful feedback from the audience. When June told me about her plans for this book, it seemed like the perfect joyful extension of her show.

It's great fun for me to find childhood friends, now well-known musicians, in these pages: the guy who teased me at music camp (Paul Dunkel); the high school friend who accompanied me home after ice-skating in Central Park, walking his bike alongside (Stephen Kates); the tall, dark, and brilliant harpsichordist who dated my cousin and whose father was my English teacher (Kenneth Cooper).

The humor, intelligence, generosity, and charm June possesses make this book unique. She serves up each personality in the most personal of all possible ways: in his or her own voice. The delightful anecdotes peppered throughout the book have as their counterpoint favorite recipes contributed by each performer. We know their music, but now we learn another side of them, and they become friends.

And as the proverbial icing on the cake, this book is graced with the incomparable caricatures of our beloved Al Hirschfeld.

It is a great honor to participate in the 150th celebration of the Philharmonic by being a part of this special book. For me, it is a deeply sentimental and personal book and I think it will prove to be so for everyone who reads it and, most of all, for anyone who cooks from it.

Introduction

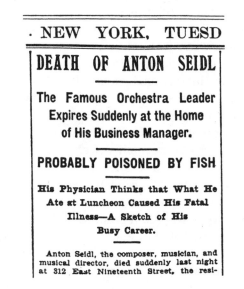

· NEW YORK, TUESD

DEATH OF ANTON SEIDL

**The Famous Orchestra Leader
Expires Suddenly at the Home
of His Business Manager.**

PROBABLY POISONED BY FISH

**His Physician Thinks that What He
Ate at Luncheon Caused His Fatal
Illness—A Sketch of His
Busy Career.**

Anton Seidl, the composer, musician, and
musical director, died suddenly last night
at 312 East Nineteenth Street, the resi-

It was a *New York Times* front page obituary. The date was Tuesday, March 29, 1898. Showers were forecast for the New York metropolitan area. Negotiations were continuing with Spain on the Cuban situation; a woman was found with a bullet in her brain in the New Amsterdam Hotel on Fourth Avenue and Twenty-first Street in Manhattan; the renowned English actress Fanny Davenport was recovering from severe illness in Chicago; and a Brooklyn grand jury was investigating the Brooklyn City Works Department.

But the big news was the death, by food poisoning, of composer and music director Anton Seidl. "Opiates were administered," the article says, "but they gave no relief, and at 10:15 o'clock . . . Mr. Seidl died in his wife's arms.

"The doctors in attendance believe that Mr. Seidl died of ptomain poison, and attribute his death to the fish he ate for luncheon. . . . He had shad roe, green peas, and mashed potatoes and a cup of custard." If Rossini had been in residence, he'd have dedicated his piece "O the Green Peas" to the maestro's demise.

Mr. Seidl was, at the time, music director of the Philharmonic Society of New York. Early programs from Carnegie Hall advertise some of his concerts: In the fifty-first season of the orchestra, on March 24, 1893 at two P.M., the maestro conducted the soprano Martha Burckard in the "Abscheulicher!" from Beethoven's *Fidelio* and Henri Marteau in the G minor Violin Concerto of Max Bruch, with the rest of the program devoted to Schumann's Second Symphony and the "Love-Death" from Wagner's *Tristan und Isolde*.

Programs nearly a hundred years later aren't so different. But food has changed greatly. In 1848, just six years after the Philharmonic had played its first notes, the Astor House in Manhattan offered a "Gentlemen's Ordinary" Thanksgiving menu: tongue, leg of mutton, a variety of turkey and oysters—all boiled—were offered to start.

The main-course selections included a galantine of turkey with jelly, cold pressed corned beef, chicken pies, and lobster salads, with side dishes of mutton cutlets, calf's head, pigeons broiled with pork, tame ducks with olives, and small oyster pies.

The desserts weren't quite so unconventional: apple, pumpkin, or mince pie, plum pudding, "maccaroons," and charlotte russe look familiar. And there's even some ice cream.

The prices aren't divulged on this menu. But the accompanying wine list gives us an idea of what we'd have paid. Bottles of claret and Sauternes are the least expensive at 50 cents each. A Pouilly, white Burgundy, goes for $1.50 a bottle. Heidsieck champagne is $2.00, as is the Cliquot. And "Prince Metternich's Celebrated Castle bottled, Gold Seal, 'Johannisbirger,' vintage 1822" comes in as the most expensive on the list at $8.00. One Madeira ("Gov. Kirby's Original Bottles 00") is a whopping $12.00, but you'd be hard pressed to go any higher.

Even by the late 1890s dinners were still holding their prices down. The Carnegie Hall Restaurant, located on Fifty-sixth Street and Seventh Avenue, for example, served a complete meal for 50 cents in 1898 and, by 1902, prices had jumped only 10 cents. Fresh game, fowl, and local seafood dominated the menus, whether meals were taken at home or in a restaurant.

Couples attending the Philharmonic would find it difficult to stroll into a local restaurant that catered to both men and women at a pretheater sitting. And planned parties, receptions, and celebrations generally did not admit women. If they did, they were placed a genteel distance from their escorts, on a balcony, behind a screen, or in an adjoining room, where they might not interfere with the whiskey and cigars of the "important" guests.

Times began to change, along with food, wine, and prices, after World War I. As women joined the work force during the war, they began taking their meals outside the home. When the men returned, the custom continued. But as more restaurants opened, prices rose and quality sank, with local game and fish becoming less available.

Don't think that the mid-1800s were days of romance and roses. At the time the Philharmonic Society was establishing its turf on East Fourteenth Street, New York City was a noisy, chaotic, filthy, and dangerous place to be. Horses with iron shoes clattered on cobblestones. Streetcars with iron wheels careened at a canter through streets unmarked by traffic lights, making the pedestrian's crossing from corner to corner more dangerous than a stroll across the FDR Drive would be today.

Gangs stalked the infamous Five Points. Wealthy families moved from lower Manhattan to Greenwich Village for the summer in order to escape the disease and vermin that spread through the fetid air in the narrow canyons of the city. Lack of ice made food a breeding ground for death. And, with more than one million people living in the area from the tip of Manhattan to Twenty-third Street in the 1870s, the overcrowding was worse than anything we can imagine today.

But the nineteenth century was also a time of great wealth. The Astors, Belmonts, Vanderbilts, Morgans, and Harrimans lined the upper portion of the city with magnificent mansions. And they competed with each other to present the finest parties and musicales in the East. It was in the midst of this cacophony and competition that the Philharmonic Society opened its doors in 1842.

Prices for tickets by the 1890s demonstrated the vast dichotomy of classes with balcony seats selling for 25 cents and multiseated boxes going for $9.00. In between, there was general admission for 50 cents, the dress circle at 50 to 75 cents, and the parquet at a dollar each.

Funding was always a factor for the Philharmonic, with underwriting coming primarily from the private sector. So what else is new? Advertising caught on at the turn of the century but in those early years very few restaurants took to the pages of the Philharmonic programs to attract their clientele. Mostly there were ads for pianos, liquor, undergarments, and wonder elixers. In 1904, for example, one Carnegie Hall program promoted "Lindsay hose supporters," "Steck pianos—the piano on which Parsifal was composed," "Drink Zoolak— invaluable for the stomach," and something new: "Victor Talking Machine, 77 Chambers Street."

Of course, by the time Carnegie Hall opened its doors in 1891, the private sector had made its statement: "Support the Arts." Andrew Carnegie, in a sermon he wrote when he retired, said, "The kept dollar is a stinking fish."

So, with those wise words from Mr. Carnegie, we come to this cookbook in celebration of the 150th year of the New York Philharmonic. In its pages you will see that music and food are complementary arts. You'll find that musicians love food, both eating it and preparing it, and you'll find some tantalizing recipes to keep you from following in Anton Seidl's fatal footsteps.

"Kitchen Classics from the Philharmonic" is arranged according to performer, rather than recipe. Chapters are titled "Singers," "Other Voices," "Composers," "Conductors," "New York Philharmonic Family," "Dancers," "Instrumentalists," and "Keyboard Artists" rather than fish, meat, bread, and dessert. If you want to find a recipe for chicken, just turn to the index. Everything is listed there to simplify your plans for lunch or dinner.

The seeds for the book came from two directions. WQXR and the New York Philharmonic. Starting in 1989, I hosted a program on WQXR-AM for about a year and a half called "Kitchen Classics." The show was broadcast for a half hour every day and featured well-known musicians who loved food and well-known chefs who loved music. We talked, gave recipes, and matched the recipes to music. One musician who told us how to make bagels, for example, got a Beethoven "Bay-ga-telle" in return. The owner of Benihana's talked about chopping, so we played music by "Choppin" with pianist Emanuel "Ax."

Meanwhile, I had already been cooking for patrons of the New York Philharmonic for fourteen years. Each year at the WQXR/New York Philharmonic Radiothon, anywhere from two to eight music lovers paid the Philharmonic about $600 and, in return, came to my home for dinner. In the course of those years, my dinners raised more than $20,000.

The 150th anniversary of the New York Philharmonic has brought these related events together. As a result of this celebration of music and food, the Philharmonic will receive 50 percent of all net proceeds from the sale of this book.

Singers

Adele Addison

Entering Adele Addison's home is like walking into a flower shop, parfumerie, and café all at the same time, for the soprano's penthouse on Riverside Drive in Manhattan radiates fragrances from peonies to pot roast. They are aromas that evoke memories of safety and excitement, childhood and sexuality, in one sweet breath.

Floral tributes and excitement were the order of the day when Adele made her first appearance with the New York Philharmonic on December 27, 1956. The handsome thirty-eight-year-old Leonard Bernstein was on the podium and the score set before the musicians was the 214-year-old *Messiah*. One of the classic recordings of this work, still available, came from this remarkable debut, which also featured countertenor Russell Oberlin, tenor David Lloyd, and bass William Warfield with the Westminster Choir.

A favorite soprano of Bernstein's, Adele Addison performed at least fourteen times with the Philharmonic in the fifties and sixties. Her attention soon became focused on teaching, though, and today she chairs the voice department at the Manhattan School of Music in New York. But it was her private teaching, in her spacious West Side apartment overlooking the Hudson, that made her students (I being one of them) realize that her talents went beyond the stage and studio to the stove. Her cooking skills are legendary.

While a pork or lamb roast was in the oven, fragrant in a unique concoction of coffee and spices, or a chicken sat stewing in an aromatic sauce over a low flame, some student in the living room slid through the stratospheric scales of Handel's "Sweet Bird" and tried hard not to drool. In earlier days, two cats, Pangur and Bili (named for the white feline in Barber's *Hermit Songs* and Debussy's sexy *Chansons de Bilitis*), whined Siamese descants from beneath the piano. And Adele's students rarely got out the front door without a doggy bag and a recipe or, best of all, an invitation to dinner.

A musical must for anything created by Adele Addison is her recording of selections from Handel's *Messiah* with the New York Philharmonic and Leonard Bernstein (CBS MYK-38481). And, to whet your appetite for the sweet, tender roasted chicken that might follow her luxurious Mushroom Pâté, listen to "Sweet Bird" from Handel's *L'Allegro ed il Penseroso*, recorded by the Musica Aeterna Orchestra and Chorus with Addison, John McCollum, and John Reardon conducted by Frederic Waldman (Decca DXSA-7165).

Mushroom Pâté

SERVES 12

1 stick unsalted butter, ¹/₂ cup
1 large onion, chopped (about 1 cup)
5 scallions (white and green parts), thinly sliced (about ³/₄ cup)
3 ribs celery, cut into ¹/₂-inch dice (about 1 cup)
3 cloves garlic, minced (about 4 teaspoons)
2 pounds mushrooms, thinly sliced (about 11 cups)
2 cups chopped walnuts
1 tablespoon dried basil, crumbled

1 tablespoon dried thyme, crumbled
1 tablespoon dried oregano, crumbled
1¹/₂ teaspoons dried rosemary, crumbled
1¹/₂ teaspoons salt
¹/₂ teaspoon pepper
12 ounces cream cheese, softened, and cut into pieces
³/₄ cup fresh bread crumbs (made from about 3 slices of white bread)
3 large eggs, lightly beaten

1 Grease a 9 × 5 × 2¹/₂″ (7 cup) glass loaf pan. Preheat oven to 350°.

2 Melt butter in a large skillet over medium high heat. Add onion, scallions, celery, and garlic. Cook until softened, stirring, about 6 to 7 minutes. Increase heat to high and add mushrooms in two batches, stirring after each addition. Add walnuts, basil, thyme, oregano, rosemary, salt, and pepper, and cook mixture about 10 minutes or until liquid from mushrooms has evaporated. Stir in cream cheese and mix well. Remove from heat.

3 Let cool briefly and purée in food processor until smooth, working in 2 batches. Stir in bread crumbs and eggs and pour mixture into prepared loaf pan. Wrap pan with wax paper and foil and bake for 1 hour 30 minutes or until a knife inserted in unwrapped center comes out clean. Cool on a wire rack and chill overnight. Remove wax paper and foil and run knife around edges. Invert onto serving dish and garnish as desired.

John Aler

Hector Berlioz and John Aler have a deal. The composer rests in peace while the tenor sings his works, and they both add up their ovations. It was Berlioz who brought John Aler to the Philharmonic on December 18, 1980. The conductor was Daniel Barenboim. And the entire program was devoted to Berlioz's *Roméo et Juliette*. Five years later, John Aler won a Grammy for Best Classical Vocal Soloist for his recording of the Berlioz *Requiem* with Robert Shaw and the Atlanta Symphony. This is not to say that the tenor is a Berlioz specialist. On the contrary, his repertoire runs the gamut of opera, oratorio, and art song.

John Aler's culinary creations also lend themselves to a variety of roles. This Celery Seed Dressing is perfect for cole slaw, but it's also a quick, easy way to bake or broil fish, chicken, or light meats such as veal. Simply brush or spoon on some dressing and either broil or bake.

To set the musical stage for a meal with John Aler and his multifaceted recipe, especially if you've chosen to use the dressing on fish, we suggest the tenor's recording of Bizet's *Les Pêcheurs de perles* (The Pearl Fishers) with the Capitole de Toulouse Orchestra (Angel 2-45003-2-ZA).

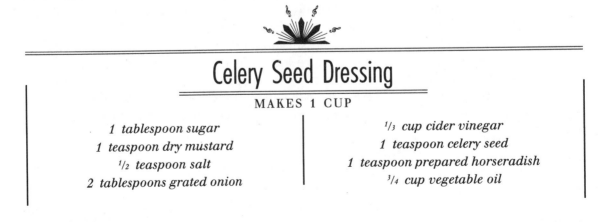

Celery Seed Dressing

MAKES 1 CUP

1 tablespoon sugar
1 teaspoon dry mustard
$^{1}/_{2}$ teaspoon salt
2 tablespoons grated onion

$^{1}/_{3}$ cup cider vinegar
1 teaspoon celery seed
1 teaspoon prepared horseradish
$^{3}/_{4}$ cup vegetable oil

1   In a small bowl mix everything except the oil. With wire whisk, slowly whisk in the oil.

Betty Allen

Betty Allen tells us that her "Cilea" con Carne is a party dish. No kidding! Anything cooked up by this energetic, ebullient emissary of music is a party. From her debut with the New York Philharmonic in 1962 to her work with the community at her Harlem School of the Arts, masses of people have surrounded Miss Allen with attention and affection, because she exudes attention and affection to them.

As if foretelling the future, Betty Allen's first major appearance with the Philharmonic involved a crowd. Far be it for this mezzo-soprano to keep the entire stage to herself. She shared the event with Adele Addison, Charles Bressler, Donald Bell, David Lloyd, William Wildermann, the Collegiate Chorale, and the Boys' Choir of the Little Church Around the Corner. The three-hour performance was devoted to Bach's *St. Matthew Passion*, with Leonard Bernstein conducting.

Actually, there were a few performances with the Philharmonic that were even earlier but, as Betty Allen explains, "they were smaller and probably insignificant by comparison."

Is a Bach motet with Glenn Gould insignificant? "It was a funny time," Betty Allen remembers. "They were redoing Carnegie Hall in the fifties. You know how they used to have just one little dressing room? Well, they were trying to fix the place up and we had all the windows wide open." For good reason, too. There wasn't any air conditioning and it was 87 degrees outside. But she adds, "Glenn Gould was cold. He was stomping around in ear muffs and mittens."

Many more performances would follow for Betty Allen, but over the years her earthy intelligence took her from the concert stage to the classroom. She had to share her passion for the arts with others. And her passion for sharing has led her to a life that is enormously exciting and rewarding. Even her recipes, written in a broad, sweeping, clear penmanship that radiates spirit, are larger than life.

Always one to share the spotlight, Betty Allen suggests that we listen to Gershwin's *Porgy and Bess* in a recording (Angel-CDS 7495682) that features two of her star students, Camellia Johnson as the Strawberry Woman, and Colenton Freeman as the Crabman. After all, we *are* talking about food!

GEORGE GERSHWIN

At the party, seat your guests for Betty Allen's "Cilea" con Carne and play the complete recording of Cilea's *Adriana Lecouvreur* (it's only got four acts) performed by Renata Scotto, Elena Obraztsova, Placido Domingo, and Sherrill Milnes with the Philharmonia Orchestra conducted by James Levine (CBS 2-M2K-34588).

"Cilea" con Carne

SERVES 8

2 tablespoons corn oil

3 large onions, chopped (about 3 cups)

1 small green pepper, chopped
(about 3/4 cup)

3 cloves garlic, chopped

1 large pork chop (about 8 ounces),
boned, cut into 1/2-inch cubes

2 pounds ground round

1 (13 3/4 ounce) can chicken broth

1 (28 ounce) can plum tomatoes,
chopped

3 tablespoons chili powder
(or less if using hot chili powder)

1 teaspoon salt

1 teaspoon sugar

1 teaspoon paprika

Dash of Yerba Buena seasoning
(optional)

2 tablespoons Worcestershire sauce

3 cans (15 3/4 ounces each) red kidney
beans, drained and rinsed

2 tablespoons chopped cilantro

2 tablespoons chopped parsley

2 scallions, chopped
(about 2 tablespoons)

1/2 ounce unsweetened baking
chocolate, chopped

1 Heat oil in a large saucepot over medium high heat. Add onions and pepper and cook stirring until soft, about 4 to 5 minutes. Add garlic and cook 1 minute longer. Remove with slotted spoon and set aside. In same saucepot, add pork cubes and bone. Cook, stirring occasionally until browned, about 3 to 4 minutes. Remove pork and add ground round to pot. Cook, stirring, until beef is browned, about 3 to 4 minutes. Return onion mixture and pork cubes and bone to pot. Add chicken broth, tomatoes, chili powder, salt, sugar, paprika, Yerba Buena, and Worcestershire sauce. Cover, reduce heat to a simmer, and cook 1 hour.

2 After 1 hour, uncover and continue to simmer 30 minutes longer.

3 Add remaining ingredients and stir until heated through, about 2 to 3 minutes longer.

Serve in soup bowls over rice, with tortillas or corn bread, green salad, guacamole, and iced tea with lemon.

Martina Arroyo

"Food is necessary for our lives. But the main ingredient is people." This is life according to Martina Arroyo. The soprano, who made her debut with the New York Philharmonic on April 4, 1963, remembers that evening clearly. She remembers it because of the people who shared it with her. She can still see the look on Thomas Schippers's face just before he began to conduct. And she still hears the silence of the audience just before the music started.

"I recall rehearsing with Tom. His wife came in and said, 'Oh, so that's how it goes. I've only heard Tom sing it.' " Martina was singing Samuel Barber's *Andromache's Farewell*, and it was more than her Philharmonic debut. There was a recording that came from that performance. And a very special gown.

"Valentina designed it for me. She worked for Greta Garbo, you know. And she used to tell me, 'Darling, take the floor with you when you walk.' "

Martina took more than the floor. She took the stage and the orchestra and the audience and swept them into the passion of the music. Then she was swept to a party. "I don't remember the food," she says with a twinkle, "but my body does. It *always* remembers the food."

There were more performances with the New York Philharmonic, of course. At least ten appearances over the years. And, while the soprano is still actively singing with major orchestras and opera companies around the world, she's also teaching "very talented graduate students" at Louisiana State University.

"You don't really get to know people until you feed them," she adds. "And students are worse than professional musicians. They're bottomless pits. At first I was cooking them things like veal cutlets. That just went over their heads. Then I tried those huge hero sandwiches. But that's not real food. That's why my Jambalaya has been such a hit. It's healthy, tasty, and *huge*."

There are about twenty students who come for dinner at Martina Arroyo's Louisiana home. "They bring their friends and they just eat the evening away." Martina sums it up with her usual earthiness: "Being together is what's important."

Martina Arroyo's LSU Jambalaya is not overly spicy but it has a tang. So Samuel Barber's *School for Scandal* Overture is the perfect accompaniment, especially since it's played by the

New York Philharmonic under the direction of Thomas Schippers (Odyssey YT-33230). After the party's over, listen to Martina's recording of Barber's *Andromache's Farewell* with the Philharmonic and Maestro Schippers (Columbia ML-5912).

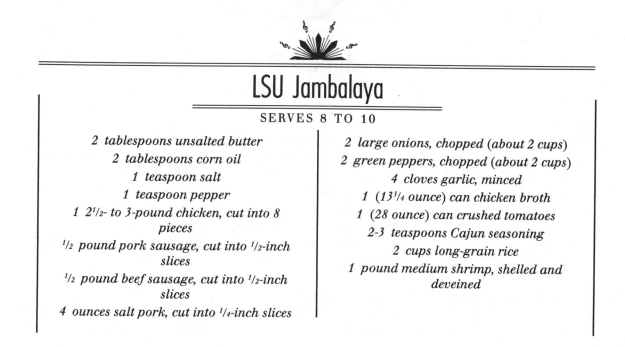

LSU Jambalaya

SERVES 8 TO 10

2 tablespoons unsalted butter

2 tablespoons corn oil

1 teaspoon salt

1 teaspoon pepper

1 2½- to 3-pound chicken, cut into 8 pieces

½ pound pork sausage, cut into ½-inch slices

½ pound beef sausage, cut into ½-inch slices

4 ounces salt pork, cut into ¼-inch slices

2 large onions, chopped (about 2 cups)

2 green peppers, chopped (about 2 cups)

4 cloves garlic, minced

1 (13¾ ounce) can chicken broth

1 (28 ounce) can crushed tomatoes

2-3 teaspoons Cajun seasoning

2 cups long-grain rice

1 pound medium shrimp, shelled and deveined

1   Heat butter and oil in a large saucepot over medium high heat. Season chicken with ½ teaspoon salt and ½ teaspoon pepper and add to pot. Brown well, about 4 to 5 minutes on each side. Remove and drain fat from saucepot.

2   In same saucepot over medium high heat, add sausages and salt pork. Cook, stirring until meat is browned and fat is rendered from salt pork. Remove sausages and salt pork and all but 3 tablespoons fat from pan. Add onions, green peppers, and garlic and cook, stirring until soft, about 4 to 5 minutes. Add chicken broth, tomatoes, remaining salt and pepper, and Cajun seasoning. Stir well and return chicken and sausage mixture to pot. Bring to a boil, add rice, stir, and cover. Reduce heat to a simmer and cook about 15 minutes, or until rice is nearly done. Stir in shrimp and cook 5 minutes longer.

Rose Bampton

"The first time I sang with the Philharmonic, Maestro conducted," Rose Bampton remembers. Which maestro? "Toscanini. There *is* no other maestro as far as I'm concerned," the Metropolitan Opera soprano says with emphasis. "I'm pretty sure we sang a Beethoven Ninth, but for some reason we rehearsed the Verdi *Requiem*. I have no idea why it got changed."

There are other little mysteries in Rose Bampton's musical memories. "I was always so excited after a performance that I could have had a feast placed in front of me and I wouldn't have remembered what it was. But I'll tell you this. I had a strange habit when I was singing. If I had a concert in the evening, I always ate a soft-boiled egg, some toast, grapefruit, and, of course, tea with lemon. But if I were singing in an opera, I had lamb chops and a baked potato. Concerts were shorter and I wasn't singing so long. But an opera could go on for hours and I needed more sustenance to get me through. It wasn't superstition. I just found eating that way worked for my body."

A much sought-after teacher, working with students from Juilliard and the Manhattan School for many years, Miss Bampton passes on much of this information to her "girls." "They have to find out what's best for them. But I do suggest that they stay away from ice cream and milk products before they sing. That kind of thing creates too much phlegm. Most of them drink hot tea with lemon, but I have one girl who insists on Coca-Cola before a performance."

If ice cream and dairy products aren't good for singers, we have to assume that Rose Bampton's Cheese Soufflé should be consumed after a performance, not before. "Oh, yes. That would be terrible for a singer before going on stage. But it's such a wonderful dish. I'll tell you how I found it.

"My Pelly (husband Wilfred Pelletier) and I were in Tel Aviv for a gathering of choral societies from all over the world. On a Sunday before we left, we watched from our hotel window as dozens of children and adults flew these magnificent kites in the park. Well, we were going on to Paris the next day and we decided to buy some of those kites and take them with us as gifts.

"The family we were visiting had children and they just went wild when they saw what we'd brought. We all had to rush right outside to try them out. But my friend, the hostess, had prepared this soufflé and I was afraid it would be ruined if we took the time. 'Oh, no,' she insisted. 'It'll be fine.' And it was. That's one of the reasons I like it so much. You can prepare it ahead of time and it doesn't drop or anything. It's just wonderful!"

You needn't wait for the end of Beethoven's *Fidelio*, with Rose Bampton, (2-Vic. LM-6025) to try this soufflé. But, if you do, it will keep. And, for the joy of the kites, we suggest Debussy's *Jeux* with the New York Philharmonic and Pierre Boulez (CBS MYK-37261).

Cheese Soufflé Supreme

SERVES 6

6 slices white bread	¹/₂ teaspoon pepper
2 tablespoons unsalted butter, softened	¹/₂ teaspoon dry mustard
5 large eggs, separated and at room temperature	¹/₂ pound cheddar or American cheese, grated, about 2 cups
1¹/₂ cups milk	¹/₂ pound bacon, cooked until crisp and crumbled
¹/₄ teaspoon salt	

1 Preheat oven to 325°. Grease a 2-quart casserole dish.

2 Spread the bread slices with the softened butter and cut into 1-inch cubes (you should have about 2 cups). Place the egg yolks in a large bowl and add bread, milk, salt, pepper, mustard, cheese, and bacon.

3 In a separate bowl, beat egg whites until stiff with an electric mixer or by hand. Lighten the bread mixture with a quarter of the egg whites and then fold in the remainder (the mixture can stand several hours in the refrigerator at this point—the flavor actually improves with standing).

4 Place in prepared dish and place dish in baking pan filled with hot water (bain-marie.) Bake 1 hour or until set. A cake tester inserted in the center will come out almost clean and the top of the soufflé will not wobble in the middle.

Judith Blegen

More than her New York Philharmonic debut, soprano Judith Blegen remembers her first encounter with the orchestra as a listener. "My father had brought me from our home in Missoula, Montana, to audition for some conservatories in the East. I was still in high school at the time. My first audition was for the Curtis Institute in Philadelphia. I auditioned and I got right in. And that's where I went.

"My father and I went up to New York to celebrate," she remembers, "and he took me to two performances, *The Music Man* and the New York Philharmonic. Erica Morini was playing the Mendelssohn Violin Concerto with the Philharmonic. When she walked out on the stage and started to play, I started to cry because it was so beautiful.

"John Corigliano was the concertmaster in those days. I remember we were sitting in the first row and he kept looking down at me all the time Morini was playing and I was crying. He must have wondered whether there was something wrong with me."

Judith's mother was a violinist and Judith was admitted to Curtis for both violin and voice. And now she's married to Raymond Gniewek, the concertmaster of the Metropolitan Opera Orchestra. But it's not just the violin section that's pulled at the soprano's heartstrings.

"When Leonard Bernstein came into my life I was so impressed, so thrilled, I almost couldn't take it. I'm just not that kind of person," she adds, explaining that she's quieter, more introspective than what the world thinks performers should be.

Of course, Bernstein and Blegen had many more live and recorded encounters over the years, and her opinion never changed. "I just thought he was thrilling. You know, of all the people I met while I was singing, he was the most unforgettable. He devastated me."

Be overwhelmed by the performance of Haydn's *Lord Nelson Mass*, with Leonard Bernstein, Judith Blegen, Gwendolyn Killebrew, Kenneth Riegel, Simon Estes, the Westminster Choir, organist Leonard Raver, and the New York Philharmonic (Columbia M-35100).

Chicken with Orange Soy Glaze

SERVES 4

1 2¹/₂- to 3-pound chicken, cut into quarters	1 clove garlic, minced
1 cup orange juice	¹/₄ cup honey
	¹/₄ cup soy sauce

1 Set oven rack 5 to 6 inches from source of heat and preheat broiler and broiling pan. When heated, place chicken pieces on pan and broil 7 to 8 minutes on each side or until cooked through.

2 Meanwhile, place remaining ingredients in a small saucepot and bring to a boil over high heat. Simmer sauce 7 to 8 minutes.

3 When chicken is cooked, place on serving dish and pour sauce over.

Elaine Bonazzi

Elaine Bonazzi, a singer who can act, too, has won ovations as the shrewish, lonely Marie in *The Most Happy Fella*, the hair-raising Mrs. Lovett in *Sweeney Todd*, and the all-knowing Madame Armfeldt in *A Little Night Music*. On the concert stage, she's seen as the vibrant redhead with a voice and musicianship to match. And, when she thinks of her appearances with the New York Philharmonic, one very special event comes quickly to mind.

"I was one of the soloists with Leonard Bernstein and the New York Philharmonic in 1976 when they did a first hearing of some of the movements from his wonderful *Songfest*," she proudly remembers. The mezzo had been assigned a strikingly rhythmic song about sleeping sickness. "In preparation, I went to the library to research this disease and, to my surprise, discovered that this particular illness only afflicts men.

"I mentioned this to the maestro at our first coaching session and found that he was as surprised at this discovery as I. 'Well, Bonazz,' he said affectionately, 'it really should be a man singing this, then, since he's talking about himself in the song. But let's do it anyway.'

"I had a sinking feeling that I'd probably never get to do the piece again and cursed my visit to the library. But, at the performance in Avery Fisher Hall, there were some hearty 'Bravas' when we finished the song. Maestro Bernstein looked down at me and gave me a broad grin and an impish wink. That somehow made up for the knowledge that I'd never sing that piece again."

Indeed, since then, the song has been assigned to a temporarily tired tenor and not a vivacious, redheaded mezzo. The resulting recording features the composer conducting the National Symphony (DG 415965-2), but even though it does not include Elaine Bonazzi, we suggest you listen while preparing the mezzo's energetic Chicken Onorina.

Chicken Onorina

SERVES 4

¹/₄ cup unbleached flour	1 tablespoon olive oil
¹/₂ teaspoon salt	4-6 garlic cloves, finely minced
¹/₂ teaspoon pepper	2 large sprigs fresh rosemary or
2 boneless chicken breasts, cut into	1 teaspoon dried
1-inch wide strips (about 10 to 12)	¹/₄ cup red wine vinegar
1 tablespoon unsalted butter	³/₄ cup chicken broth

1   Mix flour with salt and pepper and coat chicken lightly, shaking off excess. Meanwhile, heat butter and olive oil in a large skillet over medium high heat. Add chicken and cook, stirring, until lightly golden, about 3 to 4 minutes. Add garlic and rosemary and continue cooking until chicken is golden brown, about 2 minutes longer. Add vinegar and simmer 1 minute. (At this point you can let the chicken rest for 20 minutes or so before finishing.) Add chicken broth and cook covered 20 minutes longer, or until chicken is very tender.

Serve with rice pilaf.

VARIATIONS: Substitute ¹/₂ teaspoon lemon zest and ¹/₄ cup lemon juice for vinegar, and tarragon for rosemary. Or substitute dry vermouth for vinegar and use rosemary, tarragon, or sage.

Charles Bressler

harles Bressler's singing debut with the New York Philharmonic on December 17, 1959, was an auspicious occasion for the tenor for more reasons than one might think. "I was singing with Jennie Tourel that night," he recalls, "and she was an idol of mine." Also on the stage in Carnegie Hall were soprano Lee Venora, countertenor Russell Oberlin, bass Norman Farrow, the Schola Cantorum, and Leonard Bernstein. The singing contingent was performing the Bach *Magnificat*, just in time for the Christmas holiday. And, as a special holiday gift to the audience, three illustrious Philharmonic personalities were playing Bach's Concerto for Three Pianos. It would be a rare night in any month to hear Leonard Bernstein, Carlos Mosely, and David Keiser at the keyboards.

So Charles Bressler's birth with the Philharmonic that night was a truly blessed event. "I was invited to a party later at Lenny's home in the Osborne," the tenor continues. "Lenny's parents were there and so was Jennie. She told me this wonderful story about meeting Bernstein for the first time. She said that Koussevitsky had called her years before to say he was sending some music over for her to look at. About a half hour later, she opened the door to find that the messenger with the music was 'the most beautiful young man. He was seventeen years old and, oh, so beautiful!' " Beautiful Lenny, the messenger.

The year after his debut, Charles Bressler was in Italy and discovered a new idol. "It was in 1960," Charles tells us, "that I found something called Spaghetti alla Carbonara. It was pretty much unknown here in those days. I was in Rome at the time and Robert White, the tenor, called me to tell me about this fabulous restaurant called Pierluigi's Trattoria. Right near the prison.

"We all got addicted to the dish. It was so good, we kept going back to that wonderful, unassuming trattoria. We sat out on the sidewalk, ate, talked, and had a great time. Best of all, the food was terrific and very inexpensive."

And there was a perhaps apocryphal note that went with the Carbonara. Charles Bressler fills in the details. "Pierluigi said he'd found the dish because there had been a strike of coal miners in Italy. He said they were locked in and had to make do with what they had—so they created this combination.

PASTA NEVER BASTA

"A few years later we found Carbonara in a restaurant on University Place. And now it's a universal dish." So, from a strikingly dubious start in the Italian coal mines, a star was born. But times have changed. "Recently I was at a Lincoln Center restaurant where we paid twenty dollars for pasta. Imagine!"

The classic performance of Bach's *Magnificat* that began Charles Bressler's career with the Philharmonic came out on a recording from Columbia in 1959 (ML-5775). And, for a look at American vocal music while whipping up the American tenor's Carbonara, listen to his *Flowering of Vocal Music in America*, volumes 1 and 2 (New World 2 230/1).

Spaghetti alla Carbonara

SERVES 4

½ pound lean bacon, cut into ¼-inch pieces (freeze for ½ hour to make slicing easier)
1 large onion, chopped (about 1 cup)
3 tablespoons dry vermouth
1 pound spaghetti

3 large eggs, lightly beaten
⅓ cup freshly grated Parmesan cheese
½ teaspoon salt
½ teaspoon pepper
2 tablespoons chopped parsley (optional)

1 Cook bacon in a large skillet over medium high heat, stirring until cooked but not crisp, about 3 to 4 minutes. Add onion and stir until translucent, about 3 to 4 minutes more. Add vermouth and stir about 2 minutes longer. Keep warm.

2 Meanwhile, bring a large saucepot of salted water to a boil and cook spaghetti al dente, according to package directions. Drain.

3 In large mixing bowl, place eggs, cheese, salt, and pepper. Add drained spaghetti and bacon mixture. Stir well. Sprinkle with chopped parsley if desired.

"This is the original recipe from Rome 1960. All other ingredients are incorrect and are not even gilding the lily," says Charles Bressler.

Patricia Brooks

"I was studying with Martha Graham and I almost got into the company, but I injured my knees." Good thing, too, or we'd have missed one of the most beautiful sopranos of the past several decades!

Patricia Brooks seemed destined for the stage, whether it was as a dancer, pianist, actress, or singer. But the singing really came last. "I went to the High School of Music and Art in New York but I got in as a pianist. Then they assigned me the viola, so I learned that." But all the while, Pat was concentrating on a career as an actress or dancer. "I played the guitar and sang along with that, but it wasn't anything serious," the soprano admits.

It wasn't until her mother, an established voice teacher, offered Pat singing lessons that the teenager began to work on her voice. But she was still more interested in acting than anything else. "I was at the Circle in the Square in *The Iceman Cometh* when I first met Ted Mann. It was about the same time I was doing some children's shows playing my guitar and singing. I was about seventeen years old and fresh out of high school.

"Ted looked at me and said to his partner, José Canseco, 'I'm going to marry that girl.' I was terrified. I thought, my God, this older man is interested in me." Ted Mann was nine years older, but that's a big difference when you're seventeen. Obviously not too big, because they were married just two years later.

Meanwhile, the voice lessons continued, and Pat's voice progressed to the point where she got a job in the original Broadway cast of *The Sound of Music*. "I was the second nun from the left," Pat remembers. "And you know who else was in the cast? Tatiana Troyanos! We used to sit backstage when we weren't needed and sing madrigals. Then, suddenly, I turned into an opera singer. I knew nothing about opera. I'd studied French in high school. But I had to learn Italian and German and all the repertoire.

"I guess all that other training really helped, though," Pat says in retrospect. "All that time I spent learning to act and dance and be a good musician helped so much when I started to sing professionally."

Patricia Brooks was known as one of the greatest acting singers in the country. She had the musicianship to back up her voice and the beauty to back up her movements. What a combination!

Cooking was another subject altogether. "I love to cook but when I first got married I didn't know anything about it. I had to learn and it was really painful. My mother cooked at home but somehow I never picked it up from her."

And these Forgotten Cookies? Pat Brooks remembers, "I got the recipe from the mother of a redheaded boy who was a good friend of my son, Jonathan, when he was at the Trinity School." The names are forgotten, but the forgotten cookies are remembered.

For an unforgettable and chilling performance, gird yourself with a cup of hot tea and some cookies and be riveted by the New York City Opera recording with our Miss Brooks of Robert Ward's *The Crucible* (2-CRI S-168). And, lest you forget the recipe, call on Michael Feinstein to sing Irving Berlin's "Remember" (Elektra 9 60744).

Forgotten Cookies

MAKES 2 DOZEN

3 large egg whites at room temperature
Pinch salt
1 cup chopped walnuts

3 tablespoons maple syrup
2 teaspoons rum (optional)

1   Preheat oven to 350°. Grease a cookie sheet well.

2   Place egg whites and salt in a large bowl. With hand-held electric mixer beat on high speed until whites form stiff peaks. In a small bowl, combine walnuts, syrup, and rum. Fold into whites and drop by tablespoons, about ½ inch apart, onto prepared cookie sheet. Bake 5 minutes, turn off oven, and "forget" the cookies for 25 to 30 minutes, or until they are dry.

Nico Castel

Very few people have had the opportunity to perform what they wished at their debuts with the New York Philharmonic. But when Nico Castel made his first appearance with the orchestra, he was both tenor and improviser. The work, *Renga with Apartment House, 1776*, was a Philharmonic Bicentennial commission written by John Cage. The New York premiere took place on November 4, 1976, in Avery Fisher Hall. Pierre Boulez led the forces in this regular subscription concert, which included not only Mr. Castel as the Sephardic Jews—all of them—but also Chief Swift Eagle in the vast role of the American Indians.

"We each sang for the people we represented," Nico Castel explains. "John Cage came to me because I was recommended by the Sephardic Synagogue. He was looking for someone who could sing Sephardic songs. You see, he didn't write the music for me or Swift Eagle. I sang bits and pieces of Sephardic songs I knew through the twenty-two-minute piece. I learned how to interrupt my singing when the orchestra crashed in with something big or someone else did something that sounded important. Then I'd wait until I heard the next silence and I'd start again." Tenor and improviser. "We had a big Park Avenue reception after that performance," the tenor tells us, getting to the meat of the evening. "They had really terrific food."

Nico Castel's musical life is balanced between stage performances and language coaching. Since he is fluent in six tongues—German, French, Italian, English, Spanish, and Portuguese, not to mention several dialects—he is able to help other singers sound more authentic in their roles. Nico can also don different accents in English at the drop of a dictionary, switching from a Yiddish rabbinical student to an elderly Italian streetsweeper as easily as most of us flip a light switch. And his kitchen creations follow the same pattern.

"I was born in Portugal and brought up in a Sephardic household. We ate a combination of Portuguese seafood and Near Eastern dishes. When I came to New York and was on my own, I began experimenting." The result of those experiments is a cuisine with a variety of international accents, from the Portuguese coast to the Tex-Mex border.

To salute the versatility of style brought to us in food and music by Nico Castel, we suggest his recording, with Stuart Burrows, Beverly Sills, and Norman Treigle, conducted by Julius Rudel, of Offenbach's *Tales of Hoffmann* (Angel 3-4AVC-34011). And try *Tenors Any-*

one? (Sony Classical MDK 46635) for a variety of tenors singing a variety of songs they've rarely sung before (José Carreras in "Some Enchanted Evening," Placido Domingo in "Yesterday," Mandy Patinkin in "Over the Rainbow," and Richard Tucker in "What Kind of Fool Am I?").

Bacalhau a Gomes de Sa

SERVES 8

1 pound salt cod (bacalhau)
¾ cup olive oil
6 large onions, about 3 pounds, sliced thin (about 12 cups)
6 large russet potatoes, about 4 pounds, peeled and sliced thin (about 9 cups)

½ teaspoon pepper
Hard-boiled eggs, for garnish
Pitted black olives, for garnish
Parsley, for garnish

1   Place salt cod in a large bowl and cover with cold water. Place in refrigerator and soak at least 24 hours, changing water several times. Drain, place cod in a large saucepot, and cover with fresh cold water. Bring to a boil, cover, and remove from heat. Let sit 15 minutes or until cod flakes easily. Drain and flake the cod. Set aside.

2   Heat ¼ cup of the olive oil in a large skillet over medium high heat. Add onions and cook, stirring occasionally, until golden brown, about 30 minutes.

3   Meanwhile, place potatoes in large saucepot and cover with cold water. Bring to a boil and simmer until tender, about 12 to 15 minutes. Drain and set aside.

4   Preheat oven to 350°. In a 4½-quart casserole, layer ingredients starting with 2 tablespoons of the olive oil. Add half the potatoes, half the flaked cod, half the onions, 3 tablespoons olive oil and ¼ teaspoon pepper. Repeat layers. Sprinkle the remaining 3 tablespoons of olive oil on the top. Cover and bake 35 minutes. Uncover and bake 10 minutes longer, or until top is browned.

Garnish with sliced hard-boiled eggs, pitted black olives, and parsley, and serve with a crusty white bread.

John Cheek

"My debut was in 1977 with Leinsdorf conducting *Parsifal*. I sang Klingsor with Jon Vickers and Janice Martin. It was my first Wagner." The singer is John Cheek and he's not talking about his debut at the Met. The bass is recounting what he remembers as his first performance with the New York Philharmonic in Avery Fisher Hall. "There was a platform that Erich Leinsdorf had constructed so we were against the back wall—behind the orchestra—and our voices really boomed out. My agent, Thea Dispecker, said it was like Bayreuth."

The following year, John Cheek was back booming with the Philharmonic again. But this time the program was a mixed bag of orchestral and chamber works, so that John was sharing the stage not with the full orchestra, but with Kathleen Battle, Maria Ewing, Philip Creech, and the four hands of pianists Paul Jacobs and James Levine for a performance of Brahms's *Liebeslieder Waltzes.*

For any performance, orchestral, operatic, or chamber, John Cheek has very specific ways to prepare himself. "If I'm doing opera I eat a light meal of pasta a couple of hours before. For a concert I usually eat closer to the performance because I may not be on until the second part of the concert. Yes, sometimes I'm hungry after I sing, but if I give in to that too many times I blow up like a balloon." Without missing a beat, the bass adds, "I just joined a gym."

On the road, food is sometimes too good to resist. Paris is one of John Cheek's favorite places to eat. "We recently ate so well in Paris that we staggered out afterward."

Italy isn't to be sneered at, either. "On one trip to Tuscany we had a marvelous *piccione*. It was stuffed with bacon and bread crumbs and was simple and wonderful. That rich, dark meat! They served wonderful Chianti to wash it down. I'll bet that wine came from the hills I was looking at from the restaurant!

"When I was a student in Siena, Italy, I worked one year with Gino Bechi, the great singer and teacher. He had a pet name for me," the bass tells us. "He called me 'Signor Cheek to Cheek.' "

If Gino Bechi can do it, so can we. When preparing Signor Cheek to Cheek's recipe, toast it with a performance of (yes!) Irving Berlin's "Cheek to Cheek" from *Top Hat.* And, if that isn't too much for you, to accompany John Cheek's Braised Fennel Salad, play *Stars and Stripes*, Marches, Fanfares, and Wind Band Spectaculars," performed by the Cleveland Symphonic Winds conducted, of course, by Frederick Fennell! (Telarc CD-80038)

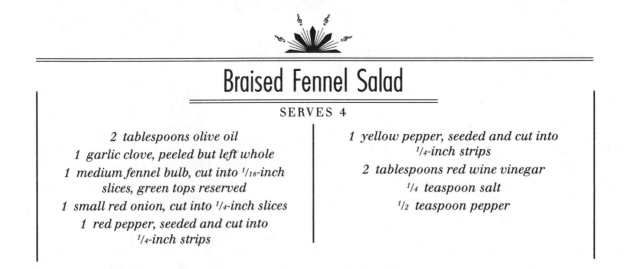

Braised Fennel Salad

SERVES 4

2 tablespoons olive oil
1 garlic clove, peeled but left whole
1 medium fennel bulb, cut into 1/16-inch slices, green tops reserved
1 small red onion, cut into 1/4-inch slices
1 red pepper, seeded and cut into 1/4-inch strips

1 yellow pepper, seeded and cut into 1/4-inch strips
2 tablespoons red wine vinegar
1/4 teaspoon salt
1/2 teaspoon pepper

1   Heat olive oil in a large skillet over medium high heat. Add garlic and cook, stirring, until golden brown, about 3 minutes. Remove garlic and add fennel. Cook, stirring, about 3 to 4 minutes. Add onion and peppers and continue to cook, stirring, about 10 minutes more. Remove from heat, add vinegar, salt, and pepper and stir well. Place in serving dish and sprinkle with fennel tops, coarsely chopped.

Barbara Cook

"It was a valentine for Leonard Bernstein," Barbara Cook remembers of her New York Philharmonic debut. The date was February 13, 1961, and the singer shared this musical valentine for Lenny with a quartet of conductors—Aaron Copland, Vladimir Golschmann, Lukas Foss, and Yuri Krasnopolsky—and eight other singers including Jennie Tourel, Betty Comden and Adolph Green, Edie Adams, Carol Lawrence, Anna Moffo, Elaine Stritch, and Richard Tucker. Quite a valentine!

"It was the first time that I had performed—maybe the only time I performed—'Glitter and Be Gay' since I was in the original cast of *Candide* in 1956. I was so nervous," Barbara Cook remembers. "I'd never sung in Carnegie Hall before and certainly never with the New York Philharmonic. I kept trying to tell myself, 'This is Indianapolis,' just to make myself feel better. When I came off I just sat down backstage in a daze. People had to lead me back for a bow.

"I was so happy, though, because Lenny was overjoyed. He thought I was even better that night than I was in the original production." She sighs as she thinks of Bernstein. "He was always so supportive. He just made me feel that I could do anything I wanted to do."

Barbara Cook's '61 coloratura in Carnegie Hall is far removed from Barbara Cook's '91 club style at the Carlyle. And so are her eating habits. "What I do now is to eat a couple of hours before my performance. I eat half my dinner then and the other half after. I'm always hungry after I sing. I try to avoid high-fat foods. And I don't eat any bread or wheat or sugar anymore. They're just not good for me. It's almost like an allergy. I don't break out or anything from wheat and sugar. But once I start to eat them, I can't stop. And I feel a lot better when I'm eating this way. I wouldn't think of eating ice cream or cookies or pie. It really is like an allergy."

That doesn't mean she's stopped enjoying good food. "I have some really favorite restaurants these days. In New York I stick to neighborhood places that serve good fresh seafood like Docks on the Upper West Side. In London, I head for Le Caprice. But my all-time favorite is Fredy Girardet in a little town called Crissier in Switzerland. They serve French food and he's the best chef in the world. Wally Harper, my pianist, is interested in gourmet food and he'd heard of him. We often make a stop in Switzerland just for dinner. It's really a picture-book little town and the restaurant is in the old city hall. I love taking people who've never been there. I took my son recently and he loved it."

Coming back to the reality of cooking it yourself, Barbara Cook tells us that the David whose pasta recipe follows is her former husband, David LeGrant. And while she rarely eats pasta these days because of the wheat, this recipe is fairly low in fat and calories. It's also easy and delicious.

To hear the different sides of Barbara Cook while cooking David's Fabulous Pasta, begin with her original-cast recording of Bernstein's *Candide* (CBS MK-38732). Then switch to her Disney album with Wally Harper conducting cartoon classics like "When You Wish Upon a Star" and "Zip-a-dee-doo-dah" (MCA Classics MCAD-6244).

David's Fabulous Pasta

SERVES 2

4 ounces spinach fettuccine

1 tablespoon olive oil (for even lower fat use 1/2 cup defatted chicken broth)

1 clove garlic, minced (about 1 teaspoon)

1/2 small red onion, chopped (about 1/2 cup)

1/2 cup farmer's cheese (or pot cheese)

1/8 teaspoon salt

1/4 teaspoon freshly ground pepper

2 tablespoons chopped parsley

1   Bring a large pot of cold water to a rolling boil and cook fettuccine according to package directions. Keep warm.

2   Meanwhile, heat oil (or broth) in a medium skillet over medium-high heat. Add garlic and onion and cook stirring about 4 minutes or until onion is translucent. (If using broth, cook until broth has reduced to about 1/4 cup.) Place pasta, cheese, salt, pepper, and parsley in a serving bowl and add onion mixture. Toss well.

Serve with crusty bread (no butter!) and a leafy salad with no-fat dressing.

Placido Domingo

"I was working on my *Cake Bible*," Rose Levy Beranbaum remembers, "and I knew that, with my musical background, I wanted to dedicate one of my cakes to a great singer. I had this wonderful chocolate cake and one day while I was playing tennis (that's when I get all my best ideas), I realized that this unnamed chocolate cake was truly the "tenor" of all chocolate cakes. This was something worthy of dedicating to one of the world's greatest tenors.

"When I got home, I called Placido Domingo and spoke with his secretary. She said that he adored chocolate but she'd have to speak with him first. She called back pretty fast and said he'd be delighted to have a cake named after him but when would he get to taste it?"

Rose reports that she was just thrilled out of her mind. She made an appointment to see the tenor at his home and bring him a sample cake. "I wore a chocolate-colored dress and really made a whole presentation of it. When I rang his doorbell and he answered it—himself—I don't know who was more surprised, him or me. You see, I was shocked to find that the world-famous Placido Domingo opened his own front door. He was shocked because his secretary had forgotten to tell him I was coming."

The surprise visit didn't seem to dissuade the tenor from inviting Rose—and her cake—into the house. "I uncovered the cake and the aroma just rose around all of us. There was silence for a moment and then his wife said, 'No calories, of course!'

"A short time later, I had my press party for the *Cake Bible*. It was held at the Rainbow Room and I wanted Mr. Domingo to be there but he was off singing in San Francisco. But he sent me a telegram. It said, 'Now that I have tasted your cake, I am so proud to have it named after me. Bravo!'

"Wait!" Rose tells us, all excited now by these memories. "There's more! His secretary called and left a message on my answering machine. I had trouble erasing it because it was so nice. I'll never forget it. She said, 'What Placido is to singing, you are to cakes.' Imagine!"

A cake dedicated to a world-famous tenor must have that world-famous tenor serenading us as we eat a slice (or two). Mr. Domingo opens his cake concert with his album *Con amore* (RCA AFL1-4265). Then, to match one of Rose's greatest hits, Domingo's *Greatest Hits* (RCA AGL1-4364).

Chocolate Domingo Cake

SERVES 10 TO 12

¹/₄ cup plus 3 tablespoons unsweetened cocoa (Dutch processed) or ¹/₂ cup nonalkalized cocoa

²/₃ cup sour cream

2 large eggs, at room temperature

1¹/₂ teaspoons vanilla extract

1¹/₂ cups plus 1 tablespoon sifted cake flour

1 cup sugar

³/₄ teaspoon baking powder

¹/₄ teaspoon baking soda

¹/₂ teaspoon salt

14 tablespoons (1³/₄ sticks) unsalted butter, softened

Confectioners' sugar and a chocolate or real red rose, for garnish

1   Preheat oven to 350°. Grease a 9 × 2″ cake pan or a 9-inch springform pan. Line with parchment or wax paper, grease again, and flour.

2   In a medium bowl, whisk together the cocoa, sour cream, eggs, and vanilla until smooth. In a large mixing bowl combine all the remaining dry ingredients and mix with an electric mixer on low speed for 30 seconds to blend. Add the butter and half the cocoa mixture. Mix on low until the dry ingredients are moistened. Increase to medium speed (high speed if using a hand mixer) and beat for 1¹/₂ minutes to aerate and develop the cake's structure. Scrape down the sides. Gradually add the remaining cocoa mixture in 2 batches, beating for 20 seconds after each addition to incorporate the ingredients and strengthen the structure. Scrape down the sides and pour into the prepared pan. Smooth the surface with a spatula. The pan will be about half full. Bake 30 to 40 minutes or until a tester inserted near the center comes out clean and the cake springs back when pressed lightly in the center.

3   Cool in the pan on a cooling rack for 10 minutes. Loosen the sides with a small spatula and invert onto a greased wire rack. Reinvert so top is up. Dust with confectioners' sugar, top with a rose for garnish, and serve hot or warm from the oven.

Maureen Forrester

There are very few singers who can say they made their official debuts at the YWCA, were heard by Otto Klemperer, and were immediately engaged by the conductor to sing Beethoven's Ninth. That's the way Maureen Forrester began her illustrious career. And she was no flash in the pan, either. Bruno Walter heard about her soon after the Beethoven performance and invited the Montreal contralto to come to New York to sing Mahler's *Resurrection Symphony* with the Philharmonic at Carnegie Hall. That was in 1957. And she's been going strong ever since.

In fact, this magnificent musician has given us more than 130 recordings, including a pop album, *From Kern to Sondheim*, and an appearance with Samuel Ramey and Barbara Cook in MCA's *Carousel*. When she's not singing, she's lobbying, as chairperson of the Canada Council, as a member of the board of the Toronto Symphony, and, in 1990, as spokesperson for the Arthritis Society. She and Glenn Gould are the only classical artists in the Canadian Hall of Fame. And the contralto has managed to collect some twenty-nine honorary doctorates.

With all that, Maureen Forrester still has time to cook. She tells us that she got her recipe for wild rice casserole "on my very first American recital tour in 1955," proving that this authentic midwestern dish has withstood the test of time and, like its contributor, is also not a flash in the pan. "I was in Decorah, Iowa, at the time," she says. "The casserole has a rather nutty quality and it can serve lots of people at a reception."

We have music for lots of people with Maureen Forrester standing out in the crowd: Mahler's Symphony No. 2 (*Resurrection*) with the New York Philharmonic (CBS 2-M2K-42032) and *Carousel* with Barbara Cook, Samuel Ramey, Sarah Brightman, Maureen Forrester, the Royal Philharmonic, and the Ambrosian Singers (MCA MCAD-6209).

Ground Beef and Wild Rice Casserole

SERVES 12 TO 16

2 cups wild rice

4 tablespoons (½ stick) unsalted butter

4 medium onions, chopped (about 3 cups)

4 ribs celery, chopped (1½ cups)

2 cups sliced mushrooms (about ¼ pound)

2 garlic cloves, minced

4 pounds ground beef

2 (10¾ ounce) cans cream of mushroom soup

2 (10¾ ounce) cans cream of chicken soup

2 (10¾ ounce) cans consommé or chicken broth

2 cans water

¾ teaspoon salt

1 teaspoon pepper

2 bay leaves

2 teaspoons dried thyme

⅔ cup chopped Italian parsley

1 cup toasted sliced almonds

Chopped parsley, for garnish, if desired

1 Preheat oven to 300°. Soak rice in hot water to cover for 15 minutes. Drain well.

2 Heat butter in a large Dutch oven or saucepot over medium high heat. Add onions and celery and cook, stirring, until soft, about 5 minutes. Add mushrooms and garlic; cook until mushrooms are brown and release their moisture, about 8 minutes. Stir in rice and remaining ingredients (except almonds). Cover and bake 2 hours, uncover, and skim off surface grease. Cover and bake 1 hour longer. Skim again and sprinkle with almonds and additional chopped parsley if desired.

Reri Grist

Soprano Reri Grist, a talented New Yorker, went off to Zurich to sing Zerbinetta and, next thing she knew, she was a star. Her debut with the Zurich Opera was such a sensation that she was signed as a regular member of the company and other houses began hunting her down.

This was back in 1959. From Europe, the soprano returned to the United States to make her debut at the Santa Fe Opera, and after that it was a life of flying from city to city, country to country, and stage to stage. Reri Grist finally came home to New York in 1966 for her Metropolitan Opera debut. But it wasn't in New York that she wanted to stay. She and her family decided to settle down and live in Berlin. The Germans know a good thing when they see—and hear—it, and they've elevated this pert coloratura to the status of a television superstar. She even appeared in an award-winning biographical portrait entitled "Reri Grist—Singer" for German and Australian TV.

Now it's time for "Reri Grist—Cook." The life of a singer never includes much leisure time, and Reri Grist's life is no exception. So the coloratura creates dishes that are both quick to prepare and delicious. Calabaza (or calabash) is a gourd in the squash family. And Reri tells us that this particular recipe is very easy to make and even easier to eat. The creamy texture of the soup and the touch of nutmeg make this a real gourmet comfort food, perfect for a cold autumn afternoon.

For some fireworks to accompany this smooth soup, listen to Reri Grist's recording of Mozart's *Der Schauspieldirektor* with the Dresden State Opera (3-DG 2709051). And, for the squash in the soup, Jimmy Durante's recording of *Comedy: The Best of MGM* (SE-4207) . . . "Good night, Mrs. Calabash, wherever you are!"

Cream of Calabaza Soup

SERVES 4 TO 6

1¹/₂ pounds calabaza squash, peeled, seeded, and cut into ³/₄-inch cubes

1 medium russet potato, about 8 ounces, peeled and cut into ³/₄-inch cubes

3 cups chicken broth

¹/₄ teaspoon salt

¹/₂ teaspoon pepper

1 cup milk

¹/₂ teaspoon nutmeg, preferably freshly grated

1 tablespoon unsalted butter

1¹/₂ teaspoons chopped fresh dill or dash of sweet paprika

1   Place the calabaza, potato, chicken broth, salt, and pepper in a medium saucepot. Bring to a boil over high heat. Lower heat to a simmer and cook until vegetables are soft, about 15 minutes. Remove from heat.

2   Purée soup in a food processor or blender. Return to saucepot and stir in remaining ingredients. Over medium heat, stir until just heated through, about 5 minutes more.

NOTE: Calabaza can be found in most Spanish markets, but acorn squash can be substituted.

Jerry Hadley

"My wife is from Iowa," tenor Jerry Hadley tells us. "Her family had a ceremonial clove of garlic. They brought it out to wave over the table once a year."

This could be a problem for a man who takes his cue from baritone Sherrill Milnes when he says his wife is Italo-Midwest. "Part of my family is from Italy," the tenor reminds us. "My grandfather spoke something that mixed several different dialects and languages together. Only about three of *his* relatives could understand him. And my grandmother cooked by the 'I feel, so I do' method. No measuring, ever. I guess that's how I learned to cook, too."

The more serious side of Jerry Hadley turned up on the morning of November 14, 1990, when the tenor appeared with the New York Philharmonic and a long list of musical luminaries—James Levine, Michael Tilson Thomas, Christoph Eschenbach, Thomas Hampson, Marilyn Horne, Mstislav Rostropovich—to pay tribute to the memory of Leonard Bernstein. It was a morning no one there will ever forget. A mourning that cut beyond a debut. Food was far from anyone's thoughts that day.

Under almost all other circumstances, however, food is right up there near the top in order of importance for Jerry Hadley. "I love to eat pasta," he says, his Italian background glowing. "And if I'm singing that night, I'll eat a plate of pasta and a salad around four thirty." When asked what cities he's sung in that have been really great for food, his eyes light up and he says, "All of them! Singers have an uncanny ability to find the best places to eat."

The tenor thinks a moment before saying, "After all, all we talk about is food, sex, and the competition." He thinks again and adds, "Not necessarily in that order."

You needn't listen in any particular order, either. But, to accompany Jerry Hadley's recipe for Penne with Summer Vegetables, we suggest something light, such as the tenor's recording of Jerome Kern's *Showboat* (Angel 3 A13-49108), and something Italian, such as his performance of Puccini's *La Bohème* (DG2-423601-1).

Penne with Summer Vegetables

SERVES 4 TO 6

12 ounces penne (or 2 ounces per person)

1/4 cup extra virgin olive oil

1 medium eggplant, cut into 1/2-inch dice

2 sprigs fresh rosemary or 1 teaspoon dried

1 medium yellow squash, cut into 1/2-inch dice

1 medium zucchini, cut into 1/2-inch dice

1 bulb fennel, thinly sliced

1 medium red onion, peeled and thinly sliced

3 garlic cloves, peeled and thinly sliced

1 red pepper, seeded and cut into 1/2-inch julienne

1 yellow pepper, seeded and cut into 1/2-inch julienne

1 teaspoon dried thyme

1 tablespoon grated orange zest

1/4 cup dry white wine (optional)

4 tomatoes, peeled, seeded, and chopped

1/4 teaspoon salt

1/2 teaspoon pepper

3 tablespoons balsamic vinegar

1   Bring a large pot of salted water to a rolling boil. Cook penne al dente according to package directions. Drain and keep warm.

2   Meanwhile, heat olive oil in a large skillet over high heat. Add eggplant and rosemary, and cook, stirring, about 5 minutes. Add squashes, fennel, onion, and garlic, and cook, stirring, about 5 minutes more. Reduce heat and add peppers, thyme, orange zest, and wine if using. Simmer 5 additional minutes. Add tomatoes and stir. Cook 3 minutes more to warm through. Remove from heat, remove rosemary stems, and add salt, pepper, and vinegar. Serve hot or at room temperature over penne.

Jerome Hines

"I married a woman who sings better than I do, so at night I feel like I'm sleeping with a critic from the *New York Times*," says Metropolitan Opera bass-baritone Jerome Hines of his wife Lucia Evangelista, who also happens to cook better than he does. "Lucia is the most wonderful cook in the world. I came home recently from a tour and she'd prepared bay scallops for me. I sat there eating them and curling my toes, they were so good. I said, 'Darling, will heaven be like this?' And she answered, 'It will if I can do the cooking!'"

Jerome Hines made his debut with the New York Philharmonic in 1955 when he appeared with Herva Nelli, Claramae Turner, Richard Tucker, and the Westminster Choir in a performance of the Verdi *Requiem* under the direction of Guido Cantelli. And the bass-baritone hasn't quit yet. "I just sang a Rossini *Stabat Mater* for an AIDS benefit and, before that I did four *Don Carlos*," he says with pride. That's not all he's justifiably proud of.

"I founded the Opera Music Theater International in 1987. Our base is in Newark, right next to Symphony Hall." In fact, Jerome Hines was responsible for saving Symphony Hall from the wrecker's ball. He's been chairman of the board of the Hall and he's currently on the advisory board of the new cultural centers in Newark and in Camden. He also spent eight years as a member of the New Jersey State Council on the Arts. "It's my nature," the singer-politician explains.

"I recently returned from Moscow, where I helped establish a cultural exchange program between young singers from Russia and my Opera Music Theater International." How was the food? "Terrible! It was terrible twenty years ago and it's worse now. Three of us went out to dinner and two ordered fish and the third asked for steak. The fish was inedible and the steak was so tough it couldn't be cut, much less chewed."

What did they eat? "Well, the soup was delicious and they've always had good ice cream. It only comes in vanilla, but it's good. And, of course, the caviar is great," he said, curling his toes again. "I have a tin right here in front of me. Beluga, I think," and I started curling *my* toes.

Does the bass-baritone have a special routine he follows before a performance? "I always eat about five hours before I sing. I like to start a performance on an empty stomach. So I have something like fish or chicken for my protein and a big, raw vegetable salad.

Then, during the performance I usually snack on coffee and some nuts or cheese."

Nuts or cheese? Don't they get stuck in your throat? "That's okay," Jerome Hines replies. "Then I have an excuse if I don't sing well." He needn't concern himself with that. Just listen to his recording of the Brahms *Requiem* to see why (2-CBS M2S-686). Then, while you're cooking up some of Lucia's Ossobuco, play the Prelude to Verdi's opera "Simon Ossobuco-negra" with the orchestra of La Scala conducted by Claudio Abbado (2-DG 415692-2).

Ossobuco Lucia

SERVES 6

2 tablespoons unsalted butter	4 garlic cloves, finely minced
6 pieces veal shank, each about 2 inches wide (about 5 pounds total)	¼ cup white wine
½ teaspoon salt	8 plum tomatoes, peeled and puréed in blender
½ teaspoon pepper	1 teaspoon dried oregano
½ pound mushrooms, thinly sliced	2 teaspoons fresh lemon juice (optional)
1 cup chopped Italian parsley	

1 In a large saucepot or Dutch oven, melt the butter over high heat. Season the shanks with salt and pepper and add them, (in batches if necessary) to the pan. Brown well on both sides, about 3 to 4 minutes on each side. Remove and add mushrooms. Cook stirring until lightly browned, about 2 minutes, and add parsley and garlic. Cook, stirring, about 1 minute longer. Add wine and stir. Stir in tomatoes and oregano and return shanks to pot. Reduce heat to simmer, cover, and cook until shanks are very tender, about 1½ hours. Remove shanks to a serving platter and keep warm. Increase heat and boil sauce 6 to 7 minutes to reduce it by ⅓, or to taste. Season with lemon juice and additional salt and pepper if desired. Pour over shanks and serve.

Marilyn Horne

"There's one thing I *don't* eat before I sing," says Marilyn Horne emphatically, "and that's Tamale Pie!" Actually, the great mezzo-soprano loves this dish, but it would not sit too well with her on stage. "I stay away from spicy foods or anything that might bloat me before a concert. Usually I eat a plate of pasta or a chicken breast. Something plain," she explains.

"This Tamale Pie is wonderful for a party. I got the recipe from my former mother-in-law," she adds. "I used to be a really dedicated cook but now that I live alone, I don't bother too much. It's so easy to make a pasta or, in New York, just to pick up the phone and order in."

When Marilyn Horne is on the road, she follows pretty much the same pattern. "I love Italian food, so when I'm singing in Italy I'm sure I'll always have great meals."

Marilyn Horne made her debut with the New York Philharmonic in 1966 when Lukas Foss conducted a program that featured three of Berg's Seven Early Songs along with excerpts from *Wozzeck*, Webern's Five Pieces for Orchestra, and Brahms's Symphony No. 1. But the performances that really stand out in the mezzo's mind are those of the Verdi *Requiem* with Leonard Bernstein. "I remember one with Lenny that had [Galina] Vishnevskaya, [Richard] Tucker, and Cesare Siepi. They were so exciting to sing with."

Of recently memorable meals, one with her family stands out for both the food and the company. "I was in California a little while ago and my daughter, Angela, came up with this wonderful pasta. She got the idea from a cookbook and it was a great combination of spaghetti, some kind of light cream sauce, saffron, and peas."

The good company of Marilyn Horne is a necessity while preparing her Tamale Pie. I suggest you start with her recording of Rossini's *Alternative Opera Arias*, arias that are usually cut from performances (CBS IM-38731). Then, for the sheer fun and beauty of it, listen to the mezzo's *Beautiful Dreamer* album of great American songs, from Copland's "At the River" to "God Bless America"—in a rousing rendition (London 417242-1).

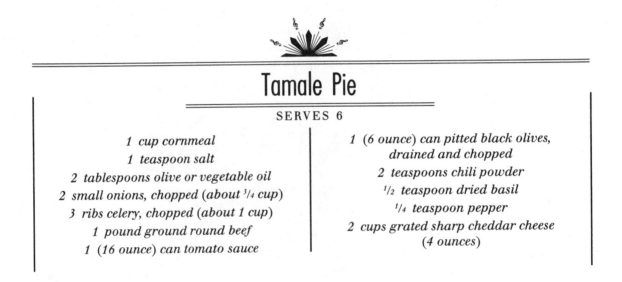

Tamale Pie

SERVES 6

1 cup cornmeal
1 teaspoon salt
2 tablespoons olive or vegetable oil
2 small onions, chopped (about ³/₄ cup)
3 ribs celery, chopped (about 1 cup)
1 pound ground round beef
1 (16 ounce) can tomato sauce

1 (6 ounce) can pitted black olives, drained and chopped
2 teaspoons chili powder
¹/₂ teaspoon dried basil
¹/₄ teaspoon pepper
2 cups grated sharp cheddar cheese (4 ounces)

1   Bring 4 cups of water to a rolling boil in a large saucepot over high heat. Stir in cornmeal and salt and cook about 20 minutes, stirring constantly to avoid lumps. Preheat oven to 350°. Grease a 2-quart casserole.

2   Meanwhile, heat oil in a large skillet over medium high heat. Add onions, celery, and ground round, and cook until meat is browned, about 6 to 7 minutes. Pour off excess fat and add tomato sauce, olives, chili powder, basil, and pepper. Bring to a boil. When cornmeal is thick and creamy, pour meat and half the cheese into the saucepot and mix together. Pour into prepared casserole and sprinkle remaining cheese on top. Bake 45 minutes. Let rest 10 minutes before serving.

NOTE: *This pie is somewhat mushy the first day it is made. The second day it is quite firm and more like a pie. Reheat it at 350° for 30 to 45 minutes.*

Evelyn Lear

If ever there were a New York home-grown soprano, it's Evelyn Lear. The internationally celebrated opera star was born in Brooklyn and educated at Hunter, New York University, and Juilliard. But she was coming of operatic age in the late 1950s and it was still the time that "home-grown" singers had to make their start in Europe. So, in 1957, with the help of a Fulbright, Evelyn Lear went off to study in Berlin.

Just two years later, she became a member of the Berlin Opera. And then, in 1960, on just three weeks' notice, the soprano took on the dreadfully difficult title role in Berg's *Lulu*. She performed it, in concert form, for the Austrian premiere. From there, it was tributes and triumphs for the soprano from Covent Garden to Chicago, with roles that varied from the stratospheric coloratura of Zerbinetta to the colorfully flamboyant mezzo-soprano of Carmen.

Being a stylish actress didn't hurt, either. Evelyn Lear went from the operatic stage to the movie screen for Robert Altman's *Buffalo Bill and the Indians* with Robert Redford and to the New York stage for a 1984 musical, *Elizabeth and Essex*, in which she played the title role.

Well known as a recitalist, in solo appearances and with baritone Thomas Stewart, Evelyn Lear made her official debut as a soloist with the New York Philharmonic on April 8, 1971, in a program of Haydn and Szymanowski conducted by Stanislaw Skrowaczewski.

One would think, with all these concert, stage, and screen appearances, that Evelyn Lear couldn't find the time to eat, much less cook. But her recipes are as varied as her repertoire. Her Black Forest Apple Strudel, especially with the schlag (whipped cream), reminds us of Strauss's *Der Rosenkavalier*, an opera in which she's appeared as Sophie, Octavian, and the Marschallin.

To properly polish off Evelyn Lear's Black Forest Apple Strudel, begin with the soprano's recording of the Marschallin's monologue (Philips 9500177). Then, for just a dollop of schlag, try the Stephen Foster recording *Beautiful Dreamer* with Evelyn Lear and Thomas Stewart (DGG 139303).

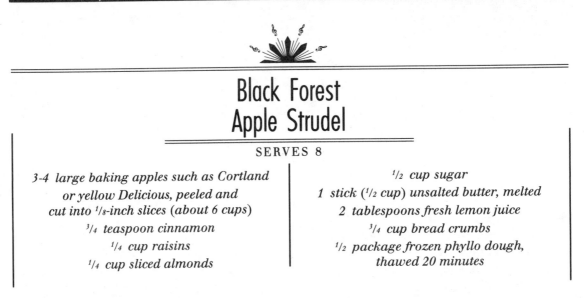

Black Forest Apple Strudel

SERVES 8

3-4 large baking apples such as Cortland or yellow Delicious, peeled and cut into 1/8-inch slices (about 6 cups)

3/4 teaspoon cinnamon

1/4 cup raisins

1/4 cup sliced almonds

1/2 cup sugar

1 stick (1/2 cup) unsalted butter, melted

2 tablespoons fresh lemon juice

3/4 cup bread crumbs

1/2 package frozen phyllo dough, thawed 20 minutes

1   Preheat oven to 375°. Grease a cookie sheet with sides.

2   In a large mixing bowl, combine the apples, 1/2 teaspoon cinnamon, raisins, almonds, 1/4 cup sugar, 2 tablespoons melted butter, and the lemon juice. Mix well and set aside. In a separate small bowl, mix the remaining sugar with the bread crumbs.

3   Lay a clean pastry or kitchen cloth on the counter and sprinkle with water. Place 2 phyllo sheets on cloth, brush with melted butter, and sprinkle with 2 tablespoons bread crumbs. Repeat 4 more times. Spread apple mixture in a line along center of dough leaving a 2-inch border on bottom and top and a 1-inch space on ends. Using pastry cloth, roll into a tight loaf (like a jelly roll). Fold dough in at borders, and seal ends by brushing with more butter. Carefully transfer to greased cookie sheet and brush with melted butter.

4   Mix remaining cinnamon into remaining bread crumbs and sprinkle over strudel. Bake 25 to 30 minutes or until golden brown.

Serve hot with schlag (whipped cream).

Robert Merrill

Robert Merrill's wife, Marion, loves to cook so much that she's thinking seriously of writing her own cookbook. "I keep thinking I should write everything down and let people know how I've kept him singing all these years."

"He loves to eat," Marion tells us. "But my concern is good nutrition. We both love food, all kinds of food—Chinese, Indian, Russian Jewish, Slavic. And we've traveled so much over the years that we've really had a chance to try just about everything."

Marion remembers one restaurant in London with particular fondness and interest. "We love Wheeler's in Soho. I could eat Dover Sole there every day. After a while, I prevailed on them to give me a copy of their menu because they list all the ingredients for each dish on it. Mind you, they don't tell the amounts. But at least you know what's in it and can reconstruct it from there."

The Merrills are amazed at the food they're finding these days in the interior states of America. "The quality of food has really improved in this country," Marion says. "We were recently in Columbus, Ohio, at a Hyatt Hotel and we had really good grilled salmon and tuna.

"For the most part, we stay with fish and vegetables. But if there's nothing worthwhile on a menu, you can't go wrong with a salad. Usually we ask for a chef's salad—we tell them to hold the ham and cheese and go heavy on the turkey. Bob likes to eat something light around four or five o'clock on the day of a performance. If we can't find anything else, we'll order fried chicken and remove the coating and the skin." There's always a way.

The way Robert Merrill met the New York Philharmonic was via the Bloch *Sacred Service.* It was April 7, 1960, presumably around Passover and Easter. And Leonard Bernstein's program followed the Jewish work with the Pergolesi *Stabat Mater.*

Remembering that event brings Marion back to food. "One holiday recently, I decided to make a brisket. Do you know it had been so long since I'd cooked meat that I'd forgotten how to make it? It's amazing how tastes change. Thirty-five years ago we lived on roasts and chops. It's very different now."

Different or not, since she does the cooking in the Merrill household, she's obviously been doing something right. After all, she *has* been keeping him singing all these years!

Marion tells us that the Vitello Tonnato recipe is her version of an Italian dish she and Robert tasted a long time ago. For this recipe, we suggest any of the many Italian opera recordings featuring Robert Merrill: Rossini's *Barber of Seville* (4-RCA LSC-6143) or Verdi's *Rigoletto* (2-RCA LSC-7027) for starters. And, of course, on the holidays or at any time of year, the beautiful and moving Bloch *Sacred Service* in the recording with Mr. Merrill and the New York Philharmonic under Leonard Bernstein (CBS MS-6221).

Vitello Tonnato

SERVES 8 TO 12 AS A FIRST COURSE OR 4 TO 6 AS A MAIN DISH

3-5 pound veal roast, boned and tied
2 medium onions, cut into ¹/₂-inch slices
2 carrots, cut into ¹/₂-inch slices
3 sprigs Italian parsley
1-2 bay leaves
2 garlic cloves, peeled but left whole
2 whole cloves
4 cups boiling water

Tuna Sauce
2 (7³/₄ ounce) cans tuna, drained
8 anchovy fillets
¹/₂ cup fresh lemon juice
1 cup olive oil
4 teaspoons capers, drained

1 Heat a large saucepot or Dutch oven over high heat and brown veal on all sides, about 10 minutes. Pour off any fat. Add onions, carrots, parsley, bay leaves, garlic, cloves, and boiling water. Cover, reduce heat to a simmer, and cook 2 to 2¹/₂ hours or until tender. Remove and chill.

2 To make sauce, place tuna, anchovies, and lemon juice in a blender and blend on low speed until smooth. With blender running, gradually add oil until mixture is the consistency of a thin mayonnaise. Remove to a bowl and stir in capers.

3 To serve, slice cold veal very thin and place in a shallow serving dish. Pour tuna sauce over meat, cover, and marinate in the refrigerator at least 24 hours before serving. Serve cold.

ANNA MOFFO AND ROBERT MERRILL

Anna Moffo

"When I sing, I don't remember parties," the vivacious Anna Moffo says. "But that's really the way I was brought up. You see, I never went to any receptions or parties after my performances until I met Bobby (husband, Robert Sarnoff). My teacher had told me that singers devote themselves to their voices and it was dangerous to go to places where people were smoking and drinking. I was taught to take care of myself and parties didn't fit into that regimen. It was Bobby who convinced me that wasn't normal."

The eminent soprano does remember her debut with the New York Philharmonic. "It was in 1961 and was a valentine to Bernstein.* Richard Tucker and I sang excerpts from *West Side Story*, and from what I remember, it was the first time operatic voices were asked to sing that music."

Anna Moffo makes a habit of studying the background of the roles she sings. "I want my costumes to come from the proper era and I want to know who my character is, where she comes from, and why she acts the way she does. To do this I study the history of her country and try to find out what was going on there at the time in which the opera is set.

"Singing is like cooking," Anna explains. "When I cook I want to know why a dish is made a certain way. For example, the southern Italian cuisine uses oil. But north of Rome, they use either all butter or a mixture of oil and butter. Well, that's from the French. I try to do the same thing when I'm learning a new role. What's in my character's background that makes her what and who she is? Who is my lover and who are his parents? I've tried to get to know my Alfredo, in *Traviata*, for instance. Now there's a man-virgin, for a change!

"I even try to find out what they ate at the time of the opera. You can't tell me that the aristocracy and even the artists in the 1800s were chewing on chicken bones and throwing them on the floor. They had knives and forks. They did drink champagne, though," she adds, thinking of a little *Bohème* here and a little *Traviata* there.

"When I'm traveling, I'm known for making my way into the kitchens of restaurants where I eat. I want to know how they cook, what goes into the food. Oh, they never really tell

---

The same valentine in which Barbara Cook performed.

you the truth. There are always secrets. But it's really helped my cooking technique to evolve."

This is a soprano who adores, loves, and is passionate about food. "They tell me I have a talent for cooking. I think I have a talent for loving to eat. In fact, I have a cookbook that's in the works. I want to share my recipes and the fact that cooking is therapeutic. It's good discipline, too." Perhaps Anna Moffo has just summed up the reasons so many musicians, especially singers, love food.

Many of the operas Anna Moffo has recorded have eating and drinking scenes. There is, of course, the magic gingerbread house in Humperdinck's *Hansel and Gretel* (2-RCA ARL2-0637). Puccini's *La Bohème* sets its second act in a restaurant (2-RCA AGL2-3969). And, what would Verdi's *Falstaff* be without food and drink? Thin! (3-Angel S-3552)

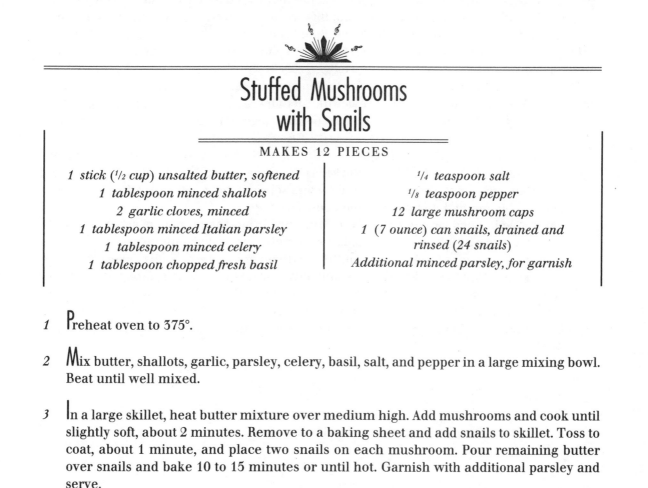

Stuffed Mushrooms with Snails

MAKES 12 PIECES

1 stick (¹/₂ cup) unsalted butter, softened
1 tablespoon minced shallots
2 garlic cloves, minced
1 tablespoon minced Italian parsley
1 tablespoon minced celery
1 tablespoon chopped fresh basil

¹/₄ teaspoon salt
¹/₈ teaspoon pepper
12 large mushroom caps
1 (7 ounce) can snails, drained and rinsed (24 snails)
Additional minced parsley, for garnish

1   Preheat oven to 375°.

2   Mix butter, shallots, garlic, parsley, celery, basil, salt, and pepper in a large mixing bowl. Beat until well mixed.

3   In a large skillet, heat butter mixture over medium high. Add mushrooms and cook until slightly soft, about 2 minutes. Remove to a baking sheet and add snails to skillet. Toss to coat, about 1 minute, and place two snails on each mushroom. Pour remaining butter over snails and bake 10 to 15 minutes or until hot. Garnish with additional parsley and serve.

Erie Mills

Erie Mills is the kind of soprano who can sing circles around high Cs, land on both feet, and come up with the audience smiling. She flits from coloratura cascades as Blondchen in Mozart's *Abduction from the Seraglio* to the bubbles of Johann Strauss's *Die Fledermaus* as Adele, and then goes on to soar through the pyrotechnics of Richard Strauss's *Ariadne auf Naxos* as Zerbinetta.

She endeared herself to New Yorkers when she appeared as a dazzling Cunegonde in Leonard Bernstein's *Candide* at the New York City Opera, a performance that's been televised on "Live from Lincoln Center" and a recorded role for which she's received a Grammy Award.

Much as we would like to think of Erie Mills as a New York treasure, the soprano has chosen to head for the peaceful hills of northern California rather than reside in the towering tumult of Manhattan. But, West Coast or East, this soprano, born in Granite City, Illinois, is obviously as at home in the kitchen as she is on the stage.

Her recipe is titled simply Pasta with Cauliflower, but the particular art of California cuisine is evident in its ingredients. Who but a Californian would combine cauliflower with clams, crushed red pepper, and garbanzos? Sherrill Milnes and Jerry Hadley may have Italo-Midwestern wives, but Erie Mills is *West*-adapted-Italo-Midwest. What a combination. Better yet, what a treat. Her recipe tastes terrific and, of course, it's healthful, too.

For good healthy singing to accompany this special dish, we suggest Erie Mills's recording of *Candide*, especially the moving finale, "Make Our Garden Grow" (2-New World NW-340/41-1).

Pasta with Cauliflower

SERVES 4

1 small cauliflower, cut into small
    flowerets (about 5 cups)
1/4 cup olive oil
1 garlic clove, minced
1/8-1/4 teaspoon crushed red pepper flakes
8 ounces orecchiette ("little ears")
    or other small pasta

1 (16 ounce) can garbanzo beans,
    drained and rinsed
1 (10 ounce) can baby clams, drained
1/4 teaspoon salt
1/2 teaspoon pepper

1 Bring a large saucepot of salted water to a boil. Cook cauliflower 5 minutes and remove with strainer. Keep water.

2 Heat olive oil in a large skillet over medium heat. Add garlic, cauliflower, and red pepper flakes and cook, partially covered, stirring frequently, for 25 to 30 minutes or until cauliflower is very soft. If necessary, add a bit of water to prevent sticking.

3 Bring the saucepot of cauliflower water back to a boil and add pasta. Stir and cook according to package directions until al dente. Drain and add pasta to skillet. Add garbanzo beans, clams, salt, and pepper, and stir. Cook just until warmed through, about 4 to 5 minutes.

Sherrill Milnes

"I know everything they say about cholesterol," Sherrill Milnes says with a swagger. "So I try not to eat steak more than four or five times a week."

You can pick yourself off the floor now. The Metropolitan Opera baritone knows his body and what makes it work. "I'm a full-stomach singer," he confides. "And nothing is as good as a steak before I go on stage. After a performance I try to be careful." That's when he eats his apple cranberry pies.

"I remember years ago when I first started singing in public, I would get to the last act of an opera and actually feel faint. That taught me to eat as close to the performance as possible and to eat as much as I could tamp in. How's that for a real Midwest term?"

A friend of tenor Jerry Hadley, whose wife is "Italo-Midwest," Sherrill says, "I agree with Jerry. My wife lived in Rome for a while but also came from the Midwest. Everything she cooks has gravy. Even pasta."

And, going beyond his family, the baritone concurs, "I think all singers just know the best restaurants in every city. It's as if we have a food compass."

Along with his operatic experience, at the Met and in major opera houses around the world, the baritone has performed with almost every important orchestra in America and abroad including, of course, the New York Philharmonic. He made his debut with the Philharmonic at one of the Promenade Concerts with André Kostelanetz in 1970, singing the good, meaty music of Mussorgsky and Tchaikovsky. At that point, he was already a star at the Met.

"For my twenty-fifth anniversary at the Metropolitan Opera we had a big party at home, but it was catered. My wife was at that Saturday matinee. When it was over, we just went home with our friends and ate." What kind of food did they have? "Everything."

Musically, we have some of everything, too. It is indeed *A Grand Night for Singing*, with Sherrill Milnes and tenor Placido Domingo (RCA LSC-3182). And, to wash all those beefy baritone and tenor performances down, we suggest a drink or two "In Taverna," from Carl Orff's sexy *Carmina Burana* with Milnes and the Boston Symphony (RCA 6533-2-RG).

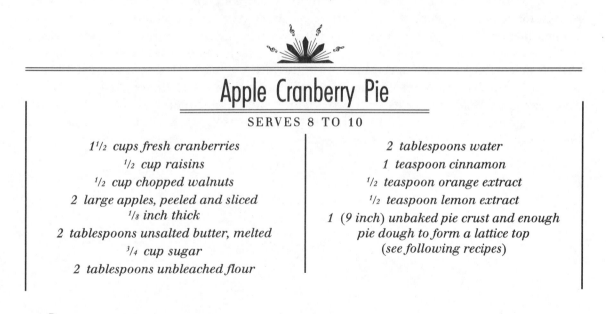

Apple Cranberry Pie

SERVES 8 TO 10

1½ cups fresh cranberries
½ cup raisins
½ cup chopped walnuts
2 large apples, peeled and sliced
⅛ inch thick
2 tablespoons unsalted butter, melted
¾ cup sugar
2 tablespoons unbleached flour

2 tablespoons water
1 teaspoon cinnamon
½ teaspoon orange extract
½ teaspoon lemon extract
1 (9 inch) unbaked pie crust and enough pie dough to form a lattice top
(see following recipes)

1 Preheat oven to 400°. In a large bowl combine all filling ingredients and mix well. Pour into crust and form lattice top.

2 Bake 15 minutes, then lower oven temperature to 350°. Bake 40 minutes longer or until fruit is cooked. Cool on a rack. Then eat.

Pie Crusts

Since Sherrill Milnes has left it to us to provide a crust for his pie, we thought we'd offer you a choice of two. The first, a particular favorite of mine, came to me from Gretal Pomex, the mother of my dearest friend, Vivian, when we were just graduating from Music and Art. I remember visiting the Pomex household as a teenager and being as fascinated with Mr. Pomex's stamp collection and the homey baking aromas emanating from Mrs. Pomex's kitchen as Vivian was enchanted by my mother's oil paint, canvas stretchers, and exotic recipes for roast pork. Pork was unheard of in the Pomex home and any pie found in our kitchen had been born in a bakery. It wasn't until I found out how easy this crust was to make—just three ingredients—that I dared to try it myself. I had a perfect pie the first time out! It's delectably buttery and reminds me of the best Viennese tart crusts I've ever tasted.

The second crust we've included comes to us from Jean Galton. It's a bit more American-traditional and, in its own way, lighter and flakier than the cream cheese and butter crust of Gretal Pomex. It reminds me of the pie crusts I've tasted in friends' homes and have never been able to recreate on my own. Now you and I have the proper recipe.

Gretal Pomex's
Viennese-Style Pie Crust

MAKES ONE 8- OR 9-INCH
SINGLE CRUST

1 stick (¹/₄ pound) unsalted butter,
softened
1 (3 ounce) package cream cheese,
softened

1 cup unbleached flour

1   In a large mixing bowl cream together the butter and cream cheese. Stir in flour. (Alternatively, put butter and cream cheese in a food processor and pulse to combine. Then add flour and pulse until dough comes together.) Chill 30 minutes. Roll out to fit pie plate.

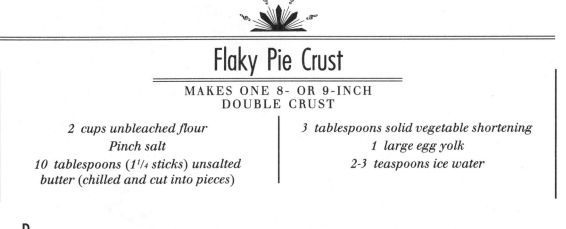

Flaky Pie Crust

MAKES ONE 8- OR 9-INCH
DOUBLE CRUST

2 cups unbleached flour
Pinch salt
10 tablespoons (1¹/₄ sticks) unsalted
butter (chilled and cut into pieces)

3 tablespoons solid vegetable shortening
1 large egg yolk
2-3 teaspoons ice water

1   Place flour and salt in a large mixing bowl and mix well. Cut in butter and shortening with a pastry cutter or knife until it resembles crumbs. Stir in egg yolk and ice water. (Alternatively, place flour and salt in food processor, pulse to mix. Add butter and shortening and pulse until mixture forms crumbs. Add egg and ice water as needed until dough comes together.) Chill 30 minutes. Divide in half and roll out to fit pie plate.

Jarmila Novotna

JARMILA
NOVOTNA
IN *HELEN
GOES TO TROY*

"Magic brought me to America," Jarmila Novotna says with a smile. "In 1937 I sang the part of Pamina in Mozart's *Magic Flute* with Toscanini in Salzburg. The next year, Hitler began his march and Toscanini left Europe in anger. When he came to the United States, he invited me to come to New York to sing.

"My manager was at the pier to meet us when we arrived from Czechoslovakia and he was in a terrible state," the great soprano remembers. "He told me that they couldn't get any singers because of the war and they needed a soprano right away for *Traviata* and *Butterfly* in San Francisco. Well, there I was with my husband, our two children, and the nurse. I told him it was impossible. But my husband and I talked it over and decided to leave the children in New York and we immediately got on the train for California.

"The day after I made my debut in *Butterfly*, the manager called again and told me that Bidu Sayao had the mumps. She couldn't sing *Bohème* in St. Louis and he wanted me to fly off to St. Louis and take her place. Well, I was afraid of flying," the soprano admits. "I'd never flown before. But my husband and I said, okay, we go. And we flew that evening, already in the dark. I settled in my seat, looked out the window after we took off and saw this flashing red light on one wing and a flashing green light on the other. I turned to my husband and said, 'This America is really something! They have traffic lights in the sky!' "

Jarmila Novotna returned to New York to make her Carnegie Hall debut on December 2, 1939, in Beethoven's Ninth with Toscanini and the NBC Symphony. Finally, three years later, she returned to the hall to sing for the first time with the New York Philharmonic. The conductor on that occasion was Artur Rodzinski and the program was devoted to Berlioz's *Damnation of Faust.* One of the other soloists that evening was Ezio Pinza.

The soprano's husband, Baron George Daubek, provided so well for his family that it was only recently that his wife had the opportunity to learn to cook. "First we stayed in hotels in New York. And then we moved to Park Avenue and the first thing my husband did was hire a cook and a maid. I was terribly busy at the time, anyway, so it's just as well. And before performances I always ate very lightly. Just some tea and perhaps some bread and butter."

But now the soprano has begun cooking. "And my husband makes the best risotto in the world." We think you'll enjoy this Christmas bread, too. And, while it's lovely to make it for the holiday, the bread is guaranteed not to explode if you make it for the Fourth of July. But no matter what time of year you choose to bake this recipe, you'll need the voice of Jarmila Novotna to accompany you. Begin with the historic 1939 recording of Beethoven's Ninth with the NBC Symphony and Arturo Toscanini (Nuova Era 6-2243/48). Then listen to a varied program of arias by Smetana, Dvořák, Fibich, Offenbach, Mozart, Verdi, and even some Czech folksongs—all sung by Miss Novotna (Pearl 2-261/2).

Vanočka
(Christmas Bread)

MAKES 1 VERY LARGE LOAF

1¹/₂ cups milk	7-8 cups unbleached flour
1 cup sugar	2 sticks (¹/₂ pound) unsalted butter,
2 packets active dry yeast	softened and cut into pieces
1 teaspoon freshly grated lemon zest	1 cup raisins
1 teaspoon salt	1 egg yolk
2 large eggs	1 tablespoon water

1   Heat milk to about 100°. Stir in sugar and sprinkle in yeast. Let sit 10 minutes until yeast bubbles. Stir in lemon zest, salt, and eggs, and mix well.

2   Meanwhile, place 7 cups flour in a large mixing bowl or the bowl of a heavy-duty mixer. Cut in butter until it resembles crumbs. Pour in milk mixture and beat until dough is smooth and stops sticking to bowl (add additional flour if needed). Knead by hand 10 minutes or with an electric dough hook 5 minutes. Place in a clean bowl, cover, and let rise 2 hours.

3   Place dough on board and knead in raisins. Knead 5 minutes more. Divide in half. Divide one portion into 4 equal parts and roll into 14-inch lengths. Braid together and place on a greased cookie sheet. Divide the remaining dough into 2 parts. Cut one portion into 3 equal parts, roll into 12-inch lengths, and braid. Place next to first braid. Divide remaining dough into 2 equal parts, roll into 9-inch lengths, and twist together. Place alongside the other braids, cover with a cloth, and let rise in a warm place 2 hours.

4   Preheat oven to 350°. Uncover and place the largest braid diagonally on cookie sheet. Place the 12-inch braid on top and anchor with toothpicks to prevent sliding. Repeat with remaining twist and again anchor with toothpicks. Mix the egg yolk with the tablespoon of water and brush over entire loaf. Bake 50 to 55 minutes or until a cake tester inserted comes out clean. Remove to a rack and cool.

NOTE: To make this into Easter bread (Mazanec), make 3 loaves out of the dough, brush with the egg yolk and cut a cross on the top of each. Bake in greased loaf tins about 50 minutes, or until cake tester inserted in middle comes out clean.

Russell Oberlin

It's certainly fitting that Russell Oberlin, world-class countertenor and musician, should send us a recipe for Iced Caviar Surprise. Caviar and "class" are somewhat synonymous and Russell Oberlin's singing is certainly in a "class" by itself. It's also very, very classy. This is a performer whose every note has been perfectly placed and whose sound is so rare, so delicious, that it's carried him through a concert and recording career that is the envy of many a singer. This is a soloist whose presence in an oratorio or cantata with the Philharmonic of the fifties and sixties was a must. Why use a female alto when you could have the rich, pure sounds of Russell Oberlin?

Countertenors are a rare breed. It's not like in the old days, thank goodness, where they removed part of a male's anatomy so he might retain the fresh, high tones that would otherwise be lost upon reaching puberty. Today's male altos are singing in that range by choice, not castration.

It is, however, surprising to hear the sound we associate with a female emanating from a male. It's a little like drinking wine from a glass when you've expected beer. It's jolting at first and then quite nice.

Russell Oberlin doesn't want us to be surprised at the high cost of caviar, so he suggests that we use "an assortment of 'cheap' caviar, though what," he asks rhetorically, "is cheap these days?

"I use black lumpfish, red salmon, and golden whitefish." He chooses these because of their different colors. It makes the dish particularly attractive.

Because this is so obviously a party dish, Russell Oberlin's recording of Elizabethan and Jacobean Ayres, Madrigals, and Dances with the New York Pro Musica seems an apt choice (MCA 2502). For the caviar, go back to the movie soundtrack of *High Society* to hear Frank Sinatra and Celeste Holm sing "Who Wants to Be a Millionaire?" Remember the words? "Who wants to drive a foreign car? I don't. Who wants to tire of caviar? I don't!" (Cap. SW-12235).

Iced Caviar Surprise

SERVES 6

1 (10½ ounce) can jellied beef
consommé
1 (8 ounce) package cream cheese
3 teaspoons each assorted "cheap"
caviars such as black lumpfish, red
salmon, and golden whitefish

Pumpernickel or dark rye triangles

1   In electric blender combine consommé and cream cheese. Blend until smooth and pour into six 4-ounce ramekins. Cover each with plastic wrap and chill at least 3 hours or overnight. When ready to serve put a small dollop of caviar—about ½ teaspoon—of each type (I use three because the different colors look nice) on top of each ramekin. Serve immediately with pumpernickel or dark rye triangles.

William Parker

It was on May 12, 1977, that William Parker made his debut with the New York Philharmonic in Berlioz's "Damnation of Faust" with Jessye Norman, Kenneth Riegel, Justino Diaz, the Westminster Choir, and a trio of boys' choirs all under the direction of Pierre Boulez. While this performance was a memorable occasion for Will, the months he spent studying with Rosa Ponselle are the real highlight of his life. They're so important to him, in fact, that he named a recipe after the legendary soprano. And, while he takes those lessons very seriously, he enjoys laughing at his creation.

"It's about as silly a concoction as one can make for dessert," he chortles. But each part of this dessert has a meaning. "The toasted almonds represent the darkness of her voice. In fact, they said her voice was pure gold.

"The red strawberries signify her rich, deep sound. She had the power of two people! And the meringue is light and fluffy, just like the cloud on which she came down from heaven."

Obviously, Rosa Ponselle was important to William Parker. "I only worked with her for six or eight months but it was a wonderful time and I loved every moment of it. She sang at every lesson. Imagine!"

Now the baritone travels from country to country and from city to city giving concerts. But he has a problem when he's away from home. "I'm allergic to onions," he protests. "Onions, shallots, leeks, and even scallions. So, when I'm out, it's very hard to order food. I've trained some restaurants to serve me food without any of these things. There's a restaurant just outside of Lyons, for instance. Madame Point knows me now and when I visit there she says, 'Ah! Naked salad and dessert.' She's right. There's not much else to eat. And I've even bribed an Indian woman to make me chutney and curry without onions.

"When I'm in New York and I order out for Chinese food, I call my local Empire Szechuan and, as soon as they hear my voice, they know—No Onions! I think one of the reasons I began cooking was out of self-preservation. I know what I put into the food." And what he doesn't, too!

When you're eating Will's Strawberries Rosa, partner this culinary reminiscence of Rosa Ponselle with music sung by the soprano. She recorded an album of arias and songs by Verdi,

Bellini, Rubinstein, Dvořák, and Foster between 1923 and 1929 and, if you can find this classic, you'll understand William Parker's admiration for the great soprano (Pearl 207). Pair Ponselle with Parker: Songs by Ives, Chanler, Dello Joio, Fine, and Ward (New World 300).

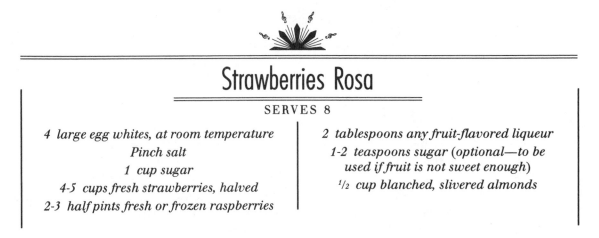

Strawberries Rosa

SERVES 8

4 large egg whites, at room temperature	2 tablespoons any fruit-flavored liqueur
Pinch salt	1-2 teaspoons sugar (optional—to be
1 cup sugar	used if fruit is not sweet enough)
4-5 cups fresh strawberries, halved	1/2 cup blanched, slivered almonds
2-3 half pints fresh or frozen raspberries	

1 Pick a nice dry day and preheat oven to 200°. Line a large baking sheet with parchment paper or brown paper and trace 8 three-inch circles about 2 inches apart. Grease baking sheet lightly to stick the paper down.

2 In a large clean mixing bowl beat egg whites and salt with an electric mixer until stiff peaks form. Slowly add sugar while beating constantly until stiff peaks form again. Transfer whites to a pastry bag fitted with a 1/2-inch star tip. Pipe 2 tablespoons of meringue in the middle of each circle and spread with a spatula (if you don't have a pastry bag use a tablespoon). Pipe two rings of meringue (one on top of each other) around the edge of each circle to form walls. Make sure the edges touch the middle to form a sealed shell (if using a tablespoon, just push middle meringue outward and heap up to form walls). Bake 1 to 2 hours or until completely dry.

3 Place strawberries in a large mixing bowl. Set a fine sieve over bowl and with a wooden spoon or ladle, mash the raspberries through, leaving the seeds behind. Mix in the liqueur and the sugar if using. Stir well and let sit 1 hour.

4 Heat a small skillet over medium heat and add the almonds. Cook stirring, until lightly browned, about 6 minutes. Remove to a small bowl.

5 Place each meringue shell on a serving plate and fill with about 1/4 cup of the strawberry mixture. Sprinkle each with 1 teaspoon of the almonds and serve immediately.

Luciano Pavarotti

Several years ago, George Lang, the Hungarian-born restaurateur, author, design consultant, and musician, gave a party in his spectacular New York apartment to prove a point. The Metropolitan Opera was premiering a new production of *La Bohème* and "the man who invents restaurants," as George has been called in *Fortune* magazine, set out to prove that when you put two or more singers together in any one place for any length of time, pasta will suddenly appear in bountiful amounts of mouth-watering configurations.

The singers he gathered included two of the *Bohème* stars, Luciano Pavarotti and Renata Scotto. And the dinner George Lang presented included recipes by these spectacularly vocal pasta buffs.

George's point got proven but, in the course of the experiment, the point was somewhat obscured by mounds of delectable dishes, magnums of fine wines, and conversation that encompassed the worlds of music and food.

The late Robert Jacobson wrote of this enriched evening in *Opera News*, "Pavarotti's origins are in Reggio Emilia, the food center of Italy, with Bologna as its capital. He was raised in Modena and savors the rich *tortellini alla panna*, twisted pasta with cream, cheese, and butter," and here he went on to quote the great tenor, who said, "but deduct the calories, please."

The world has had its pasta consciousness raised over the last ten years or so. We now know that, by itself, pasta, whatever its shape or size, needn't change our dimensions. It is not at all high in calories and it has little or no fat. It's the cream and the cheese and the butter that threaten our waistlines and blow up our hips. So the recipe we have from Luciano Pavarotti (courtesy of Jenifer Lang) is ideal for a weight reduction diet and terrific for anyone watching cholesterol.

If you want to make it even lower in calories, reduce the amount of oil. While it's true that olive oil has established itself as being good for the heart, it is still oil. And all oil has the same number of calories. Lots! I make this dish for myself very often, especially in the summer, when tomatoes are juicy and sweet. Because I am always watching my weight, I omit the oil entirely and the dish tastes great.

Best of all, since the only thing you cook is the pasta, this is an extremely easy dish. While the spaghetti or linguini is cooking, I put all the raw ingredients in an attractive bowl and then, when the pasta is al dente and drained, I spoon it on top of the "sauce," add a turn or two more of fresh ground pepper and a dash of freshly grated Parmesan cheese and that's it. Luciano Pavarotti has been known to cook this up in his hotel room when he's on tour.

To add to the pasta–Pavarotti ambience, begin with an album featuring the tenor called *My Own Story* (2-Lon. PAV-2007). If you have a fish course after your pasta, play Pavarotti's *King of the High C's* (Lon. 26373). And, for the simple pleasure and passion of pasta, try Pavarotti's *Passione* (Lon. 417117-1).

Summer Pasta with No-Cook Sauce

SERVES 2

1 large tomato, peeled, seeded, and
cut into $1/2$-inch dice
$1/4$ cup olive oil
$1/4$ cup basil or Italian parsley, shredded
1 garlic clove, cut in half

$1/2$ teaspoon salt
$1/2$ teaspoon pepper
$1/4$ pound pasta

1   In a large serving bowl, combine all ingredients except the pasta. Mix well and set aside while preparing the pasta.

2   Bring a large pot of salted water to a boil and cook pasta al dente according to package directions. Remove garlic halves from tomato mixture. Drain pasta and add to mixing bowl. Toss well and serve hot or at room temperature.

Roberta Peters

"I have a lady who cooks for us," Roberta Peters admits. "But I usually stand over her." The soprano, who made her official debut with the New York Philharmonic in 1964 when Sir Joseph Krips led her and the orchestra in an all-Viennese program that included Adele's "Laughing Song" from *Die Fledermaus*, remembers an even earlier performance. And that one had a reception.

"It was sometime in the early fifties, I think. And it was a benefit concert that Bernstein conducted. I know that Jan Peerce and Robert Merrill were there and there was a big party for all of us afterward." Both the menu and the program are long forgotten.

Meanwhile, Roberta Peters's eating habits have changed over the years. "I used to insist on eating a steak before a performance but I've come to the conclusion that it was a big mistake. Now I have some protein like chicken or fish with some vegetables about three hours before I sing. I keep it light. After a concert or an opera I love to go out and enjoy that After-Concert Glow.

"My husband, Bertram [Fields], hates big parties but I love them. So we compromise and give dinners for six or eight people and then, once a year, we go all-out and have a lot of people over."

When we spoke, Roberta was planning her son's wedding. "He's getting married in the spring and we're having the reception in our garden. We're expecting about two hundred twenty-five people." That's big. "But we just bought a home in Florida, so from now on most of our entertaining will be done down there.

"I still travel quite a bit, of course, and I have some really favorite restaurants around the country." What's her favorite city? "San Francisco," she answers immediately. "Ernie's is a terrific restaurant out there. And, of course, almost all the Chinese restaurants. I just love Chinese food.

"When I used to tour with the Met in the spring, we had some really wonderful meals because they always booked us into the best restaurants in town. San Antonio has a great Mexican restaurant right on the river. And, in Boston, we like to go to Durgin Park, or I should say 'Pahk' the way they do up there."

Roberta Peters's recipe for Noodle Pudding is better than any I've ever tasted. (Sorry,

Mama!) It's very firm but moist. And it's packed with a really delicious cinnamon flavor. This is not something to save for the holidays. And it's good warm or cold.

Roberta Peters's recording of Mozart's *Magic Flute* can also be served at any temperature and in any season (3-DG 2709017). And, just for fun, I'm sure the soprano would appreciate Joan Morris and William Bolcom as they make their way through *Yankee "Noodle" Blues*—just for us, you understand (Omega OCD 3004).

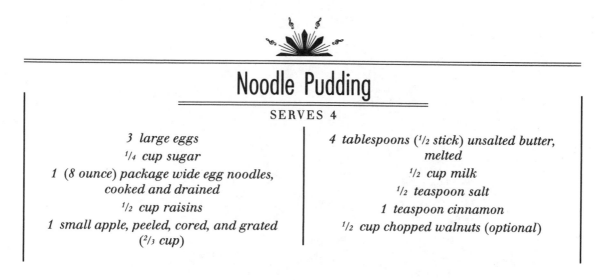

Noodle Pudding

SERVES 4

3 large eggs	4 tablespoons (¹/₂ stick) unsalted butter, melted
¹/₄ cup sugar	¹/₂ cup milk
1 (8 ounce) package wide egg noodles, cooked and drained	¹/₂ teaspoon salt
¹/₂ cup raisins	1 teaspoon cinnamon
1 small apple, peeled, cored, and grated (²/₃ cup)	¹/₂ cup chopped walnuts (optional)

1 Preheat oven to 350°. Grease a 2¹/₂-quart ovenproof casserole.

2 In a medium bowl whisk together eggs and sugar until well combined. Stir in remaining ingredients. Pour into prepared dish and bake 1 hour or until top is lightly browned and crisp. Serve warm or at room temperature.

Paul Plishka

DON CARLO WITH RENATA SCOTTO,
TATIANA TROYANOS, SHERRILL MILNES,
AND PAUL PLISHKA

"I don't know when you saw me last," Paul Plishka said recently on the telephone. "I've lost sixty-five pounds." The pride in the bass's voice is unmistakable, all the way from San Francisco. "I've become about ninety-five percent vegetarian and I really stay away from animal fat. I buy the best fruits and vegetables I can find and I grill them or stir-fry them. I stress the part about the best—the freshest, juiciest, most delicious—because I've found that when I eat something wonderful, I eat less. Give me fresh vegetables, marinated in a wonderful balsamic vinegar and then grilled on a wood fire and I'm completely happy!"

A larger Paul Plishka came to the New York Philharmonic as a soloist for the first time on January 14, 1971, for a performance of the Bruckner *Te Deum* in Philharmonic Hall with conductor Daniel Barenboim, soprano Sheila Armstrong, mezzo-soprano Janet Baker, and tenor Stuart Burrows. "That may have been my Philharmonic debut, but the event I remember best is singing Beethoven's Ninth in the parks of New York. We were sitting on the stage, waiting for the final movement to come so we'd have our turn to sing. And all these people were spread out in front of us eating these huge picnics. My throat was getting drier and drier and they were pouring more and more wine. I wanted to reach down and grab some."

Of course, Paul Plishka restrained himself and simply sang for his supper. His travels take him to many parts of the world, where he sings before and after his supper. But his favorite area, mainly because of its propensity for simple, fresh foods, is the South of France.

"At home I grow many of my own vegetables. But when I travel, I'm very choosy about what I have. And Provence is just wonderful. I still love my bruschetta. And it is made with olive oil, no animal fat. But I'd eat less of it. And I just might experiment with different kinds of oils to make it even healthier. I really feel great with those pounds off. I'm still a big man but there's a huge difference. The only thing is I'm driving the costume departments nuts!"

To accompany Paul Plishka's recipe for Bruschetta, we recommend the Overture to Rossini's *Il Signor Bruschino*, recorded by the NBC Symphony with Arturo Toscanini with other Rossini overtures performed between 1938 and 1951 (Relief CR 1884). And, for a change of pace, Massenet's *Le Cid*, recorded by Paul Plishka with the Opera Orchestra of New York in 1976 (CBS2-M2K-34211).

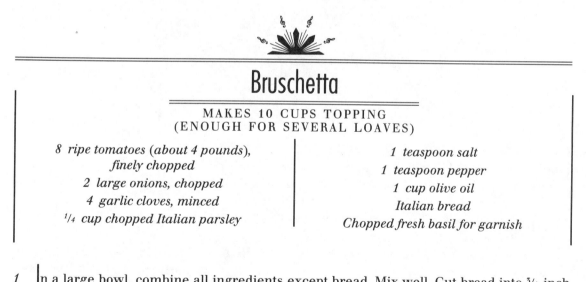

Bruschetta

MAKES 10 CUPS TOPPING
(ENOUGH FOR SEVERAL LOAVES)

8 ripe tomatoes (*about 4 pounds*), finely chopped

2 large onions, chopped

4 garlic cloves, minced

¼ cup chopped Italian parsley

1 teaspoon salt

1 teaspoon pepper

1 cup olive oil

Italian bread

Chopped fresh basil for garnish

1   In a large bowl, combine all ingredients except bread. Mix well. Cut bread into ¾-inch slices and toast or grill until brown and crispy. Spread with 2 to 3 tablespoons of tomato mixture and sprinkle with chopped fresh basil. Serve.

NOTE: This mixture stores well in the refrigerator. For best flavor, bring back to room temperature before using.

Beverly Sills

"I never met a meal I didn't like," quips Beverly Sills, soprano, fundraiser, administrator, talk show host, and author. Also known as "Bubbles," Beverly has one of those rare personalities that spreads joy to everyone around her.

"I loved singing with André Kostelanetz at the Promenade Concerts," the soprano recalls with enthusiasm. "The decorations in the hall were so pretty to sing to and everyone was so happy to be there." In fact, Beverly's debut with the Philharmonic was conducted by Kostelanetz, but it wasn't at a Promenade. It wasn't even in Philharmonic Hall. The date was February 4, 1961, and the place was Carnegie Hall, but it could easily have been a Promenade program: Chabrier's *España*, three dances from Falla's *Three-Cornered Hat*, Rimsky-Korsakov's *Capriccio Espagnol*. Lots of upbeat, toe-tapping music, familiar and fun, including "Una voce poco fa" from *The Barber of Seville*, sung, of course, by Beverly Sills.

But as festive as Beverly's debut with the Philharmonic may have been, nothing could beat the soprano's farewell concert some eighteen seasons later. Along with the performers who crowded the New York City Opera's stage, from Mary Martin and Carol Burnett to Beverly herself, there was an enormous, festive postconcert supper in a tent outside the New York State Theater at Lincoln Center. "It was so warm and festive with all the balloons and confetti." It's something the soprano will never forget, yet—typical of the spirited Beverly Sills, who puts the past behind her and steps right into the future—when asked when her farewell took place, she's a little vague. "I think it was 1979 or 1980."

There are, of course, parts of the past that aren't vague at all. "My mother did all the cooking when I was a child," is one indelible detail in Beverly's memory. And she's very clear about the person responsible for feeding her today. "Ona Power has been my 'everything' for thirty years," she tells us. "And, for formal parties, I have Remi Gautier."

Beverly Sills loves the food in New York City, at home and at restaurants. But, on the road, there's one city that's her favorite and she makes it very clear: "Paris, Paris, Paris." Any questions?

As to the Dutch Babies we've chosen for this book, Beverly Sills is a little unsure about the origin of the recipe. "I'm not really sure where it comes from," she confesses, "but it certainly makes for cozy Sunday breakfasts."

To accompany your Dutch Babies, listen to something sweet: music by Victor Herbert sung by Beverly Sills (Angel CDC-47197). And, after breakfast, for a spicy afternoon: *Mad Scenes and Other Bel Canto Arias* (Angel 4AV-34016).

Dutch Babies

SERVES 4

3 large eggs
¹/₂ cup unbleached flour
¹/₂ cup milk

¹/₂ teaspoon salt
3 tablespoons unsalted butter, melted

1 Place an 8- or 10-inch iron skillet in the freezer. Preheat oven to 450°.

2 Combine all ingredients except butter in blender. Blend at low speed 1 minute or until well combined. Pour melted butter in chilled skillet and swirl to coat. Pour in batter and bake 15 minutes. Reduce oven temperature to 350° and bake 10 minutes longer.

Serve with jam or stewed fruit, or with butter and maple syrup.

Gregg Smith and Roz Rees

The New York Philharmonic is always coming up with innovative and interesting ideas for presenting music, new and old. Over the last few decades, they've given us the Promenades, Rug Concerts, and Horizons. And, it was the Horizons '86 series, under the artistic direction of Jacob Druckman, that brought the Gregg Smith Singers to the Philharmonic. The conductors in Avery Fisher Hall the night of May 30 were Gunther Schuller and Gregg Smith, and the Singers performed *Trois Poèmes d'Henri Michaux* by Witold Lutoslawski.

The Gregg Smith Singers, a small ensemble of impeccably trained musicians who can read anything—upside down, sideways, and always on perfect pitch—specialize in choral music most other ensembles are afraid to touch. From the music of early America to works written the day before a performance and handed them with the ink still wet, this group has given us a legacy of choral literature.

Gregg Smith and Roz Rees, his wife and first soprano, have also given their friends a tradition. The couple was married in the late 1960s on Christmas Eve. Church jobs, for singers, conductors, and organists, often mean the disruption of home and hearth. But Gregg and Roz worked around their carols to take their vows. Thank goodness!

Every year since the wedding, a day or two before Christmas Eve and their anniversary, they've celebrated by throwing a party for an intimate hundred or so of their closest friends and colleagues. We're told that there will be a late supper. So, we arrive around nine P.M., vaguely hungry, having had a light, early dinner at home. A huge punch bowl filled with sparkling, lethal holiday cheer is the only thing in sight. So, by ten, we're gulping down cup after cup. We're stacked up on the couch, floor, piano bench, and against the walls—anything that serves to hold us up. And, somewhere around midnight, happily reeling from champagne and hunger, an enormous, seemingly bottomless pot of something smelling delicious comes out of the kitchen.

The resulting queue looks like a gigantic conga line with plates. Soon there's silence as we slurp down the dish of the year, prepared alternately by Gregg or Roz. But the highlight is yet to come.

Somehow, a pianist has freed the bench for himself. Gregg has found a place to stand

and be seen near the tree, we've all been given candles to hold and, between bites and swallows, one hundred or so voices—*good, professional* voices—are raised in "Joy to the World," "O Come All Ye Faithful," Handel's "Hallelujah Chorus" and, with tears to salt candle and stew, "Silent Night."

This celebration takes place every year. The food and the company change but the spirit is always the same. And the musicmaking is magnificent.

Sing along with the Gregg Smith Singers as they present songs by Stephen Foster with the New York Vocal Arts Ensemble (Vox/Turnabout CT-6409).

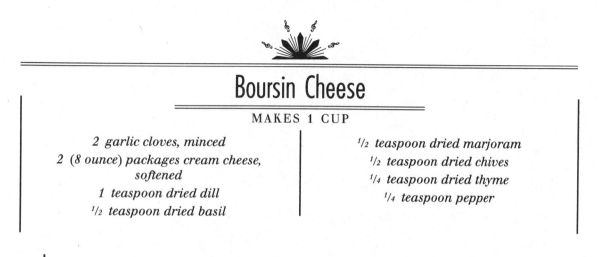

Boursin Cheese

MAKES 1 CUP

2 garlic cloves, minced

2 (8 ounce) packages cream cheese, softened

1 teaspoon dried dill

¹/₂ teaspoon dried basil

¹/₂ teaspoon dried marjoram

¹/₂ teaspoon dried chives

¹/₄ teaspoon dried thyme

¹/₄ teaspoon pepper

1 In a food processor or blender combine all ingredients. Pulse until well combined and refrigerate, covered, until ready to serve.

Risë Stevens

RISË STEVENS AND DARREN McGAVIN
IN *THE KING AND I*

"I'm a very good cook," Risë Stevens acknowledges with pride. The world famous mezzo-soprano has good reason to be a good cook. "I learned by absorbing what a lot of other really fine cooks did in their kitchens. I watched my father when I was a child. He was Norwegian and he did some really wonderful, fancy things with salmon and smorgasbord and cheese. My mother was no great cook, but she could get by with simple dishes like roasts.

"Later, when I got married and lived in Europe, I had a chance to watch my mother-in-law, and she made all sorts of Viennese and Hungarian dishes. I guess I learned from a lot of different places and put them all together. The important thing is knowing the way people like to eat and then catering to that style."

Like so many others, Risë Stevens's way of eating has changed over the years. "I used to eat the same thing before every performance, a nice steak and salad. And I'd follow that up with a great big piece of chocolate cake. Don't forget, I would lose five or six pounds every time I went on the stage and I just felt that eating that way gave me the energy I needed." Things are different these days. But her tastes haven't changed. "I love European cuisine, especially Czech and Hungarian. Yes, I like Chinese food but I can't stand Japanese. It's funny, too, since Norwegians use so much fish. But I'm used to a smoked flavor and the Japanese raw fish just doesn't suit me. I guess it's just a matter of taste."

Risë Stevens made her first appearance with the New York Philharmonic as a soloist in the Bach B minor Mass. "I was still a student at Juilliard at the time," she recalls, "and I don't remember too much else about it." But the mezzo-soprano will never forget another appearance she made with the orchestra. "I sang for the ground-breaking at Lincoln Center and that was quite an event. Eisenhower was there and so was my mother. It was very exciting. Leonard Warren was also singing," Miss Stevens remembers, "and I did excerpts from *Carmen.*

"I love people," the mezzo continues. "So events where I have a chance to meet others are very special to me. Of course, on tours when things got very hectic, I would skip the parties and receptions after performances. All I wanted was a glass of hot milk to make me relax. But if I didn't feel too tired I'd go out and enjoy myself. The parties they gave in the South always had Southern fried chicken. They make it in a way that's different from anyplace else and it's really wonderful."

Along with her work at the Metropolitan Opera and the Philharmonic here in New York, Risë Stevens also had the opportunity to make movies. She recalls her days playing opposite Bing Crosby. "Oh, he was a charming man but he was terribly nervous about playing the part of a priest. He wasn't sure how the public would accept him and it was very important to him. So he was kind of reserved and concentrated while we were actually filming. We got to know each other after the movie was over and I really enjoyed him. He was funny. He'd hear me sing and tell me that he'd better take voice lessons from me."

The Metropolitan Opera Guild has put out a series of red-jacketed records called *Great Artists at the Met.* Each disc features a legendary star of the Met in best loved roles with the company. The Risë Stevens recording includes, of course, her renowned performance of *Carmen* with excerpts from Acts 1, 2, and 4 dating back to early summer, 1951. There's also a duet with Ezio Pinza from Thomas's *Mignon* recorded on February 7, 1947. And, for the Viennese Boiled Beef and Miss Stevens's predilection for Viennese and Hungarian cooking, there's a legendary performance of excerpts from Strauss's *Der Rosenkavalier* with soprano Erna Berger and the RCA Victor Orchestra with Fritz Reiner dating from April 5, 1951. This record is probably very hard to come by and I apologize for whetting your appetite, but if you look for it, the number is MET-114. Good luck!

Viennese Boiled Beef

SERVES 8

3 carrots, cut into ¹/₂-inch chunks

2 onions, unpeeled, 1 cut in half

6 celery ribs, cut into 1-inch chunks

2 teaspoons salt

4 sprigs parsley

1 bay leaf

6 whole peppercorns

4 whole allspice

2 pounds chicken parts (necks, backs, wings)

4 pounds beef brisket

HORSERADISH SAUCE

3 tablespoons unsalted butter

3 tablespoons all-purpose flour

1¹/₂ cups beef bouillon or broth, heated

2 tablespoons prepared horseradish

1 tablespoon chopped fresh dill

1 Place carrots, the halved onion, celery, salt, parsley, bay leaf, peppercorns, allspice, and chicken parts in an 8-quart saucepot and cover with water (about 8 to 10 cups). Bring to a boil, skim off any scum, and simmer 2 to 3 hours.

2 Meanwhile, preheat oven to 350°. Place whole onion in a baking pan and bake 50 minutes or until soft.

3 When stock has simmered 2 to 3 hours, place beef in a large Dutch oven and strain stock over it. Add more water if necessary to cover beef. Add the baked onion, cover, and simmer 3 hours or until beef is very tender. Remove, slice, and serve with Horseradish Sauce, boiled potatoes, and creamed spinach.

4 To make sauce, melt butter in a small saucepot over medium heat. Whisk in flour and cook, stirring, about 1 minute. Add the heated bouillon and whisk until smooth and thickened, about 2 minutes. Stir in horseradish and dill.

Richard Tucker

B arry Tucker remembers, "My father loved good food and some of his favorite cities were Chicago, for the beef, Cincinnati, for the chili, and Miami for the ribs. *Beef* ribs, of course."

Richard Tucker, the great tenor, made his New York Philharmonic debut singing Mendelssohn's *Elijah*, with Mitropoulos conducting on April 10, 1952. His sons were small children at the time, but Barry remembers what his father did before a performance. Any performance. "Before singing, my father always drank hot tea. He'd have a light breakfast around eleven the morning of a performance and then just have tea all day. While he sang, he sucked on Vicks cough drops."

And after? "Well, after was when he really went to town. We all did. We'd leave the theater and go out for a big dinner. He loved spicy food," Barry adds. "He was crazy about the Cajun cooking in New Orleans. But when he sang out in the Northwest, San Francisco or Seattle, he'd send us these huge crates of fresh salmon. The fish were enormous."

The tenor was a man of enormous zest. He told big, funny stories. He entertained royally. And he never sang at home. Barry and his two brothers heard their father in concert halls, opera houses, and on the radio and television. "But home was home," Barry assures us. "He never mixed the two."

There was, of course, plenty of publicity. And, at times, the family would get caught up in it. "I remember one time," Barry says, "in those days when they put recipes up in trains and buses, they asked my mother for a dish under my father's name. She gave them something, but she inadvertently left out one of the ingredients." Barry smiles and adds, "Did we get a lot of mail!"

There are no ingredients left out of this recipe, provided by Barry with the assurance that this was one of his father's favorite things to eat. We suggest that if you listen to Richard Tucker's performance of *With These Hands* (MS-6767), you hold your face away from the food. Tears are salty! When you've recovered from that recording, move on to an entire album of nostalgia, also well worth the tears: *Richard Tucker in Memoriam: A Portrait of the Artist*, featuring live performances of thirteen arias recorded between 1950 and 1972 (Odyssey YT 35498).

Sweet and Sour Meatballs

MAKES ABOUT 100

2 *pounds ground round beef*
2 *large eggs*
²/₃ *cup plain bread crumbs*

1 *(10 ounce) jar grape jelly*
1 *(12 ounce) jar chili sauce*

1 In a large mixing bowl combine the ground round, eggs, and bread crumbs. Form into 1-inch ("quarter-size") meatballs. In a large saucepot combine the grape jelly and chili sauce. Over medium heat, stir until jelly has melted and add the meatballs. Stir gently, cover, and cook until done, about 45 minutes.

Dawn Upshaw

Dawn Upshaw has a very well-organized life. "When Michael [Nott] and I got married," she tells us, "we decided that each of us would take on certain responsibilities. We split the housekeeping and household chores, but, when it came to the cooking, Michael decided he wanted that one for himself. My reaction? Good!

"I don't cook very often," the soprano explains, "and when I do get into the kitchen it's mostly to do cakes and dips." Sounds like a song from *A Chorus Line*!

Dawn and Michael met while they were attending Illinois Wesleyan University. "He's a musicologist," she tells us. "Now we have a little girl, Sarah, who was born in 1989. I usually take my whole family with me when I travel, so I'm pretty lucky. There was only one time that I went away alone and that was for ten nights.

"I've done quite a bit of traveling. Can you imagine, I never had sushi before I went to Japan! It was really fun, too. I took one taste and I was just wild about it." Other places the soprano is wild about include Austria, for the desserts, "and everything in Italy," she confesses. "I eat normally before a performance because I like to get on stage feeling satisfied. I know some singers wait until after but, well, I guess I do both. I eat before *and* after. I just like to eat."

Dawn's debut with the New York Philharmonic came in 1991, during the Gala Concert that began the Mozart Year. "I sang an aria from *Idomeneo*. It was very exciting and a little strange, too, because Zubin was supposed to conduct but it was during the Gulf War so he went to Israel. Raymond Leppard took his place and it all went very well." In fact, that was quite an evening for everyone concerned. The concert officially opened the year's celebration of the music of Mozart and it was all televised on "Live From Lincoln Center." That's the way to make a debut!

Getting back to food, Dawn's dip recipe came to her from one of her closest friends in college. "Ann is a cellist and now she lives in Baltimore."

Dawn was the 1985 Naumburg Vocal Award Winner and, as a result, the Naumburg Foundation presented the soprano in recital on a recording from MusicMasters. There are a lot of lovely songs to "Dip" into on this disc, from a whole set by Hugo Wolf to a pair by Kurt Weill (MMD 60128L). Then there's Dawn Upshaw's performance of Barber's *Knoxville:*

Summer of 1915, but don't stop there. On the same recording, you'll find the sensuous, passionate aria "Steal Me, Sweet Thief," from Menotti's *The Old Maid and the Thief* (Elektra/Nonesuch 79187-1).

Dawn's Dip

SERVES 6

1 cup mayonnaise
1 cup grated Parmesan cheese
1 (9 ounce) package frozen artichoke hearts, thawed

¹/₄ teaspoon salt
¹/₂ teaspoon pepper
Whole wheat crackers

1 Preheat oven to 350°. In a small mixing bowl combine all ingredients except crackers. Place mixture in a 9-inch pie plate or small casserole and bake 30 minutes or until browned and bubbling. Serve hot or warm with whole wheat crackers.

Robert White

It was back in 1959 that the New York Philharmonic commemorated the 200th anniversary of the death of George Frideric Handel. The festival, with concerts in Carnegie Hall, included Handel's *Passion According to St. Paul.* And one of the singers scheduled to sing was countertenor Russell Oberlin. Mr. Oberlin, however, was indisposed. Enter Robert White.

"I was still a college student at Hunter," the tenor tells us. "I was walking down this long corridor at the school, about to go into the men's room, when I heard the dean shout, all the way from the end of the hallway, 'Robert White, Robert White, you can't go in there. You have to go to Carnegie Hall!' So I shouted back, 'Why? Do they have better bathrooms at Carnegie?'

"Anyway," Robert continues, "she told me that I had to go right to the hall to see Leonard Bernstein. 'They're doing the St. Paul Passion of Handel and Pontius Pilate is sick.' Well, that was a bombshell! She gave me a dollar for a taxi (you can see how long ago this was) and I reported right to Lenny in his dressing room."

The performance took place the following night. Robert got a fantastic review and caused quite a sensation as the countertenor of the day. But the occasion also had some bittersweet moments. "My father had died just three weeks earlier," Robert explains. "And the day before he died he said to me, 'I only hope I live long enough to hear you sing at Carnegie Hall.'"

Robert White's father was born in 1891, the same year Carnegie Hall opened. "Dad sang there dozens of times and, of course, he was one of the great pioneers of radio." Joseph White, also known as the Silver Masked Tenor, was quite a legend.

Robert's debut with the Philharmonic was certainly an auspicious occasion, but singing countertenor was not what he planned to do forever. "I gave it about two years and then decided it just wasn't for me. I was a tenor and I was afraid I'd hurt myself singing in a way that was just unnatural to me. In 1965, as I stood packing to leave for Fontainebleau on a full scholarship to work with Nadia Boulanger, the phone rang and it was Lenny. He said, 'I know you're working to sing like a manly tenor, but I want you to sing the high part in my *Chichester Psalms.*' I was flattered but I told him no. 'Not even for you, Lenny.'"

Enter Robert White, tenor. Major recording artist and concert singer with a wonderful command of language and music that makes him one of the most intelligent and exciting singers of the day. All this and he cooks, too. In fact, Robert is quite an entertainer. And his Green Sauce is a real treat with chicken, fish, or veal.

While cooking, serving, and eating Robert White's Green Sauce, the ideal musical accompaniment is almost any song from his recording of *Favorite Irish Songs of Princess Grace*. He starts with "Danny Boy" and serenades us with eighteen more, including "I'll Take You Home again, Kathleen," "My Wild Irish Rose," and a rousing rendition of "McNamara's Band" (Virgin Classics VC 7-90705-2). If you're having a more classic evening, turn to Robert's performance of Beethoven and Weber settings of Irish, Scottish, and Welsh songs with pianist Samuel Sanders, violinist Mark Peskanov, cellist Nathaniel Rosen, and flutist Ransom Wilson. Fittingly, the album is called *The Gallant Troubadour* (EMI CDC-7 47420 2).

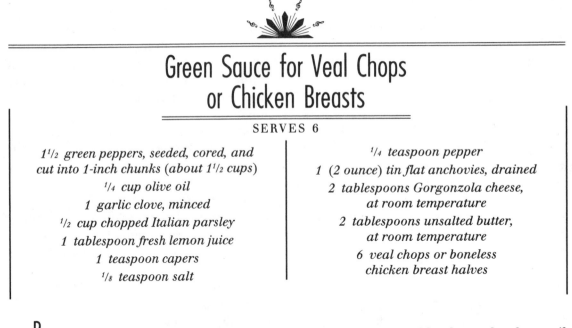

Green Sauce for Veal Chops or Chicken Breasts

SERVES 6

1¹/₂ green peppers, seeded, cored, and cut into 1-inch chunks (about 1¹/₂ cups)
¹/₄ cup olive oil
1 garlic clove, minced
¹/₂ cup chopped Italian parsley
1 tablespoon fresh lemon juice
1 teaspoon capers
¹/₈ teaspoon salt

¹/₄ teaspoon pepper
1 (2 ounce) tin flat anchovies, drained
2 tablespoons Gorgonzola cheese, at room temperature
2 tablespoons unsalted butter, at room temperature
6 veal chops or boneless chicken breast halves

1   Preheat broiler. Place first 9 ingredients in food processor or blender and pulse until smooth and well blended. In a small bowl, cream together Gorgonzola and butter.

2   Broil veal chops or chicken breasts 2 to 3 inches from source of heat, about 4 to 5 minutes per side or until done (depending on thickness of chops). Place about 1 teaspoon of Gorgonzola butter on each piece of meat and top with sauce.

Earl Wrightson and Lois Hunt

Earl Wrightson and Lois Hunt, the sensational singing pair, made careers both together and separately in the operatic arena and on the Broadway stage. Their recordings of love songs made them household legends in the years after Jeanette MacDonald and Nelson Eddy captured our ears and our hearts.

Wrightson and Hunt made their New York Philharmonic debut outdoors at the old Lewisohn Stadium at City College. Those were the days when the Philharmonic played its summer concerts in the confines of that outdoor arena, rather than in the parks. And the soloists and performances from those evenings under the gargoyles of the college made the series a legend.

Today, New Yorkers pride themselves on being seen with their picnic hampers on the Great Lawn of Central Park. It's not what you wear, it's what you eat. But in the earlier days of the Lewisohn Stadium concerts, you ate before or after the performance and you got dressed for the occasion. Outdoors or not, you got dressed to the teeth!

Although symphony concerts had taken place in the stadium as early as 1918, the Philharmonic was not officially ensconced as the orchestra of note until 1922. "Minnie" Guggenheimer was, if you'll excuse the expression, instrumental in raising the funds for these low-price outdoor concerts. In fact, as Howard Shanet writes in *Philharmonic: A History of New York's Orchestra*, Mrs. Guggenheimer continued "to raise money for season after season of Stadium Concerts throughout almost half a century."

Shanet also recalls a stadium concert that was attended by the Crown Prince of Sweden. "Minnie," as she loved to be called as she grew older, was preparing to introduce him to the audience. Shanet writes, "She invited him onstage by snapping her fingers and calling, 'Here, Prince, Prince!' "

Earl Wrightson and Lois Hunt were not introduced to the Lewisohn Stadium audience in quite the same manner. But they were roundly applauded and appreciated then, as they are to this day. The pair is currently singing and teaching the art of musical theater, something they know well, at the 92nd Street Y in New York. They impart their wisdom about diction, stage deportment, and movement and the necessity of appearing realistic on stage while singing a tune about the moon and a spoon.

Singing of spoons, it seems that Earl drives Lois a little crazy in the kitchen. "He's a typical male in that room. He goes to the market, buys everything we don't need, and then empties it, with great pride, all over the counters for me to put away." "But I'm a great cook," Earl counters. It makes you wonder how they ever crooned to each other so lovingly for so many years.

But they each have their specialties and they both love food. These Maryland Crab Cakes are favorites. They're light, slightly spicy, and hearty. While you sample one or two, take heart and listen to Earl as he sings "Stout-Hearted Men" (GPWH-5013). Then, if the food isn't enough to entice a wayward sweetheart back to your heart and hearth, play Lois Hunt's performance of "Lover, Come Back to Me" from this recording of songs by Sigmund Romberg and Rudolf Friml.

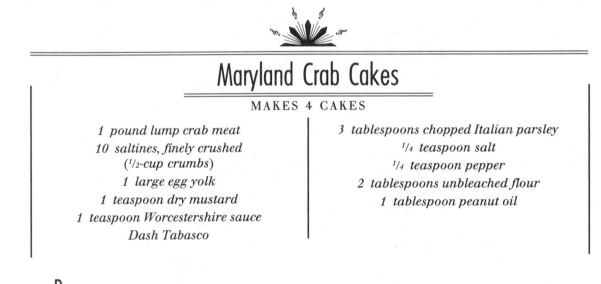

Maryland Crab Cakes

MAKES 4 CAKES

1 pound lump crab meat
10 saltines, finely crushed
(½-cup crumbs)
1 large egg yolk
1 teaspoon dry mustard
1 teaspoon Worcestershire sauce
Dash Tabasco

3 tablespoons chopped Italian parsley
¼ teaspoon salt
¼ teaspoon pepper
2 tablespoons unbleached flour
1 tablespoon peanut oil

1   Pick over crab meat, discarding any shell and cartilage. Place in a large mixing bowl and add the saltines, mixing well. In a small bowl, combine the egg yolk, mustard, Worcestershire, Tabasco, parsley, salt, and pepper. Mix well and gently stir into the crabmeat. Form into 4 cakes and dust with the flour.

2   Heat the peanut oil in a large skillet over medium high heat. Cook the cakes until golden brown, about 4 to 5 minutes, and turn with a spatula. Cook another 4 to 5 minutes and serve.

Other Voices

Martin and Janet Bookspan

There's a way that Martin Bookspan has of saying "the New York Philharmonic" that makes it sound different from anything else. Any other orchestra, any other city.

Martin Bookspan was the radio voice of the New York Philharmonic from 1975 until 1988, when the broadcasts were discontinued owing to lack of funding. We still hear him on the televised presentations "Live from Lincoln Center," of course. And his very sound will always be identified with the sound of the orchestra.

"The broadcasts didn't really change in style over the years. I tried to create a sense of being in the hall. Naturally I know what the program is going to be. But otherwise I never know what I'm going to say until I open my mouth," Marty explains, assuring us that during those minutes he fills while there's applause or the orchestra is tuning up, there is no script.

Neither was there a script one year when the Philharmonic traveled to Europe. "We were in Lucerne during the Jewish high holy days," Marty recalls. "Several of us went to Synagogue. It was Orthodox with the men downstairs, the women up. After the service, a lovely lady invited fourteen of us to eat at her house. Imagine! She found out we were from the United States and part of the New York Philharmonic. And she managed to feed fourteen more mouths on the spur of the moment."

This was not just some little impromptu snack, either. It was the traditional end of the fast. "We had chicken soup with matzo balls, chopped liver, brisket, fruit compote. The whole thing. And there were fourteen of us. Julius Baker, Manny Zegler, Nat Goldstein from the orchestra. Our daughter. It was spontaneous and we'll never forget it."

Closer to home, there was the party that introduced Marty's wife, Janet, to Syllabub. Janet Bookspan, a director and narrator in her own right, explains, "We were up in the Berkshires. Mary Thorne was in charge of Bernstein's household. And she ran Serenak, which was Serge and Natalie Koussevitsky's home at Tanglewood. She was a fantastic hostess and a really great cook. She knew I'd narrated a recording of the Walton *Façade* and she knew that one of the sections was titled 'Syllabub.' So she played it for the guests that night and then she served Syllabub for dessert!"

Follow Mary Thorne's example with Janet Bookspan's recording of Sir William Walton's *Façade*, conducted by David Epstein (Vox CT2257).

Syllabub

SERVES 10

2 (10 ounce) cans almond macaroons,
broken into pieces (about 5 cups)
6 tablespoons sugar
1/2 cup sweet sherry
1/2 teaspoon almond extract
1/2 teaspoon cinnamon
1/2 teaspoon grated lemon zest

1/4 cup lemon juice
2 cups heavy cream
1/2 cup toasted, slivered almonds
(optional garnish)
1/4 cup chopped candied cherries
(optional garnish)

1   Line a glass 5- to 6-cup serving bowl with the broken macaroons.

2   In a medium mixing bowl, combine the sugar, sherry, almond extract, cinnamon, lemon zest, and juice. In a separate mixing bowl with electric beaters or whisk, beat the cream until stiff. Fold cream into sherry mixture and pour over macaroons. Cover and refrigerate overnight. Decorate with almonds and cherries and serve.

"This recipe lends itself well to adaptations and additions—but what makes it special is the mixture of flavors of lemon, cinnamon, sherry, and almond," says Janet Bookspan.

Margo Feiden

Margo Feiden's book *The Calorie Factor*, published in 1989 by Simon & Schuster/Fireside, acknowledges among others, William Shakespeare and Ludwig van Beethoven for helping Margo "hold the fabric of my life together" in the twelve years she took to write the book. The fabric of the author's life is now woven intricately into the work of Al Hirschfeld, whose art she has represented and sold in the Margo Feiden Gallery for more than twenty years. The path that led her to that gallery is as unusual as her acknowledgments.

One day in 1969 she was on her way to meet a friend for lunch in Greenwich Village. She was walking on Tenth Street when she suddenly spied a space for rent. "What a wonderful spot for a gallery," she thought, and she made a mental note of the rental agent's phone number. As soon as she got to her friend's home she rushed to the phone, made an appointment with the landlord and, forty-five minutes later, had herself an art gallery. Or the space for one.

At first she showed photographs by her friend Diane Arbus. Then the artist Raphael Soyer moved in with a retrospective of his work. It was at this point that Al Hirschfeld came to the gallery to see the Soyer exhibition. According to an article in *The West Side Spirit*, a small New York newspaper, Hirschfeld was sidetracked from the art by a photograph of Margo "wearing goggles, an aviator scarf and standing in front of an airplane." The famous Hirschfeld asked her about the picture and Margo replied, "That's my hobby—I fly airplanes." He paused a moment to think and then said, "Any woman who can fly an airplane can sell my art." That proclamation began a long-term relationship between Hirschfeld and Feiden. The gallery remained in the Village for a while and then moved uptown to Madison Avenue.

Meanwhile, back at *The Calorie Factor*, Margo proceeded to practice what she'd printed and lost 150 pounds in fourteen months. "Calories are it," she swears. "Fat doesn't exist independent of calories and calories are the indicator of how much fat exists in food."

In 1988, calories, gallery, poetry, and music all came together when Margo married Julius Cohen, a Madison Avenue jeweler. "We flew our wedding guests out to the Southwest for a weekend," Margo tells us. "Our wedding took place at six A.M. under a eucalyptus tree in the desert surrounded by fifty human friends and a hundred and fifty coyotes. We chose to be married at sunrise because the desert is at its most magnificent then. We had a whole orchestra of doves and coyotes and all the morning prairie animals in full chorus.

"I wore a white Renaissance gown, train and all, and Julius was dressed in a beautiful light blue seersucker suit." There wasn't any calorie counting that weekend, though. "The night before the wedding we had a wonderful party with a Mexican-Southwestern flavor. And after the wedding we had a full breakfast that I had flown out from Murray's Sturgeon and Eli Zabar's EAT in New York."

To sing along with all those doves, coyotes, and humans at the sunrise wedding breakfast, we suggest Grofé's *Grand Canyon Suite* performed by the New York Philharmonic with Leonard Bernstein (CBS MY-37759). And, to sum it all up: "Food, Glorious Food" from *Oliver* (RCA AYL1-4113).

Lower-Calorie Guacamole

MAKES 8 SERVINGS OR 2 CUPS

2 cups chopped, steamed asparagus
  or green beans
2¼ teaspoons lemon juice
3 tablespoons chopped onion
1 large tomato, chopped
¾ teaspoon salt (optional)
½ teaspoon chili powder
¼ teaspoon cumin

¼ teaspoon black pepper
¾ teaspoon minced garlic
Dash Tabasco
⅓ cup sour cream (preferably
  reduced calorie)
8 large lettuce leaves
16 cherry tomatoes, halved

1 Combine all ingredients except lettuce and tomatoes in a food processor or blender. Process until smooth. Transfer to a bowl and chill several hours or overnight.

2 To serve, line 8 salad plates with lettuce leaves. Add ¼ cup guacamole and garnish with 4 cherry tomato halves. Serve with tortilla chips.

Nimet Habachy

The name Nimet is as soothing as decaffeinated coffee to New York night owls and insomniacs who must have their classical music to make it through to dawn. This Egyptian-born Scheherazade serves radio audiences more than the usual menu of musical fare on WQXR's "New York at Night." More often than not the program is interspersed with colorful readings in fluent French, Italian, or British-accented English pouring from a deep cello-like voice tinted with a touch of honey.

Nimet weaves her music around a nightly theme, such as colors (*The Red Poppy*, *The Blue Danube*, *The Love for Three Oranges*, and an opera by Joseph Green, aka Giuseppe Verdi); or travel (*Calm Sea and Prosperous Voyage*, *Années de pèlerinage*, *España*, the *Grand Canyon Suite*, and a *New England Tryptich*); or, quite often, historic events such as wars and revolutions (*Andrea Chénier*, *War and Peace*, *1812 Overture*, and *The Battle of the Huns*).

WQXR'S SHEHERAZADE OF THE NIGHT

As befits the Pearl Mesta of WQXR, Nimet's parties also have themes. There are bicycle brunches, elegant evening soirées, play readings, and old-movie marathons, with occasional sit-down dinners for an "intimate" eighteen at a new and highly polished antique-style table. "It has too many legs," Nimet complains. "When I seat people, I ask them to raise their hands if they have a leg. Seventeen hands shoot up."

But every meal shares one item: Baba Ghannoush. Like the Rahadlakum that Hadj the Beggar sings about in Wright and Forrest's *Kismet*, Nimet's Baba Ghannoush is "the kind of confection that drives a man out of his Mesopotamian mind." If you like garlic, you'll be wild about this recipe. Just don't eat it before attending a Philharmonic concert or you'll find yourself alone with your Mesopotamian breath.

For Nimet, the spinner of night-time music, we suggest the New York Philharmonic's recording of Rimsky-Korsakov's *Scheherazade* (Bernstein—CBS MY-38476). And, to accompany you while preparing Nimet's Baba Ghannoush, we recommend the Philharmonic's performance of "Baba Yaga" (a distant cousin, by marriage, twice removed from Baba Ghanoush) from Mussorgsky's *Pictures at an Exhibition* (CBS MYK 36726).

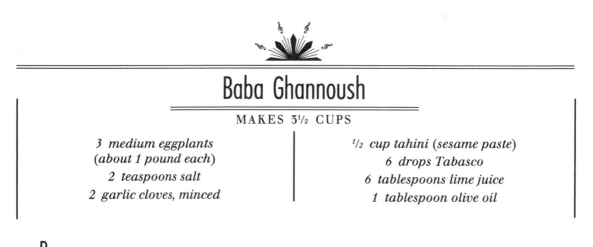

Baba Ghannoush

MAKES 3½ CUPS

3 medium eggplants	*½ cup tahini (sesame paste)*
(about 1 pound each)	*6 drops Tabasco*
2 teaspoons salt	*6 tablespoons lime juice*
2 garlic cloves, minced	*1 tablespoon olive oil*

1   Preheat oven to 400°. Cut eggplants in half lengthwise, place on baking sheets, and sprinkle with 1½ teaspoons salt. Bake 45 minutes or until very soft. Cool on sheets. Scrape pulp from skins and reserve.

2   In a food processor or blender, place garlic, tahini, remaining salt, Tabasco, lime juice, and olive oil. Process until well mixed and add eggplant. Pulse until mixed but do not purée (baba tastes better if it is not too smooth).

Serve with heated pita bread or on grilled meats.

Kitty Carlisle Hart

"I don't know where the kitchen is in my house. I'm a singer and actress, not a cook," says Kitty Carlisle Hart without a trace of remorse in her voice. And without any guilt she adds, "I love to eat, though." The singer, actress, author, sought-after speaker, and chairman of the New York State Council on the Arts hails from New Orleans, so when it comes to food, she's not been kept from the best.

"My mother was born on a cotton plantation and, when I was growing up, we had ladies cook for us who were from that plantation. They really knew how to cook. We used to have these wonderful long French baguettes, sliced lengthwise and filled with fried oysters. In those days we still had river shrimp because nothing was polluted. On Sundays we'd have great big soup plates with cracked ice underneath just filled to the brim with fresh river shrimp.

"We had an icebox but there wasn't much in the way of refrigeration, so there were lots of sauces. Of course, most of the food was based on French recipes anyway, so the sauces were there. And the shellfish!" she exclaims. "We had wonderful crawfish bisque, very spicy and rich and delicious. The coffee was strong in those days. My mother used to say that if the spoon didn't stand upright it was no good."

With all those mouth-watering memories of meals, it's amazing that Kitty Carlisle Hart isn't as round as a cotton ball. "I have to watch my weight," she admits. "I weigh myself every morning and, if I'm a little off, I just watch it."

Mrs. Hart's association with the New York Philharmonic is both business and pleasure. While she's never performed—that is, sung or acted—with them, she has appeared countless times to host an event, make a speech, fundraise, or introduce a performance. "Since I'm chairman of the New York State Arts Council, I almost always introduce the opening concert in the city parks. I welcome people and tell them how wonderful it is for the city to have this cultural gem and how important it is to continue these free outdoor performances."

In addition to the wonderful picnics enjoyed by the crowds at these summertime events, there are often receptions held before or after the opening concert for friends and family of the Philharmonic. Salmon mousse à la Hart would be perfect at one of these events, and it would certainly set the right tone for any indoor party you were planning. This recipe comes to us from Pilar Miguel, Mrs. Hart's cook and housekeeper since 1973.

The proper music for this celebration should include a recording of the Marx Brothers' *A Night at the Opera*, with Kitty Carlisle. It's no longer in print but if you can find it, or a video of the movie, that should be the centerpiece of your party. With Kitty's mousse, serve music by Modest "Moussorgsky" (which happens to be the way his name is spelled in several older texts). Since the mousse may be served as a prelude to the meal, I suggest the Prelude to *Khovanshchina* (London 414139-2). And, in honor of Kitty Carlisle, opera singer, a taste of the opera she's performed so often, Johann Strauss's "Die Fleder*mousse*" (Eurodisc 258-369).

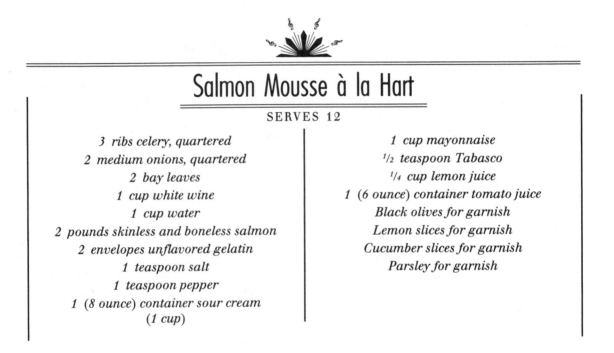

Salmon Mousse à la Hart

SERVES 12

3 ribs celery, quartered	1 cup mayonnaise
2 medium onions, quartered	1/2 teaspoon Tabasco
2 bay leaves	1/4 cup lemon juice
1 cup white wine	1 (6 ounce) container tomato juice
1 cup water	Black olives for garnish
2 pounds skinless and boneless salmon	Lemon slices for garnish
2 envelopes unflavored gelatin	Cucumber slices for garnish
1 teaspoon salt	Parsley for garnish
1 teaspoon pepper	
1 (8 ounce) container sour cream	
(1 cup)	

1   In a large saucepot over high heat, place celery, onions, bay leaves, white wine, and water. Bring to a boil, cover, and reduce heat to low. Simmer 10 minutes. Add salmon, cover, and barely simmer 8 to 10 minutes or until salmon is just cooked. Remove salmon with a slotted spoon and set aside.

2   In a small bowl soften gelatin in 1/4 cup cold water. Strain hot stock into medium bowl and stir in softened gelatin. Place all ingredients (including stock) in a food processor and pulse until smooth. Ladle into an 8-cup fish mold and chill 4 hours or until firm. Unmold onto serving plate and decorate using olive rounds for eyes, lemon and cucumber slices as gills and scales. Garnish with fresh parsley and serve with bread or crackers.

George Jellinek

Geeorge Jellinek, music director of WQXR for many years and the creator and host of the syndicated, award-winning "Vocal Scene" since the first Thursday of 1969, is, in his wife Hedy's words, "typically Hungarian."

Hedy tells us, "I grew up in Vienna and Bavaria and we had all the traditional food of the area. As a child I had coffee for breakfast. We came home from school at one o'clock and had our big meal of the day. Too big," she adds. "We had lots of meat, poultry, roast goose for holidays. Venison was indigenous to the area. And my father, a conductor with his own orchestra, loved Norwegian fish. My mother couldn't stand it."

George, on the other hand, was much more Hungarian. "He ate lots of pasta and noodle-type dishes. And his favorite dish of all time is still poppy seed noodles." Hedy will give only an approximate rendition of the recipe: "You've got to butter the noodles and then cover it all with a mixture of poppy seeds, sugar, and lemon rind."

Better than poppy seeds, even with sugar and lemon rind, is the way George and Hedy met, fell in love, and married. Hedy divulges that story without any hesitation.

"George arrived in the U.S. on my birthday, March 17, 1941. He came with my two cousins and they brought him to my house that very day. He didn't speak much English then but we got along." They must have gotten along very well, indeed, because they were married one year later, on July 29. "Our wedding was in St. Louis. He was in the army."

The Jellineks have been a team ever since. And they are ones of a kind. George is probably the only person in a radius of five hundred miles who owns a Spanish-Hungarian dictionary and Hedy is certainly the only person I've ever met who knows all the words to the choruses in the Triumphal Scene from Verdi's *Aida* in Hungarian. "And I'm not even Hungarian," she adds.

The Jellineks travel quite a bit, from the American West Coast to a variety of European capitals. "We both love the food in Italy," George tells us. "Rome, Florence, Milano. And Switzerland has very good food, too. Of course, the Vienna State Opera has elegant buffets during the intermissions where you can get some wonderful food."

George Jellinek's life revolves around his wife and the voice. Whose voice? No one voice in particular, but he's fascinated with the instrument itself—with singers, with the music for singers. His record collection is both legion and legendary. And his association with singers is cherished by every performer he's met. Of course, singers' passion for food is as famous as the Jellinek archives.

"Sandor Konya was a particularly terrific cook. He made highly spiced Hungarian food," George says with a look of regret. "I used to like spicy food, but now I stay away for health reasons. I must have had an iron stomach."

Poppy seed noodles don't sound spicy. "Poppy seeds are a passion," exults George. "Not a hobby."

For George's passion, try Glière's *The Red Poppy* with the Bolshoi Theater Orchestra (Melodiya MCD-202). And, for Hedy's Paprika Chicken, Kodaly's *Peacock Variations*, with the Hungarian State Orchestra and Antal Dorati (Hungaroton SLPX-11392).

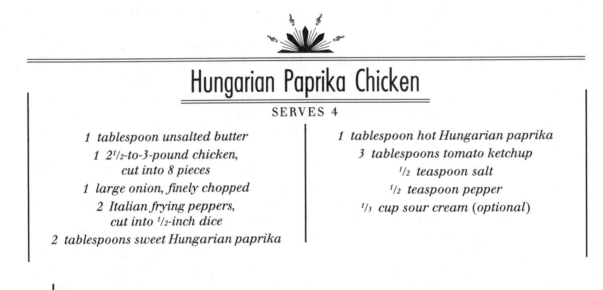

Hungarian Paprika Chicken

SERVES 4

1 tablespoon unsalted butter

1 2¹/₂-to-3-pound chicken,
cut into 8 pieces

1 large onion, finely chopped

2 Italian frying peppers,
cut into ¹/₂-inch dice

2 tablespoons sweet Hungarian paprika

1 tablespoon hot Hungarian paprika

3 tablespoons tomato ketchup

¹/₂ teaspoon salt

¹/₂ teaspoon pepper

¹/₃ cup sour cream (optional)

1 In a large skillet, heat butter over medium high heat. Add chicken and brown well, about 4 to 5 minutes per side. Remove and add onion and peppers. Cook, stirring, until soft, about 4 minutes. Return chicken to skillet and add all remaining ingredients except sour cream. Add ¹/₂ cup water, stir well, and cover. Lower heat to a simmer and cook until chicken is tender, about 40 minutes. If desired, stir in sour cream and remove from heat.

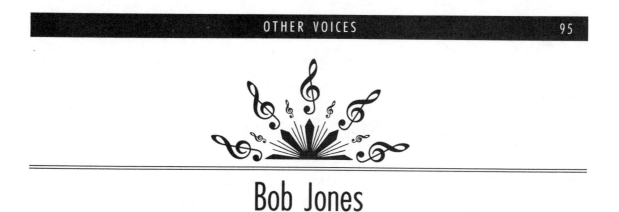

Bob Jones

"Congratulations! You're taking a walk toward wisdom." Those were the words that Tony Bennett bestowed upon Bob Jones when the well-known announcer arrived to take his position behind the microphones of WQXR in 1987. "I'd spent years playing classic American popular songs on 'The Milkman's Matinee' and 'The Make-Believe Ballroom,'" Bob says. "Now I was leaving Rosemary Clooney and Woody Herman and Count Basie behind and taking up with Beethoven and Shostakovich and Massenet. I think it's super, indeed."

Each day, when Bob Jones reports to WQXR, he somewhat reluctantly leaves behind an adored family. If there were some way to take them with him or broadcast from home, that's what he'd do. But his wife, Rae Ann, has her duties as an executive with the World Trade Center. And two of the three children, George Christian and Katharine Ruth, have to go to school. Little Marie R., called Zee-Zee after Bob's mother, was born on December 19, 1990, and she's been part of WQXR ever since. Her birth was documented on the airwaves of the station, with baby music that included Brahms's famous Lullaby and Stravinsky's *Variations on Happy Birthday.*

Bob and Rae Ann share the cooking duties. "I do steaks, pastas, burgers, and breakfasts, except pancakes, waffles, and French toast," Bob boasts. "Rae Ann does everything else."

The recipe for Steak au Poivre, which is from Mary and Vincent Price's *Treasury of Great Recipes*, holds historic associations for the Jones family. "It was the first steak that George and Katharine ever ate. They were very little at the time and, after they tasted the steak au poivre, they told me it was very good, but could I please leave off the pepper next time?" The children have grown and so have their taste buds. Pepper is in and their favorite restaurant is Peter Luger's steak house.

When they're not home cooking, Bob and Rae Ann can be found at the Cellar in the Sky at the World Trade Center or on New York's Restaurant Row at Le Rivage. "I love French food," Bob tells us. But he quickly adds, "Don't forget about Italian. I liked red sauce all along. I didn't know you weren't supposed to be eating it."

Because Bob Jones is so in love with his family, we suggest Count Basie's album *Yessir, That's My Baby* (Pablo 2310-802); and for the Steak au Poivre, the Beatles' recording of *Sgt. Pepper's Lonely Hearts Club Band* (Capitol SMAS-2653).

Steak au Poivre

SERVES 4 (GENEROUSLY)

2 tablespoons whole peppercorns
1 3 pound sirloin steak
(1¼ inches thick)
3 tablespoons unsalted butter

1 tablespoon canola or vegetable oil
⅔ cup white wine
1 tablespoon brandy (optional)

1 Crush peppercorns coarsely in a mortar and pestle or place in a heavy paper or plastic bag and crush with a rolling pin. Dry steak with a cloth or paper towel and pound crushed pepper into sides with flat of a knife or cleaver. Place on platter and refrigerate at least 2 hours.

2 In a heavy skillet over medium high, heat 1 tablespoon of the butter and the oil. Cook steak until well browned, about 5 to 6 minutes per side for rare. Remove to a serving platter and keep warm.

3 Deglaze pan with white wine and brandy (if using), boiling rapidly and scraping pan drippings with a wooden spoon. Remove from heat and swirl in remaining butter. Pour over steak and serve.

Werner Klemperer

Any television fan, seeing the name Werner Klemperer, will immediately think "Klink!" But Colonel Klink, the bungling Nazi commandant who blustered and flustered and fumed in the TV series "Hogan's Heroes," is a far cry from the stately gentleman on the stage of Avery Fisher Hall being accompanied by the New York Philharmonic and Erich Leinsdorf as he reads parts of *Egmont* with incidental music by Beethoven. The actor has performed this work with orchestras around the world. And he eats up those concerts.

"I love to work with orchestras because it gets you to different places with wonderful food. San Francisco is number one for me. That city has great gourmet food of all kinds. What a choice!

"Next comes Chicago. Milwaukee has an area with terrific German restaurants. It's too fattening," Werner Klemperer admits, "but I love it. Washington, D.C., has really come up over the past few years. They seem to have more and more of those healthy places for the young crowd. And Seattle kind of combines West Coast nouvelle with a foreign touch. I had a wonderful meal recently in a Japanese-French restaurant in Seattle. It really works!"

Getting back to music, the son of the great conductor Otto Klemperer tells us about another great conductor, Zubin Mehta. "I went to an amazing party at Zubin's home in Brentwood." So much for the music. "His wife's niece was getting married and Nancy Mehta somehow found this unbelievable catering service. There must have been a thousand waiters. She planned the whole thing and I've never seen such a mixture of foods. And it was all delicious."

Was it spicy, the way Zubin likes it? "No, and that probably annoyed him. But I'm sure Zubin had his little bags of spices at hand to adjust it to his needs."

We needn't adjust the music to our needs, since it comes so naturally to suggest excerpts from Beethoven's Incidental Music to *Egmont* performed by soprano Birgit Nilsson with the Philharmonia Orchestra conducted by Otto Klemperer (Angel CDM-63358). And, for the stuffed artichokes, Italian style, Bach's *Italian Concerto* with harpsichordist Igor Kipnis (CBS MGT-39802).

Italian-Style Stuffed Artichokes

SERVES 4

3 tablespoons dry unflavored bread crumbs

1/4 cup chopped Italian parsley

1 garlic clove, minced

1/2 cup grated locatelli cheese

1/2 teaspoon salt

3/4 teaspoon pepper

1/3 cup olive oil

4 artichokes, washed and trimmed, with stems and 1/4 inch of the top removed

1   In a small mixing bowl combine all ingredients except artichokes. Mix well and place stuffing between leaves of artichokes. Place in steamer basket and set over boiling water. Steam about 1 hour, depending upon size of artichokes.

June LeBell

Music in New York City's parks keeps this city sane. Every year, hundreds of thousands of people turn out to hear the Philharmonic in the parks, and those free performances are perfect examples of the meeting of music and food.

New Yorkers, especially those attending concerts in Manhattan's Central Park, have a style of picnicking unlike any other group. Tanglewood may have its lawn devotees and the Hollywood Bowl may provide seat-side tables for early parkers, but only in New York will you find a variety that runs the gamut from nuns nibbling peanut butter and jelly to black-tie parties complete with candelabra, caviar, and champagne.

From the avid listener to the picnic maven, the audience stakes out seating turf long hours before the music begins. With their blankets and chairs, they bring tablecloths and their own culinary creations, hot or cold. Some take advantage of the diversity of the area surrounding Central Park: gourmet Chinese take-out, Thai, Japanese, Indian, and Moroccan cuisine, the Silver Palette and, of course, Zabar's to the west and EAT to the east.

While my official debut with the Philharmonic was in 1960, when I sang Aaron Copland's *The Second Hurricane* at Carnegie Hall with Leonard Bernstein conducting the orchestra and my chorus from the High School of Music and Art, I'll never forget a choral performance I did of Orff's *Carmina Burana* several years later in the parks. We were at the Bronx Botanical Gardens that night and, as the orchestra crashed around us and we sang "O Fortuna!" the skies above us opened with a torrential downpour that was most *un*-Fortuna.

The orchestra, at the front of the stage, moved back without missing a beat. And the audience merely reversed their blankets, putting them over their bodies instead of under them, so that we were singing to a bunch of sodden lumps strewn across the field in front of the stage. The rain didn't last long but those moments of faceless, woolly hills on the ground proved the stuff of which New Yorkers are made.

When I make a picnic, I have three thoughts in mind: the taste of the food, how it can be carried without disaster, and how it will endure the elements. While the first two are important, the last is really the first to consider because you don't want to poison your guests by serving food that spoils easily. I stay away from anything with mayonnaise or cream. I'm wary of chicken and turkey that might turn foul after just a few minutes of exposure. I want food that I can *put* out and *leave* out without worrying about Death at the Philharmonic.

Attractively sliced fresh vegetables, without a dip, are perfect to start. If you must have something to go with them, choose cheese. And don't leave it basking in the late-setting sun.

My Wild Rice Salad can be a meal in itself and it won't spoil. If you want to add a meat to the menu, I'd go with something smoked like ham or turkey. But, again, keep it on ice and take it out only to serve. Put it back in the cooler quickly. And use mustard, not mayo! If you want to get very elegant, a whole poached fish with a side sauce of soy, ginger, scallions, and sesame oil is lovely. But serve it and ice it. Don't give it a chance to swim away!

Brownies are always perfect for dessert. They're eaten before anything can happen to them and they're pretty indestructible, anyway. I think you'll find these easy to make and extremely successful. They're very chewy and chocolaty, so be sure to make enough.

The Philharmonic will provide the music from the stage. But, while preparing your feast, get in the mood with Ives's "*Central Park in the Dark* performed by the New York Philharmonic and Leonard Bernstein (CBS MPT-38777) and follow it with Tchaikovsky's *1812 Overture* (but leave the fireworks for the *real* thing in the park), again with the Philharmonic and Bernstein (CBS MYK-36723).

Poached Fish

SERVES 4

1 whole salmon, red snapper, or sea
  bass (about 3 pounds), cleaned
Water or good white wine

CHINESE-STYLE SAUCE
½ cup light soy sauce
2 tablespoons sesame oil
1 scallion (white part only),
  finely chopped
1 tablespoon peeled and finely chopped
  fresh ginger

1 garlic clove, smashed with flat of knife

GARNISH
2 scallions, cut into 2-inch-long
  fine julienne
1 rib celery, cut into 2-inch-long
  fine julienne
Fresh ginger, peeled and cut into
  2-inch-long fine julienne

1 Fill fish poacher or wok with water or white wine to 2-inch depth or to just cover fish. Bring to a boil and add fish. Cover and turn off heat. Let stand about 6 to 8 minutes per pound or until the flesh will just flake when knife is gently inserted. Carefully remove fish and put on large serving platter (I pack paper towels around it for a minute or two to soak up additional liquid).

2 To make the sauce, combine soy sauce, sesame oil, chopped scallion, chopped ginger, and garlic in a small bowl. Mix well and drizzle over fish. Sprinkle with the julienned scallion, celery, and ginger and serve.

If taking on a picnic, carry fish, sauce, and garnish in separate containers and assemble just before serving.

Wild Rice Salad

SERVES 24

7 cups water

1 cup chicken broth (preferably homemade)

3 cups (16 ounces) wild rice, rinsed and drained

1 cup balsamic vinegar

2 teaspoons cream sherry

1 garlic clove, smashed with flat of knife

1½ cups olive oil (optional)

1 (10 ounce) package frozen baby peas, thawed, or 2½ cups fresh peas, cooked, drained, and cooled

24 cherry tomatoes, cut in half

3 ribs celery, cut into 2-inch-long batons

4 heads Belgian endive, cut into ½-inch rounds

½ cup chopped Italian parsley

½ cup chopped cilantro

2 cups sliced almonds, toasted briefly in skillet

1½ cups golden raisins

1 In a large saucepot over high heat, combine water and chicken broth. Bring to a boil, add wild rice, stir, and cover. Lower heat to a simmer and cook 50 to 70 minutes, checking for doneness after 50 minutes. Remove from heat and cool completely.

2 In a medium bowl, whisk together balsamic vinegar, sherry, and garlic. Slowly whisk in olive oil. (Olive oil can be omitted if desired—just use a good balsamic vinegar. It tastes great and amazes everyone who asks. Honest!)

3 Place cooled rice in a large attractive salad bowl. Arrange all vegetables, parsley, cilantro, almonds, and raisins on top (you can refrigerate up to 4 hours at this point). About 15 minutes before serving, add dressing. *Do not toss until you present this work of art.* Let people ooh and aah first.

FOR PICNIC: *Put rice salad into a large plastic container, adding dressing just before leaving home. This keeps well without refrigeration. It's great for large parties—indoors and out.*

NOTE: *These vegetables are suggestions—use any combination of raw veggies you think will look attractive.*

June's Dark Brownies

MAKES 24

4 ounces unsweetened chocolate,
  finely chopped
6 tablespoons unsalted butter,
  cut into pieces
2 cups sugar

3 large eggs, lightly beaten
2 teaspoons vanilla extract
1 cup all purpose flour
1 cup mini–chocolate chips

1 Preheat oven to 350°. Grease a 9 × 13″ baking pan.

2 In a heavy 2-quart saucepot set over low heat, melt chocolate and butter together (alternatively, place chocolate and butter in a microwavable bowl and microwave on high power 2 to 3 minutes, stirring twice, until melted). Stir in sugar, eggs, and vanilla and mix well. Stir in flour, mix, and stir in chocolate chips. Pour into prepared pan and bake 35 to 40 minutes or until a cake tester inserted in middle comes out almost clean. Cool in pan and cut into squares.

NOTE: Nuts can be substituted for chips (or added with them), and rum, brandy, or your favorite liqueur can be substituted for the vanilla extract for a more sophisticated flavor.

Andrew Porter

Andrew Porter, the music critic, came to America from South Africa. "But I was raised and trained in England," he says, "and before I worked for *The New Yorker*, I wrote music criticism for the *Financial Times* in London. That's sort of like the *Wall Street Journal* but they care more about music," he adds.

An organ scholar at University College, Oxford, Andrew Porter picked up more than musical knowledge. He also developed a taste for fine food. When he came to America in 1972 to take up his responsibilities at *The New Yorker*, he also took up some American recipes, including this Italo-American pasta recipe. "It comes from a friend of mine, Floriano Vecchi, who's an artist and lives in Greenwich Village. When I started making it, I named it after him."

Andrew didn't have to wait until he came to New York to hear the New York Philharmonic. "I first attended their concerts at the Albert Hall," he remembers. "I heard them in England under both Mitropoulos and Walter when I was just a student." Now here's the important part. Even before he did it for a living, Andrew Porter was listening with a critical ear. "I thought they were absolutely marvelous. Mitropoulos had fire and energy and Bruno Walter conducted with classic grace." There's a student worth quoting!

For Andrew Porter, student, we raise a recording of Brahms's *Academic Festival Overture* played with classic grace by the New York Philharmonic under the direction of Bruno Walter (Odys. Y-35222). And for Pasta Flori, an aria or two sung by Zinka Milanov as Floria Tosca in the Puccini opera (2-RCA AGL2-4515).

Pasta Flori

SERVES 1

1 tablespoon olive oil (preferably
extra virgin)

1 medium onion, chopped

1 garlic clove, minced

1 cup finely shredded iceberg lettuce

2-3 ounces spaghettini, vermicelli,
or capelli d'angelo

2-3 tablespoons freshly grated
Parmesan cheese

Pinch salt

1/4 teaspoon pepper

1 Heat olive oil in a large skillet over medium high heat. Add onion and garlic and "rosolate" them (*rosolare*—to cook, stirring) until they smell delicious and are soft and translucent, about 5 minutes. Meanwhile, bring a large saucepot of salted water to a boil and cook the pasta just until done. Drop iceberg lettuce in the skillet with the onion. Drain the pasta quickly and place on top of the lettuce. Add the Parmesan, salt, and pepper, and mix well. Serve at once.

Tony Randall

Tony Randall's multifaceted career has taken him from the legitimate stage to the movie screen to the television screen to the concert stage. He found his way to the stage of the New York Philharmonic in 1971 when André Kostelanetz presented a Promenade called "June Celebration of Marriage." Part of this program was devoted to "A Carnival of Marriage," with verses by Ogden Nash. Tony narrated the piece with his own particular style of sarcasm and spice, of course, while the orchestra played Strauss's "Champagne Polka," Dohnanyi's "Wedding Waltz" from *The Veil*, Saint-Saens's *Wedding Cake Fantasy*, *La Belle* [no relation] *excentrique*, and the Liszt arrangement of Mendelssohn's "Wedding March" from *A Midsummer Night's Dream*.

Although many of Tony Randall's television and movie characters have placed him in the role of a fastidious gourmet and cook, nothing could be further from the truth. "I am represented in half a dozen or more cookbooks," Tony tells us, "and I always give a jokey recipe because I actually don't know a thing about cooking. So I tell how to boil an egg, how to make toast, how to make tea with a tea bag," and, for us, "how to make peanut butter."

Not realizing at first that he was teasing, I asked, "From scratch?" He told me to get a pencil and paper and write down the following instructions:

"Take a few peanuts. Take a fork. Mash the peanuts. Voilà . . . peanut butter."

Later, in an explanatory note, he wrote, "I thought the peanut butter bit, off the top of my head, was pretty fair. But if you don't like it, I'll give you another: Hot dogs. Take hot dog out of freezer, put in frying pan or boiling water or anything hot." He added, "Good in bun."

Well, Tony, buns notwithstanding, we'll stick with peanut butter. And we'll give our readers a choice. They may use your recipe, or the one that follows, created in your honor by Jean Galton. While you're chewing on this proposal, we suggest this performance of Percy Grainger's *Gum Sucker's March* with the Michigan State University Symphonic Band (Delos DE 3101).

Cinnamon Honey Peanut Butter

MAKES ABOUT 2 CUPS

1 pound blanched raw peanuts
6 tablespoons canola oil
½ teaspoon salt

6 tablespoons Tasmanian honey
(or any other fragrant honey)
¾ teaspoon cinnamon

1   Preheat oven to 300°. Toss peanuts in a large mixing bowl with 2 tablespoons of the oil and the salt. Mix well and spread on a cookie sheet. Roast, shaking pan every 10 minutes, about 25 to 30 minutes or until peanuts are golden brown. Remove to a food processor and add remaining ingredients. Process, pulsing, until smooth.

David Randolph

O f all the people contributing recipes to this book, David Randolph has the distinction of being the only one in the *Guinness Book of Records.* The conductor made the record book for having conducted the most complete performances of Handel's *Messiah.* As of December 1990, he had led the oratorio 152 times and was still going strong.

None of these 152 performances have been with the New York Philharmonic. But David is still part of the family. In the late 1940s, he wrote the scripts for the Sunday afternoon New York Philharmonic broadcasts that were then carried live on CBS radio. He was also the intermission commentator for the Lewisohn Stadium concerts on WNYC in the late fifties. And he's something of a fixture at the pre-Philharmonic Friday morning lectures at Avery Fisher Hall.

David Randolph also loves food. His wife, Mildred, does most of the cooking at home, "but we share the eating duties," David adds with a laugh. For this music and food duo (Mildred is a singer) we suggest you listen to Mozart's String Quartet No. 17, K. 458 ("The Hunt") with the Emerson String Quartet (DG 427657), in honor of Mildred's Chicken Chasseur.

Chicken Chasseur

SERVES 4

1/4 cup unbleached flour

3/4 teaspoon thyme

1/2 teaspoon salt

1/2 teaspoon pepper

1 fryer chicken (about 3 1/2 pounds),
cut into 4 pieces

1 tablespoon olive oil

1 tablespoon unsalted butter

1 large onion, chopped

2 garlic cloves, minced

1/2 pound mushrooms, thinly sliced

1/2 cup white wine

1 (14 1/2 ounce) can stewed tomatoes

2 tablespoons chopped Italian parsley

1/4 teaspoon dried tarragon

1   In a shallow bowl or paper bag, combine the flour, 1/2 teaspoon thyme, salt, and pepper. Coat chicken lightly, shaking off excess flour. Heat olive oil and butter in a large skillet over medium high heat. Brown chicken on both sides, about 8 minutes. Remove to plate.

2   Lower heat to medium. Add onion and garlic and cook until softened, about 5 to 6 minutes. Add mushrooms and cook, stirring, until they release their moisture, about 8 minutes. Add wine, raise heat to medium high, and reduce by half. Add tomatoes, parsley, remaining 1/4 teaspoon thyme, and the tarragon. Bring to a boil and return chicken to skillet. Spoon sauce over chicken, cover, reduce heat to a simmer, and cook 45 minutes or until chicken is done.

Serve with boiled rice.

Anna Russell

Anna Russell, the Prima Vocerina of Comedy in Music, has been singing and writing about music and food for years. She made her debut with the Philharmonic at a 1954 Young People's Concert performing "Once Upon an Orchestra" by George Kleinsinger (of "Tubby the Tuba" fame) and singing an aria from Rossini's *Les Soirées Musicales.*

Food is tossed about with abandon on Anna Russell's recordings. "I gave my love a cherry without a pit," she intoned in one of her English folksongs. And she even cooked up Scottish "Haggis" in a musical melodrama. Of course, her forte has always been giving her recipe for rarefied performances with advice "For singers with tremendous artistry but no voice" which she calls "Schlumph; je n'ai pas la plume de ma tante." And another for the dramatic soprano called "Schreechenrauf."

Anna Russell is now in retirement at her home on "Anna Russell Way" in Canada. But she's still in the position to dish out such spicy advice, that it's impossible to resist reprinting her letter to me in its entirety.

Dear June LeBell,

You have really put me on the spot. The sad fact is that I have never learned to cook.

In England, when I was young, we had the family cook, who owned the downstairs, and you went there at your peril.

When I was first married (to a French horn player), we lived in a musicians' boarding house, and you ate what you were given (musicians were not paid so lavishly then as they are now).

When I married my second husband my mother-in-law lived in. She was a star cook and did it all magnificently. Although I loved her dearly, and was her greatest fan, she never would let me cook as she said I had no talent.

From then on I was on the road, mostly in hotels until I retired five years ago at the age of seventy-five.

I now have a senior's apartment, with a great little kitchen all to myself, and have spent the last five years trying to hide from the neighbors the fact that I don't know how to cook.

NOT EVERYONE COOKS

Recipes are no good. Either I don't have half the ingredients needed, or while I am reading what to do, it has either boiled over, burned or exploded, the smoke detector goes off, and the neighbors look at me in a most peculiar fashion.

By now I can do a steak, a salad, boil an egg, and that's about it. Except for Chinese soup, which you might call a recipe for non-cooks.

Go to your supermarket and get packets of frozen won tons, pork dumplings, all kinds of little one-mouthful goodies. They come in packets of ten, all decorated with Chinese pictures and characters in lovely colors. Put them in a saucepan of boiling water, and boil like mad for ten minutes. At the same time heat up some Campbell's Chicken Broth (full strength) and slice in some water chestnuts, mushrooms, chives, bits of cooked pork, or whatever. Strain the dumplings, or whatever you have chosen, and dump them in the soup.

All you need for this is two saucepans, a strainer, and a bowl.

The whole thing, including eating and washing up, can be done in twenty minutes.

I'm sorry this is the best I can manage for cooking. Should you ever write a treatise on clearing up, I am a masterly dish washer.

All the best,

Anna Russell

If you can't find the colorful little packets of pork dumplings and one-mouthful goodies that come with Chinese pictures, try freshly packaged cheese or meat ravioli.

While cooking and eating, you must accompany this "recipe" with the newly issued *Anna Russell Album*, featuring nine of the musical comedienne's finest performances (Sony MDK 47252).

Noé Tanigawa

New not only to WQXR but also to New York, announcer Noé Tanigawa was born in Honolulu, Hawaii, where food is a wonderful mix of Japanese, Chinese, Asian, and ... Hawaiian. Just what *is* Hawaiian food? "It's lots of raw stuff," Noé begins. "We have poke, which is made of cubes of raw fish mixed with seaweed, salt, and kukui nuts which are roasted and crumbled. Then," she continues, "there's poi. A lot of visitors taste this because they've heard about it, but they don't like it at first. I guess it's an acquired taste.

"Poi is a tuber. We steam it and pound it into a sticky paste. I like it really thick and we call that 'one finger.' In other words, you measure the thickness that way. One-finger poi is really thick and sticky. Two finers is looser. And the taste changes the longer you keep it. It sort of ferments. It's really good for children who are allergic to milk," she adds.

Noé's mother did the cooking at home. In fact, her recipe for Japanese-style shrimp comes from her mother's kitchen. And Noé's husband, Terry Lau, is a wonderful cook. "Chinese men are famous for cooking at home. He's also very interested in French food and he wants to take a course to learn the techniques so he can apply them to his style of cooking.

"In Honolulu we both worked on community fundraisers. Terry ran luaus for five thousand people at his church. The food was really terrific, especially the pig they cooked in the ground."

Before coming to announce at WQXR, Noé worked in Hawaii at a rock station and then went on to jazz and pop. But her real passion is painting. In fact, she came to New York primarily to work as an artist and, while she's painting and studying, she's continuing her career in broadcasting. From time to time she holds a painting up to the microphone, so keep watching your radio.

Meanwhile, stay tuned for Jean-Pierre Rampal's album *Japanese Folk Melodies* (CBS MK-35862).

Japanese-Style Shrimp Fry

MAKES 18

18 large shrimp, shelled and deveined but
with tails left on
½ teaspoon salt or garlic salt
2 large eggs
3 tablespoons water

¼ cup unbleached flour
2 cups Japanese "Panko" bread crumbs
Corn oil for frying
Grated daikon (Japanese radish)
Soy sauce or lemon juice

1 Make 3 evenly spaced cuts about ¼-inch deep along the underside of the shrimp. (These will keep shrimp from curling up when fried.) Sprinkle salt or garlic salt on shrimp.

2 In a small bowl, beat eggs and water together. Place flour on one plate and bread crumbs on another. Dip each shrimp into egg mixture, then into flour, again into egg mixture, and then into bread crumbs. Roll and coat each shrimp well with bread crumbs and place on a plate. Shrimp can sit 15 minutes in refrigerator at this point.

3 In a large skillet, pour corn oil to depth of ½ inch. Heat over medium high to about 375°. Fry shrimp until golden brown, about 2 minutes on each side. Serve with daikon and soy sauce or lemon juice.

NOTE: *Other vegetables and seafood can be prepared this way.*

Composers

Clarence and Richard Adler

The Adler family boasts two generations of musicians. Two very different kinds of musicians. Clarence Adler was the illustrious pianist and teacher of the early twentieth century. His son, Richard, is the composer of the Broadway smash hits *Pajama Game* and *Damn Yankees*.

It was Clarence Adler who made his debut with the New York Philharmonic in 1923 under the direction of Willem Mengelberg. That all-Beethoven Carnegie Hall program opened with the *Coriolan Overture* and closed with the *Eroica Symphony*. And between these two masterpieces, keyboard giant Clarence Adler joined forces with the Philharmonic, Scipione Guidi, and Cornelius Van Vliet for a performance of the Triple Concerto.

This revered and awe-inspiring teacher of Aaron Copland and Richard Rodgers was the father of a very different musical personality. Richard Adler's autobiography, *You Gotta Have Heart* (featuring drawings by Al Hirschfeld, by the way), sums up the composer-lyricist's life in a song. From the seductiveness of the stage to the tragedy of the loss of his dear friend and collaborator, Jerry Ross, to Richard Adler's winning bout with cancer, having heart is the soul of this musician.

Songs like "Steam Heat," "Hernando's Hideaway," "Hey, There," and "Whatever Lola Wants," performed on the original-cast recordings, add even more zip to Richard Adler's spicy and sweet Paradise Kraut. A great accompaniment for ham, sausage, pork, or a good, savory meat loaf, this recipe was originally contributed by the composer to the American Cancer Society's *Gourmet Guide for Busy People By Famous People.* Its tangy sauciness speaks worlds of words for a man who has had more than his share of heart!

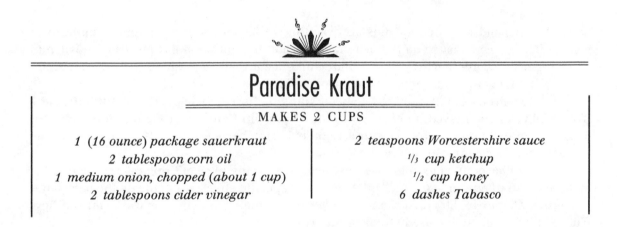

Paradise Kraut

MAKES 2 CUPS

1 (16 ounce) package sauerkraut
2 tablespoon corn oil
1 medium onion, chopped (about 1 cup)
2 tablespoons cider vinegar

2 teaspoons Worcestershire sauce
$^1/_3$ cup ketchup
$^1/_2$ cup honey
6 dashes Tabasco

1   Drain sauerkraut and rinse well with cold water.

2   Heat oil in a large skillet over medium high heat. Cook onion, stirring until translucent, about 4 to 5 minutes. Add sauerkraut, vinegar, Worcestershire, and ketchup. Stir well and cook over medium low heat for about 10 minutes to blend flavors. Add honey and Tabasco and stir well. Continue cooking until mixture is heated through, about 4 to 5 minutes.

Dave Brubeck

Orchestras and opera companies all over the world have always sought to build their audiences. One way to do that is to incorporate the more popular pieces of music into their repertories. Another way to stimulate audience growth is to give listeners something new, something different, something controversial.

While patron-commissioning has been going on for centuries, it wasn't until the New York Philharmonic moved into its new home at Lincoln Center in 1962 that the orchestra began commissioning new works on a regular basis, thereby setting the stage for a new concept in music composition around the world.

The Philharmonic has commissioned works from the likes of Copland and Cage, Hindemith and Barber and Sessions. And, before this specific effort was made on the part of the orchestra, Gershwin, Stravinsky, and Schuller had come forth with new works for the New York Philharmonic to feature in their premieres.

Of course, commissions aren't the only way to bring novel concepts to the Philharmonic. Styles of music such as folk, jazz, and even rock have begun to infiltrate the supposedly staid stands of the musicians. And that brings us to Dave Brubeck. It was in December 1959 that Leonard Bernstein brought the famous jazz musician and his quartet into Carnegie Hall for a Philharmonic concert that featured Brubeck's *Dialogues for Jazz Combo and Orchestra* (Col. CL-1466) on a program with a Bach Brandenburg Concerto, a piece by Mozart, and a new work by Robert Starer. Even today this would be called innovative programming.

Dave Brubeck has had fun with music, whether you call it jazz or classical or just plain good. He's taken rhythms and thrown amusing curves into normal patterns so that a rollicking square-dance tune has become his "Unsquare Dance." What may once have been new has, because of Brubeck, become the basis for tomorrow's composers and improvisers.

Dave Brubeck's recipe for Russian Cream may also be called the basis for tomorrow's improvisers. If any of the cream is left! "This recipe was given to me by Juliet Gerlin, my assistant, friend and neighbor," Dave tells us. He says it can be served with fresh fruit, especially raspberries. And he adds, "Russian cream needs to jell in the refrigerator for at least three hours, but overnight is even better. It will keep for a week tightly covered, making it an ideal emergency dessert."

Lots of luck, Dave! This stuff wouldn't last more than two minutes after the obligatory three hours of jelling in my icebox. It's lovely to dream of this Russian Cream accompanying fruits and simple sponge cake, but eaten by the spoonful, it can't be beat. It's addictive.

So is Dave Brubeck's music. His recording *Jazz Impressions of Eurasia*, a "classic" (Col. CL 1251), includes a piece called "Thank You (Dziekuje)" and is a fitting accompaniment for glomming down Dave's Russian Cream. He played it once when his quartet made a trip to Poland in the late fifties, and as he writes on the recording's liner notes, "the students of Poznan took us to the Music Museum where we saw a collection of instruments from all over the world. Of special interest was a room dedicated to the memory of Chopin. With these impressions fresh in my mind, we performed that night 'Dziekuje.' I thought I had insulted the audience by linking the memory of Chopin to jazz. Then came the applause and I realized with relief that the Polish audience had understood that this was meant as a tribute to their great musical tradition, and as an expression of gratitude."

Dave, for your music and your food, *dziekuje*!

Russian Cream

SERVES 8

2 cups heavy cream or half and half
1 cup sugar
2 teaspoons unflavored gelatin

¹/₂ cup cold water
2 cups sour cream or plain yogurt

1   In a small saucepan over medium high heat combine cream and sugar. Stir until sugar is dissolved, about 3 to 4 minutes.

2   In a glass measuring cup stir together gelatin and water until gelatin has softened. Pour into cream mixture and stir over medium heat until gelatin is fully dissolved (feel it with your fingers—you shouldn't feel any gelatin grains). Stir in sour cream or yogurt and mix until smooth. Pour into a serving bowl or decorative mold and refrigerate at least 3 hours or overnight.

Serve with fresh raspberries, strawberries, or rhubarb sauce. "Your guests will think that you are serving them ice cream and will be totally surprised," says Dave.

John Corigliano

There are two John Coriglianos. They both have been part of the New York Philharmonic. They both have had long and important musical careers. And they are father and son.

The elder John Corigliano was familiar to Philharmonic audiences for some forty-five years. Actually, he first appeared with the orchestra as a soloist in the Bruch G minor Concerto with Josef Stransky conducting in 1921. Then, in 1935, he joined the Philharmonic as assistant concertmaster. And, in 1943, he moved into the first chair to hold the position of concertmaster until he retired in 1966. During that time, he played more than thirty concertos with the Philharmonic. And he was the first concertmaster with the orchestra to have been born and trained in the United States.

The younger Corigliano has made his mark as a composer. "I grew up with all those wonderful musicians coming to our home. Many of them were like uncles to me." *Uncle* John to then *Little* John, for example, was better known to outsiders as *Sir* John (Barbirolli). But it was, truly, all in the family.

"The first time the Philharmonic performed one of my pieces it was absolutely traumatic for me," the composer remembers. "It was my Clarinet Concerto and I had written it specially for the Philharmonic. Stanley [Drucker] was the soloist and I made sure there were parts for every single one of the principals of the orchestra. I didn't want to leave anyone out. This was a commission and it meant so much to me personally. It really gave me a chance to express what I felt for every member of the Philharmonic. It really was entirely based on my feelings."

John Corigliano, the composer, has very strong feelings for food as well as for the Philharmonic. "I love Italian food. In fact, I could eat it every night. My mother cooked wonderful Italian food at home and, even though my father didn't cook, he certainly loved to eat.

"I remember going out to dinner years ago with Mitropoulos. We went to the Italian restaurant in New York called La Scala. In fact, it was his visits to that restaurant that made it famous among musicians. But he was a very austere man. While we were sitting at the table putting away piles of pasta, he'd order steak tartare and add these large beans that he'd bring with him. Seriously! He'd bring his own container of beans and just pour them into the dish next to the tartare and eat that. Every time!"

John composes for the dining table as well as the clarinet or flute or oboe or voice. "I like to improvise at the stove. That's how I came up with this recipe for pasta and beans. I hate to follow recipes and I usually just throw in whatever I have in the house and see how it tastes." The kitchen creator pauses a moment and adds, "It's usually very good."

After all this talk about John's Clarinet Concerto, that has to be the first choice for listening while preparing a Corigliano creation. This is the recording with the New York Philharmonic and Stanley Drucker (New World NW-309). And, because John's friends follow him anywhere he improvises a dish, we suggest the most obvious "following" music: John Corigliano's *Pied Piper Fantasy* with James Galway leading the rats (RCA 6602-1 RCD-9).

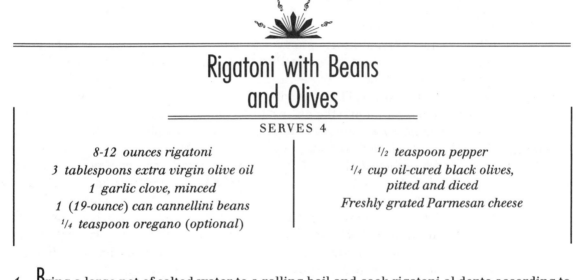

Rigatoni with Beans and Olives

SERVES 4

8-12 ounces rigatoni
3 tablespoons extra virgin olive oil
1 garlic clove, minced
1 (19-ounce) can cannellini beans
¹/₄ teaspoon oregano (optional)

¹/₂ teaspoon pepper
¹/₄ cup oil-cured black olives,
pitted and diced
Freshly grated Parmesan cheese

1 Bring a large pot of salted water to a rolling boil and cook rigatoni al dente according to package directions.

2 Meanwhile, heat olive oil in a large skillet over medium high heat. Add garlic and cook until lightly golden, about 1 minute. Add beans and their liquid, oregano (if using), and pepper, and cook, stirring, until liquid has thickened and beans are quite soft, about 5 to 6 minutes. Stir in olives. Place hot drained rigatoni in large serving bowl, add sauce and Parmesan, and toss. Serve at once.

David Del Tredici

"The Philharmonic gave a wonderful reception on the Grand Promenade of Avery Fisher Hall after they performed one of my pieces," David Del Tredici recalls. "They served very tonal foods. Tonal foods are delicious and have a high fat content. Atonal foods are composed of grains and macrobiotic inclinations." That's definitely a composer's definition.

Actually, David's food-feted composition was *All in the Golden Afternoon*, performed in 1983 at one of the New York Philharmonic's Horizons concerts. But the composer's real premiere piece with the orchestra was *Syzygy*, and that was played eleven years earlier with conductor Michael Tilson Thomas. "I was terrified," David remembers. "I sat in the audience absolutely thrilled because it was the biggest thing that had happened to me. I'd always dreamed of having the New York Philharmonic perform one of my pieces, so in a way I was thinking, Be careful what you want, you may get it."

Get it, he did. And it made a difference in the life of the composer. "In a way it validated my work. A major organization took my music seriously and that meant a lot to me and to others, too."

One of David Del Tredici's most successful scores is his "Alice" series, based on texts from *Alice in Wonderland.* "My *Final Alice* was a commission for the Bicentennial by the Chicago Symphony. [Sir Georg] Solti knew a soprano named Barbara Hendricks and thought she'd sound good in the work. She turned out to be better than perfect."

It was Barbara Hendricks who sang *Final Alice* with the Philharmonic when the work came to New York. And it is Barbara Hendricks's voice we'll be hearing as we set out to make David's recipe.

"Actually, this zabaglione comes from my grandmother. We all called her Noni and she lived to be a hundred! I guess this recipe must be very good for you," David drawls. "I asked Noni for a copy when I left California, where I'd been brought up, and started school at Princeton. I couldn't bring Noni with me, but I could bring her zabaglione."

Wait until you taste this traditional and definitely tonal dessert. I only meant to take a teaspoon or two and wound up devouring the entire pot. It's easy to make and a real treat.

David Del Tredici tells us, "The Philharmonic has played a lot of my music, from the severely atonal to the shamelessly lush." Grandma's Zabaglione is, without question, in the last stages of the final category. And, to accompany it, turn to the original edition of *Final Alice* with Barbara Hendricks and the Chicago Symphony conducted by Sir Georg Solti (Lon. LDR-71018). Since you're bound to have all your friends clamoring for this dessert, play them Del Tredici's *I Hear an Army* (CRI S-294).

Grandma's Zabaglione

MAKES 4 CUPS

4 large egg yolks
¼ cup sugar
Pinch salt
½ cup Marsala wine
(cheapest brand okay)

½ teaspoon unflavored gelatin
1 tablespoon cold water
1 tablespoon boiling water
1 cup heavy cream

1 Combine egg yolks, sugar, and salt in the top of a double boiler or a bowl set over simmering water. Beat on high speed with a hand-held electric mixer until pale and thick, about 3 to 4 minutes. Add Marsala and continue beating 3 to 4 minutes longer. Remove from heat.

2 Meanwhile, soften the gelatin by mixing it with 1 tablespoon cold water. When soft (about 1 minute), stir in boiling water, and stir into egg mixture. Beat 2 to 3 minutes longer. Cool to room temperature, then chill about 20 minutes in the refrigerator.

3 In a large mixing bowl, whip cream until stiff with a hand-held mixer on high. Fold into pudding and chill until ready to serve.

Jacob Druckman

Contemporary music is often an acquired taste. Jacob Druckman is a composer who, with the New York Philharmonic, has helped thousands of people develop a taste for what's new in music. In 1983, Jacob was the artistic director of the Philharmonic's Horizons Festival. Each program on this special summer series introduced audiences to new works performed by musicians who more or less specialized in contemporary music. One evening, for example, featured works by Morton Subotnick, Barbara Kolb, and John Adams with a whole roster of performers including Tony Randall, Ursula Oppens, and Mr. Subotnick under the direction of conductors Larry Newland and Jacob Druckman.

Since the early 1960s, the New York Philharmonic has made an intensive effort to commission new works and to play contemporary music both at regular season concerts and in special series like Horizons. And Jacob Druckman has been one of the driving forces both on stage and behind the scenes. After all, he is a composer and it's important to him, personally, that his music be heard. But it's equally important that the audience's ears be trained to understand, appreciate, and—yes—even like new works.

Jacob Druckman seems to be both impresario and composer in his kitchen, too. He describes his lobster recipe in musical terms, stressing the roots of its name: Madécasses. "The fact that this recipe originated on the Isle of Madagascar is less important than the idea that it *should* have," the composer tells us, somewhat in the style of his music. "It began with a prohibition of both butter and salt. What's a lobster addict to do? Thus, my recipe.

"After the meal is over," the composer instructs, "clear the table of all the shells and debris, but *do not discard*! I like to sneak into the kitchen in the dead of the night and wrap all the leftover shells in cheesecloth. Then I cook them to death for about an hour and out comes this broth that I use for seafood and pasta dishes the next day or the next week." He says that the broth freezes well.

I suggest that if you follow Jacob's instructions for the second part of this lobster feast, you use your own shells or those of someone you love dearly. I chew and lick shells in the privacy of my own home and I'm not sure how licked shells do in other people's broth.

According to the dictionary, the word "animus" can mean both "an animating force or underlying purpose" or "a feeling of strong ill will or hatred; animosity." For our purposes, we'll take the first meaning and suggest Jacob Druckman's *Animus III for Clarinet and Tapes* (Elektra/Nonesuch H-71253). To do honor to the origin of the recipe, I suggest Ravel's "Chansons madécasses" performed deliciously by Gérard Souzay (Philips Seq. 6527154). And, for the poor *homard*, "The Lobster Quadrille" from Irving Fine's *Alice in Wonderland*, in a performance by the Gregg Smith Singers (CRI S376E).

Homard Madécasse

SERVES 2 SYBARITES

2 large red onions, peeled and quartered
4 large carrots, scrubbed and quartered
2 green peppers, cut into 1-inch chunks
4 star anise
1 tablespoon red pepper flakes
1 tablespoon herbes de Provence or choice of oregano, marjoram, thyme, basil, or sage

2 1¹/₄-pound lobsters or one 2¹/₂-pound lobster
Lemon wedges
Cilantro or parsley leaves

1   In a food processor, combine onions, carrots, and peppers and process until finely minced. Fill a saucepot large enough to accommodate lobster(s) with water (at least 6 quarts) and add minced vegetables and herbs and spices. Cover and bring to a boil. Cook mixture 25 minutes and add lobster(s). Cook for 5 to 7 minutes per pound. Remove lobster(s), drain and split. Serve with lemon wedges and parsley or cilantro leaves.

Morton Gould

From his *Philharmonic Waltzes*, recorded in 1950 with Dimitri Mitropoulos, to his "official" performing debut with the New York Philharmonic and Paul Paray in 1961, Morton Gould has been a New York composer with an international reputation. We can't, however, say the same about his cooking.

"I don't cook," the composer admits. But he does eat. "And my favorite dish is, oh you know, that 'blown up' spaghetti." After a few minutes of picturing pasta exploding on the ceiling, we figure out that "blown up" spaghetti is more commonly known as "perciatelli."

"I like it pretty plain," Morton Gould explains, "with butter and grated cheese. But my favorite is with tomatoes and maybe some anchovies."

The simplicity of Morton Gould's taste in food is carried over to his music. He tells a story of conducting one of his works several years ago. "I conducted it the way I wrote it. But the piece had become very popular over the years and, the more popular it got, the faster it got. Well, I went ahead, not even thinking one way or the other, and led the band in my original tempo. And wouldn't you know, one of the musicians stopped me and said, 'That's too slow. It doesn't go like that.' "

Jean Galton, our food composer, has created a recipe for Morton Gould's favorite perciatelli dish. We trust that he won't turn the tables and tell us, "It doesn't go like that."

For a bit of musical nostalgia, we turn back to an early recording of Morton Gould's *Suite for Orchestra*, "Spirituals," written in 1941 and recorded by the New York Philharmonic and Artur Rodzinski on April 9, 1946 (Columbia XCO-36253-1 [on 78 rpm] and ML-2042 [10″ LP]). And whether Morton Gould goes into the kitchen himself or not, he did cook up these *Apple Waltzes* (RCA RCD1-5019).

Perciatelli with Escarole Sauce

SERVES 4

1 pound perciatelli
3 tablespoons olive oil
2 garlic cloves, minced
2 plum tomatoes, chopped (about 1 cup)
1 (2 ounce) tin rolled anchovies with
capers, drained and finely chopped

Pinch red pepper flakes
1 medium head escarole, washed and
coarsely chopped (about 6 cups)
$1/4$ cup water
$1/2$ teaspoon pepper

1 Bring a large pot of salted water to a rolling boil and cook perciatelli al dente according to package directions.

2 Meanwhile, heat olive oil in a large skillet over medium high heat. Add garlic, tomatoes, anchovies, and red pepper flakes, and cook, stirring, about 3 to 4 minutes. Add escarole, water, and pepper, and stir well. Cover and cook 5 to 6 minutes longer, stirring once or twice. Add to hot drained perciatelli and toss. Serve immediately.

Peter Schickele

Peter Schickele holds the distinction of being the only bicycle soloist ever to have made his debut with the New York Philharmonic. The concert took place on May 2, 1987, and featured members of the orchestra with a surprise guest, Joseph Polisi, president of Juilliard, joining the ensemble. Professor Schickele conducted the opening work, P.D.Q. Bach's *Abduction of Figaro.* But later in the program, he took to the bicycle for the *Pervertimento* by the same composer, while Andrew Davis led the orchestra from the podium. (There's a recording of this important work with the Royal P.D.Q. Bach Festival Orchestra conducted by Jorge Mester: Vanguard VBD-79223.)

Four years after this landmark Pension Fund (!) concert, the following manuscript of a recipe by P.D.Q. Bach was found by the Philharmonic:

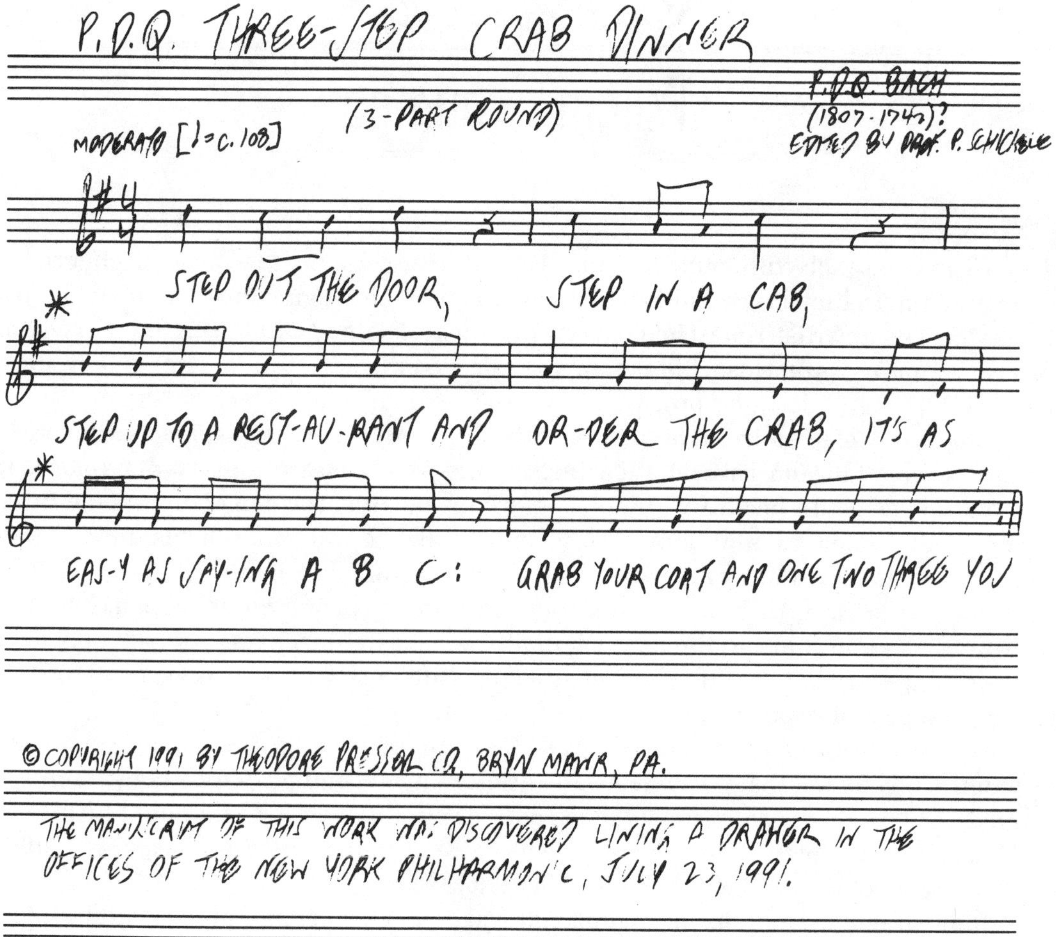

P.D.Q. THREE-STEP CRAB DINNER
P.D.Q. BACH
(1807-1742)?
EDITED BY PROF. P. SCHICKELE
(3-PART ROUND)
MODERATO [♩= c. 108]
STEP OUT THE DOOR, STEP IN A CAB,
STEP UP TO A REST-AU-RANT AND OR-DER THE CRAB, IT'S AS
EAS-Y AS SAY-ING A B C: GRAB YOUR COAT AND ONE TWO THREE YOU
© COPYRIGHT 1991 BY THEODORE PRESSER CO., BRYN MAWR, PA.
THE MANUSCRIPT OF THIS WORK WAS DISCOVERED LINING A DRAWER IN THE
OFFICES OF THE NEW YORK PHILHARMONIC, JULY 23, 1991.

William Schuman

American composer William Schuman, a legend whose music is performed, cheered, and revered internationally, managed to divide his time between composition and community service with an artistry matched only by his music. From his *American Festival Overture* to his variations on "America," Bill Schuman endeared himself to audiences and orchestras alike.

While he devoted so much of his life to these important creations, he also devoted his time to the creation and care of such institutions as Lincoln Center and Juilliard. In a telephone conversation just a few months before his death at the age of eighty-one in 1992, the composer looked back at some of the more difficult moments of his administrative career. "I remember standing in front of an audience of young students at the High School of Music and Art in New York and telling them that their school would someday join with Performing Arts and move to the as yet unbuilt Lincoln Center. I was roundly booed," Bill winced. Change isn't easy for anyone, old or young. But those with a clear vision of the future fight for change and make us all grateful for their struggles.

After Lincoln Center was built, opened, and functioning, Bill Schuman served as its president. When he left that post in 1969, he assisted a pair of the center's constituents, and assumed the position of chairman of the executive committee of the Chamber Music Society and a board member of the Film Society. (He had already left his post of president of Juilliard before the school took its place at Lincoln Center.)

Administrator, creator of culture and cultural centers, and champion of children ("they are the future of music," he insisted), William Schuman was always courteous and courageous, humorous and humble, alive with ideas and passionate about their implementation. He was also extraordinarily well organized. Since his life was so full, he had to make sure that his primary passion—composing—was fulfilled. The *New York Times* wrote in William Schuman's obituary, "Even at his busiest times at Lincoln Center, he composed a minimum of 600 hours a year, keeping track with a detailed diary."

With that kind of pace, one might wonder when there was time for food. He and his wife, Frances, outgoing, going-out people, made time. Bill told me he had a favorite local restau-

COMPOSERS   131

rant, La Panetiere in Rye, New York. "I know the owner and proprietor, Jacques Loupiac, and Jacques knows what I like," Bill said with joy. "He understands my tastes."

La Panetiere is a serene, country restaurant, surrounded by trees and grass. The seating for ninety is based on restaurants of Provence in France and the menu changes according to the season. Along with this Gratin de Framboises, they also specialize in a dessert called Chaud-Froid, Hot and Cold Fudge. In other words, William Schuman liked the serene decadence of a charming French restaurant in the American countryside, close to home, friendly and abounding with good food.

On the musical menu for William Schuman is his *American Festival Overture* played by the Los Angeles Philharmonic with Leonard Bernstein (DG 413324-2) and his Symphony No. 3, written in 1941 and performed by the New York Philharmonic with Bernstein (CBS MS-7442).

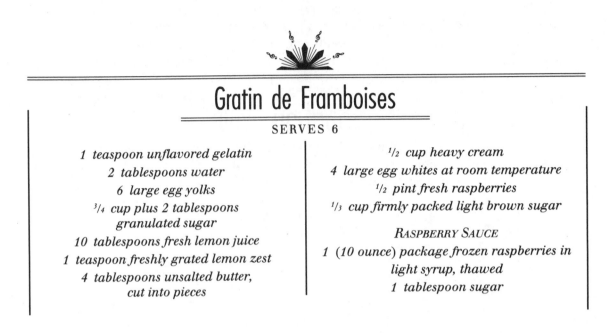

Gratin de Framboises

SERVES 6

1 teaspoon unflavored gelatin

2 tablespoons water

6 large egg yolks

³/₄ cup plus 2 tablespoons
granulated sugar

10 tablespoons fresh lemon juice

1 teaspoon freshly grated lemon zest

4 tablespoons unsalted butter,
cut into pieces

¹/₂ cup heavy cream

4 large egg whites at room temperature

¹/₂ pint fresh raspberries

¹/₃ cup firmly packed light brown sugar

RASPBERRY SAUCE

1 (10 ounce) package frozen raspberries in
light syrup, thawed

1 tablespoon sugar

1   In a small cup, sprinkle gelatin over water to soften. Let stand 5 minutes. Meanwhile, in top of double boiler set over simmering water, whisk together egg yolks, ³/₄ cup of granulated sugar, lemon juice, and zest. Stir in butter and cook, whisking constantly, until mixture begins to thicken, about 5 minutes. Remove from heat and gradually whisk in the gelatin until completely dissolved, about 1 minute. Whisk in heavy cream and transfer to a bowl to cool, whisking occasionally.

2   In a large mixing bowl or the bowl of a heavy-duty mixer, beat egg whites to soft peaks on high speed. Gradually beat in remaining 2 tablespoons granulated sugar and beat until stiff peaks form. Fold half the whites into the lemon mixture with a rubber spatula until well mixed and carefully fold in remaining whites. Pour half the mixture into a shallow 2-quart ovenproof gratin dish. Sprinkle with raspberries and top with remaining lemon mixture. Cover and refrigerate 4 hours or overnight.

3   Preheat broiler. Press brown sugar evenly through a fine sieve over top of lemon mixture. Broil gratin 3 inches from source of heat for 1 minute or until sugar just melts. Serve immediately with raspberry sauce.

4   For the Sauce, purée raspberries in food processor or blender until smooth. Strain through a fine sieve into a bowl to remove seeds. Stir in sugar until dissolved.

Ursula Vaughan Williams

Ralph Vaughan Williams, one of England's great composers, had the good fortune to have been married to a woman of many talents. Poet, hostess, cook, and historian, Ursula is a charming collection of captivating memories of life with the composer and their friends.

"I didn't disturb him while he worked," she assures us. "But I was always interested in his creations."

She was also interested in the many musicians who made their way into the Vaughan Williamses' home. "We would gather in the kitchen, you see. For some reason it was always the gathering place for everyone. And I'd chop away while we would chat." Many of those chats were with composer Gerald Finzi. "I cooked so many dinners for him, for years and years and years. He introduced me to yogurt and I absolutely loathed it.

"The Finzis had a beautiful garden. I cooked for them anything I could get. It was during the war, mostly. But it must have taken me through the whole repertoire of everything I knew.

"One composer I knew, Ross Lee Finney, loved Summer Pudding. I'd put as much fruit in it as possible. But it was Gerald Finzi who grew so much fruit. All those apple trees! You talk about the likes and dislikes of composers. Well," Mrs. Vaughan Williams says with a grin, "there was always Sibelius. But he lived mostly on brandy."

The chicken Ursula Vaughan Williams cooked up for us has quite a pedigree. She found the recipe in the London Museum, which is probably better than finding it in the Tower.

While preparing this dish, we suggest you get ready for a chat in your kitchen. A musical chat. Ralph Vaughan Williams set many of his wife's poems to music. He also set Shakespeare. One of the most beautiful pieces—a true inspiration with or without a chicken in the pot—is *Serenade to Music*. And one of the most beautiful recordings comes to us from opening night at Philharmonic Hall back in September 1962. Each part was taken by a soloist—Adele Addison, Richard Tucker, Shirley Verrett, and Lucine Amara, among others. Leonard Bernstein led the New York Philharmonic and the music and words floated over the hall. The recording is difficult to come by, but worth the search.

Of course, Vaughan Williams's *real* food music comes in his Incidental Music, after Aristophanes, to *The Wasps*. This work includes a movement called "The March of the

Kitchen Utensils" and will come in handy while preparing almost any meal (Angel CDC-47216).

And, just for fun, you must hear a song called "Place Settings" by Jeremy Nicholas. Try the performance by Sarah Walker and Roger Vignoles on Hyperion (CDA66289). It goes something like this: "Sheila's next to Andrew, and Andrew's opposite Marge. Rita can have the window seat because she's rather large. Clive can flirt with Kay so put Sally on the right, but Kath must be with Ian 'cos he's bound to end up tight." Get the idea?

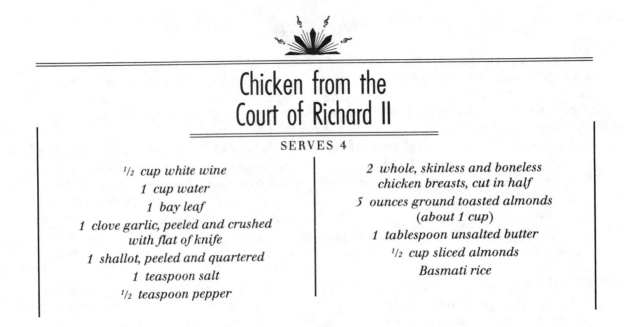

Chicken from the Court of Richard II

SERVES 4

½ cup white wine
1 cup water
1 bay leaf
1 clove garlic, peeled and crushed with flat of knife
1 shallot, peeled and quartered
1 teaspoon salt
½ teaspoon pepper

2 whole, skinless and boneless chicken breasts, cut in half
5 ounces ground toasted almonds (about 1 cup)
1 tablespoon unsalted butter
½ cup sliced almonds
Basmati rice

1   In a large skillet, combine wine, water, bay leaf, garlic, shallot, salt, and pepper. Bring to a boil over high heat and add chicken. Lower heat to a simmer and cook until done, about 18 minutes. Remove chicken to plate and keep warm.

2   Strain poaching liquid into a small saucepot and stir in ground almonds. Let stand 30 minutes. Meanwhile, melt butter over medium high heat in a small skillet and add sliced almonds. Cook, stirring, until lightly browned.

3   To serve, heat almond sauce over medium high heat until hot and thickened. Top chicken breasts with sauce and sprinkle with sliced almonds. Serve with basmati rice.

Conductors

Marin Alsop

Marin Alsop's conducting debut with the New York Philharmonic puts her into a very special category. After all, how many conductors do you know who can boast that they led their first performance with this illustrious ensemble at Valhalla? Never mind that it was Valhalla, New York.

Marin is also one of that special group of musicians who were friends, colleagues, or students of Leonard Bernstein. She treasures her memories of the maestro. "I admired his dedication and his commitment," she remembers. "He always stood up for what he believed, in newspapers, on television. He never ran from an issue."

He never ran from the dinner table, either. "He loved to talk after a concert. We'd go out to eat and we'd never even get to the entree until two A.M. because he was so busy talking. He did everything with that kind of passion. Talking, eating, conducting. He lived in the moment and I think he was excited until the moment he died.

"We were in Japan on the Fourth of July the month before my debut with the Philharmonic in 1990. After the concert he had managed to put together this enormous feast. A lobster feast." Marin doesn't know where the lobsters came from. "Maybe he had them flown in from Maine. That would be like him."

There were firecrackers, too, that night. And exactly one month later, Marin Alsop made her debut with the Philharmonic at the first of two Parks Concerts conducting an American-style program that included Three Dance Episodes from Leonard Bernstein's *On the Town*, followed by Dvořák's tribute to America, the *New World Symphony.*

Where does a young conductor take the New York Philharmonic after they've seen Valhalla? Parks Concert number two took place in Brooklyn. Of course.

The two works we suggest to accompany Marin Alsop's Chicken with Rice are Leonard Bernstein's recording with the New York Philharmonic of the ballet music from *On the Town* (CBS MK42263) and Dvořák's Symphony No. 9 (*From the New World*) in the historic first Bernstein–Philharmonic collaboration of this work (Columbia ML-5793), released on December 17, 1962.

Microwave Chicken and Rice Pilaf

SERVES 4

2 whole skinless and boneless chicken
breasts, split in half
1/2 teaspoon pepper
2 tablespoons chopped pimento
3 cups cooked rice

2 tablespoons onion soup mix
2 tablespoons dry sherry
1/2 teaspoon paprika
2 tablespoons unsalted butter, melted
2 tablespoons water

1 Place chicken on a 9-inch glass pie plate, narrow ends facing in. Cover with another plate and microwave on high power 2 minutes. Turn the dish 180 degrees and cook 2 minutes longer. In a medium bowl, combine remaining ingredients and mix well. Uncover chicken and spread rice mixture over it. Re-cover and microwave 4 minutes on high power. Uncover, stir, and cover again. Microwave on high 4 minutes longer. Let sit 3 minutes and serve.

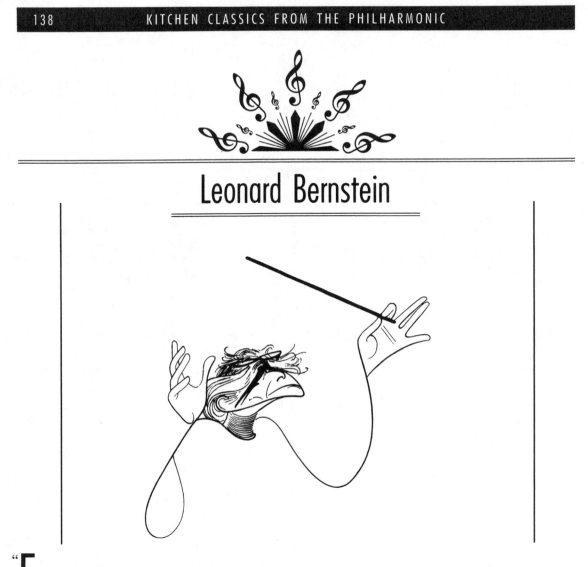

Leonard Bernstein

"**F**or Jennie Tourel, the only begetter of these songs" reads Leonard Bernstein's dedication for his song cycle *La Bonne Cuisine*, a series of four recipes.* The French is from *La Bonne Cuisine Française*, by Emile Dumont. And the English version is by "L.B."

If L.B. had tried to make these songs any harder, he'd have had to hire Julia Child to cook them. They are fast, strangely accented, and peculiarly pitched for the voice, with a wild, virtuosic piano partnering.

The recipes are, well, not to be served. But the songs, when sung as mezzo-soprano Jennie Tourel originally sang them, were always eaten up by the audience. The cycle opens with "Plum Pudding," marked "Allegro molto; matematico." And you'd better count that first

Recorded by Roberta Alexandra and Tan Crone (Etcetera Etc 1037).

measure or you'll be left on the plate. The recipe, as sung, calls for "eleven pounds of juicy Concord grapes combined with equal parts of extra fine Tokays." Okay!

Next, "Ox-Tails" (Queues de Boeuf). "Are you too proud to serve your friends an ox-tail stew?" we're asked legato-ly. "You're wrong! . . . Remove the tails which you have used to make the stew, and then you can bread them and grill them, and prepare them with a sauce." Finally, we're assured, "You'll find them delicious and different and so tempting."

After ox-tails, we're treated, musically, to "Tavouk Gueunksis," as hard to say as it is to sing. "So Oriental," Leonard Bernstein tells us. And how is it made? In 5/8 time, Allegretto alla Turca: "Put a chicken to boil, young and tender and sweet. Then—like you should know this—"in the Arab manner, slice it up into pieces. Then boil flour and water, and add to it the chicken. . . . Tavouk gueunksis, a Turkish heaven."

Now that we've whetted your appetite for Leonard Bernstein's *La Bonne Cuisine*, we come to the pièce de résistance: "Rabbit at Top Speed." And we serve it up to you with thanks to the publishers, Boosey and Hawkes. When you finish singing, try Jean Galton's interpretation of Civet à Toute Vitesse—a quick rabbit stew.

IV Civet à Toute Vitesse
(Rabbit at Top Speed)

Rabbit with 40 Cloves of Garlic

SERVES 4 TO 6

3 tablespoons olive oil

1 2¹/₂-to-3-pound rabbit cut into 7 or 8 serving pieces

¹/₂ teaspoon salt

³/₄ teaspoon pepper

¹/₂ cup dry vermouth or white wine

40 garlic cloves (give or take a few), peeled but left whole

2 branches fresh rosemary or 1 teaspoon dried

1 cup chicken broth

¹/₂ teaspoon lemon juice

1 tablespoon unsalted butter

1 Heat oil in a large (at least 6 quart) saucepot or Dutch oven over medium high heat. Meanwhile pat rabbit pieces dry and sprinkle with the salt and pepper. Brown rabbit pieces well (about 5 to 6 minutes on each side), working in batches if necessary. Remove pieces when browned and add wine, scraping up brown bits. Add garlic, rosemary, broth, and rabbit. Cover tightly and reduce heat to medium. Cook 40 minutes or until rabbit is tender. Remove rabbit to a serving dish and keep warm. Raise heat to high and reduce sauce 3 to 4 minutes longer. Stir in lemon juice and butter and pour over rabbit.

Serve with a green salad and warm bread to spread with the softened garlic.

Sergiu Comissiona

Sergiu Comissiona is a true conductor of the twentieth century. His life is spent in jets, with one foot on the podium in Houston while his baton is leading an ensemble in New York. Zigzagging from Jerusalem to Vancouver with stops in Baltimore, Madrid, and Helsinki might make the most seasoned traveler dizzy. But this maestro seems to rejoice in his journeys.

One stop in 1975 brought the Romanian-born conductor to the New York Philharmonic for the first time. It was an all-Tchaikovsky program that featured pianist Earl Wild in the B-flat minor Piano Concerto, along with the Overture to *The Queen of Spades*, the Cossak Dance from *Mazeppa*, and the Symphony No. 5. A perfect program for this conductor for several reasons.

Take the *Queen of Spades* Overture. Much of Sergiu Comissiona's career has been spent in the opera house, where he's conducted with sensitivity and understanding of the voice. And the dance sequence from *Mazeppa* takes him full circle, since the conductor's wife, Robinne, is a former ballet dancer.

With so much time spent traveling from city to city, there's not too much time for cooking. But Sergiu and Robinne have the best of all possible worlds when it comes to eating. From the east and west coasts of the United States to the tables of Sweden and Finland for fresh seafood, their diets have been at once healthy and entertaining. But Romania and its hearty fare are never too far away.

For the uninitiated, Mamaliga may well be dubbed the Romanian national dish. Even its name sounds homespun. Simple, rib-sticking food, Mamaliga is to Romania what grits are to the American South. It goes with almost anything and can be eaten at almost any time— breakfast, lunch, or dinner. Served with Romanian Stuffed Cabbage, it's the perfect dish for a gala feast or a family gathering.

When sitting down to a plate of stuffed cabbage, open the meal with Enescu's *Romanian Rhapsody No. 2* with maestro Comissiona and the Baltimore Symphony (Vox Unique VU 9006). Luciano Pavarotti's recording, "Mamma" accompanies the mamaliga (London 411959-1 LH).

Sarmele with Mamaliga
(Romanian Stuffed Cabbage)

SERVES 8 TO 10

1 large green cabbage (about 2 pounds),
cut in half and cored, leaves separated

2 pounds ground round beef

1 (11 ounce) can onion soup

3 tablespoons uncooked rice

2 large eggs, lightly beaten

2 tomatoes, chopped

1 teaspoon salt

1 teaspoon pepper

¼ cup chopped Italian parsley

1 (16 ounce) package sauerkraut,
rinsed, drained, and squeezed dry

1 (16 ounce) can tomato sauce

1 (16 ounce) can stewed tomatoes

1 cup water

MAMALIGA

7 cups cold water

2 teaspoons salt

2 cups cornmeal

1   Bring a large pot of water to a boil and add cabbage leaves. Stir and cook until tender, about 3 to 4 minutes. Drain well and set aside until leaves are cool enough to handle.

2   Meanwhile, in a large mixing bowl, combine meat, onion soup, rice, eggs, chopped tomatoes, salt, pepper, and parsley. Mix well. Fill each cabbage leaf with about 2 table-spoons of the stuffing, wrapping each leaf around filling to form a roll. Place seam side down in a large (6 to 8 quart) saucepot and spread sauerkraut on top. Pour tomato sauce, stewed tomatoes, and water on top, cover, and bring to a boil over high heat. Lower heat to a simmer and cook for one hour. Let cool and refrigerate overnight. The next day, remove from refrigerator and let stand 30 minutes.

3   Preheat oven to 350°.

4   Bake Sarmele covered for 30 minutes or until hot. Serve with mamaliga.

5   To make the mamaliga, bring 6 cups water to a boil in a medium saucepot. Add salt. Mix the cornmeal with the remaining 1 cup cold water and slowly add, stirring constantly, to the boiling water. Cook, stirring, 12 to 15 minutes or until smooth and thickened.

James Conlon

It took James Conlon a mere twenty-four years to go from the cradle to the New York Philharmonic podium. In between, he studied at New York's High School of Music and Art and Juilliard. But it was after his debut with the Philharmonic in 1974 that his career really accelerated. From New York, he went to Chicago, Boston, Philadelphia, Cleveland, and Washington to lead the major orchestras of America. And, in Europe, he conducted the London Philharmonic, the London Symphony, the BBC Symphony, l'Orchestre de Paris, l'Orchestre National de France, and—well, you get the idea. James Conlon is a well-established and well-traveled conductor.

Does he like to cook? "No," he answers flatly. "I'm a lousy cook. I never cooked as a child. My mother and grandmother took care of that. But I love to eat." When he finds the time, that is.

Obviously, this is a conductor who doesn't like to settle in any one place for any length of time. Sure, he's led more than a hundred performances at the Metropolitan Opera. And he's recently renewed his contracts with both the Cologne Opera and the Gurzenich Orchestra until 1996. His title? Generalmusikdirektor of the City of Cologne. Jimmy Conlon is, in fact, the first American ever to hold either position and the first person since 1945 to hold both posts.

But try to find James Conlon and you find yourself chasing from city to city, country to country, and podium to podium. Still, he can choose his favorite city for eating out and, without hesitation, that city is Paris.

James Conlon's recipe for Abuelo's Pound Cake came to us in just the way you might expect—faxed from overseas. In fact, it's hard to imagine this bustling and vigorous musician having the time to do anything *but* fax a recipe. At this stage in his career, if he suddenly developed a passion for cooking, he'd have to take the oven with him in the orchestra pit.

We caught up with Jimmy by telephone in France. He explained that Abuelo is his father-in-law. "Actually," he clarified, "it's what we all call him. Abuelo is Spanish for 'Grandfather' and that's become his name over the years. This is his recipe."

It's a recipe Abuelo must be proud of, too. This is a really good, simple way of making one of the most popular and versatile of all desserts. The honey glaze that goes with the cake makes it perfect eating by itself or with fresh berries. If you choose to omit the glaze, this pound cake sits beautifully under the ice cream of your choice. And, since pound cake freezes so well, you can store several of these for unexpected company or solitary binges. Try defrosting it first, though. While chocolate cakes and cookies straight from the freezer may be some people's passions, iced pound cake is just a yellow rock.

Because there's so much movement in James Conlon's life, the musical accompaniment for his pound cake recipe must be something that takes us traveling along with him. The first thing that comes to mind is Liszt's "Procession Nocturne" (Erato ECD 88235), which could cover his nighttime wanderings across the world or our nighttime perambulations to the kitchen to sneak a little more of this pound cake. And, on the same recording with the Rotterdam Philharmonic, James Conlon conducts the "pounding" rhythms of Liszt's "Dance in the Village" from *Mephisto Waltz.*

Abuelo's Pound Cake

SERVES 10

2 sticks (¹/₂ pound) unsalted butter or
  margarine, softened
2 cups sugar
1 teaspoon vanilla extract
6 large eggs, at room temperature
Pinch salt
2 cups all-purpose flour

GLAZE
¹/₄ cup honey
1 tablespoon unsalted butter, melted
2 tablespoons sugar

1 Preheat oven to 350°. Grease and flour a standard bundt pan.

2 In a large bowl, cream butter until light with an electric mixer, about 4 minutes. Slowly beat in sugar and vanilla. Beat in eggs one at a time, beating well after each addition. Beat in salt and flour until well mixed, and pour into prepared pan. Bake 1 hour or until cake tester inserted in middle comes out clean. Cool 10 minutes in pan.

3 Meanwhile, stir together all ingredients for glaze. Invert warm cake onto a plate and brush with glaze. Let cool completely.

Antonio de Almeida

Antonio de Almeida's name may sound Spanish, but the conductor was born in France and trained at Yale. That dual life has prompted this French citizen to maintain homes in both France and the United States. But while his conducting has taken him all over the world, the maestro's heart is in France. Just look at his roster of recordings and you'll see names like Canteloube, Thomas, Massenet and Offenbach. He may not call himself a specialist, but if there's any conductor around today who knows his Offenbach, it's Antonio de Almeida. Even the French government has honored him with the orders of the Légion d'Honneur and Arts et Lettres.

But enough of this podium patter. It's food and Philharmonic we're interested in. And Tony is happy to fill in the details on both. "I remember making my debut with the New York Philharmonic at Lewisohn Stadium. Rudolf Firkusny was the piano soloist in the Mendelssohn Concerto and Eugene Ormandy's brother was part of the orchestra. In fact," Tony remembers, getting to the good part, "after the concert was over, he and I went out to get some good, Czech food."

It may have been Czech after the Mendelssohn, but Tony de Almeida's recipe is definitely French and, if the French government were to taste it, they might present these crêpes with an award for delicacy. Since Maestro de Almeida won the 1989 Grand Prix du Disque for his recording of Offenbach's original, unedited overtures and ballet music, this is our first choice to accompany the maestro's Gâteau de Crêpes. You might even kick your legs in a Cancan when you hear these lively, very French overtures (Phil. 422 057-2).

Tony de Almeida has also worked with Frederica von Stade on two volumes of the beautiful songs of the Auvergne. The lush orchestral accompaniment and the sweetness of both music and words make these the ideal accompaniment for Gâteau de Crêpes (CBS MK 37299).

Gâteau de Crêpes

SERVES 6

CRÊPES
1 cup milk
1 cup cold water
4 large eggs
2 cups all-purpose flour
5 tablespoons unsalted butter, melted
Pinch salt
1/4 teaspoon pepper
Unsalted butter for crêpe pan

BÉCHAMEL AND SPINACH FILLING
3 tablespoons unsalted butter
3 tablespoons all-purpose flour
1/2 cup chicken broth
1/2 cup heavy cream
3/4 cup milk
1/2 teaspoon salt
1/2 teaspoon pepper
Pinch freshly grated nutmeg
Pinch cayenne pepper
2 (10 ounce) packages frozen chopped spinach, thawed, drained, and squeezed (or 1 1/2 cups steamed spinach)

1   In a blender or by hand, whisk together milk, water, and eggs. Add flour and blend or whisk until smooth. Add butter, salt, and pepper and set aside in the refrigerator for at least 1 hour (or up to 4 or 5).

2   To make crêpes, heat about 1 tablespoon butter in a crêpe pan over medium heat. Add about 3 tablespoons of batter and swirl in pan to spread evenly. Cook about 2 to 3 minutes or until bottom is browned and flip to brown the other side. Turn out onto a plate and cover with wax paper. Repeat until batter is finished. (You should have about 15 crêpes.) Keep warm.

3   Meanwhile, in a medium saucepot over medium heat, melt butter for béchamel sauce. Whisk in flour and cook, stirring constantly, for 3 to 4 minutes (do not let mixture brown). Whisk in broth, cream, milk, salt, pepper, and spices. Cook until thickened, about 6 to 7 minutes. Place spinach in a small bowl and stir in 3/4 cup of the béchamel.

4   Preheat oven to 350°. Place 1 crêpe on an ovenproof serving plate and spread with about 2 tablespoons of the spinach. Place a crêpe on top and repeat until all crêpes and spinach are used. Pour remainder of béchamel over gâteau and place in oven. Bake just until heated, about 10 minutes.

Paul Dunkel

"Playing the flute made me exhausted. Conducting made me hungry," says Paul Dunkel, flutist turned conductor. "I was too critical of myself as a flutist but I was hungry to conduct." And that's exactly what he's doing these days. From principal flute with the American Symphony under Leopold Stokowski, Paul now stands on his own podium facing his New Orchestra of Westchester.

During his "fluting" days, however, he faced the music for his New York Philharmonic debut with Pierre Boulez in one of the early contemporary concerts at Cooper Union. This was just right for Paul, whose taste in music has always run to the modern. "I perform and program all kinds of music, but I love contemporary works," he adds with emphasis.

His family's culinary tastes reach back to old Russia, the birthplace of his grandmother and aunts on his father's side. "They came to this country armed to the teeth with recipes that were tried and tested for centuries in Mother Russia," he remembers.

Paul's father, a scenic artist, opened the world of art to his young musical son. After classes at the High School of Music and Art, where he majored in music, Paul spent weekends and vacations in his father's studio painting skies. "I painted clouds for *Rodeo*, *Swan Lake*, *Candide*—my clouds appeared regularly on Broadway, television, and at the Metropolitan Opera."

And after the music and the art, there was the food. "Lunch was often a special affair as I got to know the ethnic restaurants around my father's studio in Greenwich Village." Paul recollects that in those days (the late fifties), "ethnic restaurants were places that didn't serve hamburgers." And he developed a non-Russian, non-American taste for the paella at El Faro. "They wouldn't give me the recipe when I started going there as an adult, so after much experimentation I came up with one of my own."

Paul has no doubts about the dish. "The ultimate test came when I prepared it for Maestro Pablo Casals at an international dinner at the Marlboro Music Festival. Both he and his wife pronounced it authentic."

Have Paul Dunkel's eating habits changed since he's landed on the podium? After all, in addition to lungs, a flutist uses lips that might be coated with crumbs or singed with spices. Was there anything that, as a flutist, he had to avoid prior to a concert? "I had to stay away from martinis before performances. Especially sake martinis." There is a slight pause as the ex-flutist reminisces. Or tries to. "I vaguely remember two concerts where I had too many of them before the curtain." What happened? "I don't remember."

Lest we forget, we have a memory medley for Paul Dunkel. It starts with Robin and Rainger's "Thanks for the Memory," sung by Michael Feinstein (Parnassus PR-0101-CD), continues with "Carried Away" from Bernstein's *On the Town* (CBS MK 44760), and ends with "I Didn't Know What Time It Was," by Rodgers and Hart, performed by William Bolcom and Joan Morris (Omega OCD 3004).

And don't forget the music for the paella! Chabrier's *España* with the New York Philharmonic and Leonard Bernstein (CBS MY-377769).

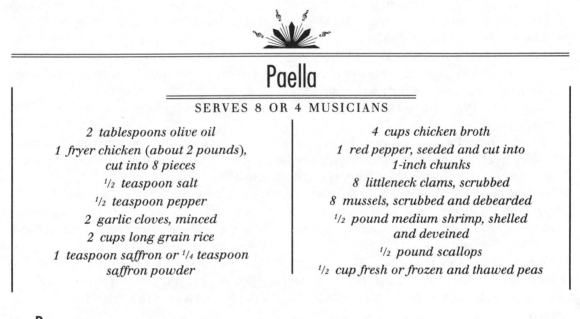

Paella

SERVES 8 OR 4 MUSICIANS

2 tablespoons olive oil	4 cups chicken broth
1 fryer chicken (about 2 pounds), cut into 8 pieces	1 red pepper, seeded and cut into 1-inch chunks
½ teaspoon salt	8 littleneck clams, scrubbed
½ teaspoon pepper	8 mussels, scrubbed and debearded
2 garlic cloves, minced	½ pound medium shrimp, shelled and deveined
2 cups long grain rice	½ pound scallops
1 teaspoon saffron or ¼ teaspoon saffron powder	½ cup fresh or frozen and thawed peas

1   Preheat oven to 350°.

2   In a 6- to 8-quart saucepot, heat oil over high heat. Sprinkle chicken with salt and pepper and cook about 4 to 5 minutes on each side or until golden brown. Remove and drain off excess fat. Add garlic and cook 1 minute. Stir in rice and cook, stirring, until just starting to brown. Dissolve saffron in broth and add to rice. Stir in red pepper and return chicken to pot. Cover and place in oven for 20 minutes.

3   Uncover and stir in clams. Return to oven for 10 minutes. Stir in remaining ingredients and cook 6 to 7 minutes, or until all the fish is cooked.

Philippe Entremont

Although Philippe Entremont has a dual career as pianist and conductor, the New York Philharmonic first met him at the keyboard with Leonard Bernstein on the podium. It was on Saturday, January 4, 1958, at a time the Philharmonic still began their concerts at 8:45 and the pianist wasn't scheduled until the second half of the program. Before him were the Schumann *Manfred Overture* and Richard Strauss's *Don Quixote*, featuring two members of the orchestra, William Lincer and Laszlo Varga. About an hour after the opening notes of the performance, Mr. Entremont took his place at the piano for a performance of the C Major Concerto of Prokofiev.

These days, Philippe Entremont has the distinction of being the lifetime music director of the Vienna Chamber Orchestra. And, when he's not in Vienna, you'll find him appearing as a guest conductor or pianist, or both, from Atlanta to Tokyo.

This recipient of Austria's First Class Cross of Honor for the Arts and Sciences is also a Knight of the Légion d'Honneur. His Crème Brûlée is also worthy of honors for its simplicity and taste. Even though a little bit goes a long way, we don't recommend it for a weight-reduction diet. And, as Paul Plishka tells us in this book, eating a little of something wonderful is much more satisfying than a lot of junk. So, if you want a special treat, pour this luscious Crème Brûlée into eight, rather than four, small, elegant ovenware dishes. You'll come out with only a few extra calories and you'll feel that you've been awarded a knighthood of your own.

A really good crème brûlée is always a hit at elegant dinner parties. To add to the atmosphere, we propose Philippe Entremont's album *Greatest Hits: Music of Chopin, Debussy, Beethoven, Schumann, and Rachmaninoff* (CBS MT-31406) and, with the New York Philharmonic and Leonard Bernstein, the pianist's recording of Rachmaninoff's Piano Concerto No. 2 (Odyssey MBK 46271).

Crème Brûlée

SERVES 4

2 cups heavy cream
2¹/₂ tablespoons light brown or
maple sugar
¹/₈ teaspoon salt
3 large egg yolks

³/₄ teaspoon vanilla extract
4-5 tablespoons brown sugar
for topping

1 In the top of a double boiler or in a bowl set over simmering water, heat cream almost to a boil. In a separate bowl, add sugar and salt to egg yolks and beat lightly to combine. Stir about ¹/₄ cup of the hot cream into the yolks and then pour back into hot cream. Stir constantly until mixture thickens slightly (about 5 minutes). Stir in vanilla. Pour through a fine sieve into 4 shallow ovenproof serving dishes (4 to 6 ounces each). Chill in refrigerator 4 to 6 hours.

2 Preheat broiler 15 minutes. Sprinkle each dish with about 1 tablespoon brown sugar, covering top completely, and broil 2 to 3 inches from source of heat until burnt and bubbling, about 1 to 2 minutes. Serve immediately or chill if desired.

Skitch Henderson

"Ruth does most of the cooking indoors and I do the honors outside," reports Skitch Henderson, director of the New York Pops and co-author, with his wife, of *Ruth and Skitch Henderson's Seasons in the Country.* "We live on a farm in Connecticut and the photographs in our book give you an idea of the beautiful surroundings. When you look at that amazing countryside, you can't help being inspired.

"The only problem with living so far from New York is that when I'm at work in the city, I can't go home for lunch or dinner. So I do the next best thing—I live at the Russian Tea Room. Faith Stewart Gordon, the owner, is a good friend."

When they are at home, Skitch and Ruth have been known to entertain lavishly. "We've cooked for as many as a hundred," Skitch says. "Isaac Stern, Henry Kissinger, and our friends from the neighborhood come over and I do a cookout. But what I like best is the wintertime, when we have just six or eight to a quiet dinner and Ruth does the cooking."

The New York Pops Orchestra has really come into its own in the more than ten years since its inception, and Skitch Henderson looks forward to more tours, more concerts ("we're sold out now"), and some television shows. The orchestra has already toured Japan, where their music director was treated to a Kobe steak dinner. "I was very disappointed. The meat is just too rich for me. I found it bland and so soft it was like whipped cream. You can cut it with your hands."

Skitch Henderson's association with the New York Philharmonic has been far from bland. "It's a unique affiliation," Skitch begins. "I was guest conductor for the very first program that contained popular music other than Gershwin. It was in Lewisohn Stadium and we did a tribute to Irving Berlin. I was told that I had to do classical repertoire for the first half of the concert and the Berlin would be relegated to a short second half. After the intermission, the heavens opened and the rain poured down. The concert was never completed or re-scheduled."

There have been other concerts since, of course. "I've done special projects with the Philharmonic, from a disastrous concert performance of *Oklahoma* for the show's twenty-fifth anniversary to the better days of New Year's Eve galas. And, during my tenure at Columbia Records, I recorded both light classical and popular material with the Philhar-monic."

If people are critical of concerts, Skitch Henderson suggests that we stop a moment and think of kitchen critics. "Whether asked for their opinion or not, people come into our house and become very astute critics of our cooking. 'This is underdone. Why don't you try a little more spice?' They wouldn't say a word if it were catered!"

But they do eat up the results. And why not, considering the expertise of the chefs and the charm of the creation. "Stew in a 'Punkin' was an experiment because we were growing these huge 'punkins' at the farm. You have to say 'punkin,'" Skitch reminds us, "because it makes them sound more like what they are. Punkin," he repeats with a punch. "And it worked so well that we put it in the book." Along with its taste and creativity, Stew in a "Punkin" has another great advantage: no tureen to scrub after dinner. In fact, if you're up to your knees in punkins—smaller punkins, that is—why not use them as individual bowls and just toss the whole thing when you're finished? Call it an Ichabod Crane party!

To accompany Skitch Henderson's Stew in a "Punkin" we begin with Vernon Duke's "Autumn in New York" played by the New York Pops (Sefel SEFD5026), and then turn to a recent recording on EMI-Angel by the Pops and Henderson called *Berlin to Bernstein* (EMI CDC7-542742).

Stew in a Pumpkin

SERVES 8 TO 10

3 tablespoons vegetable oil
1 large onion, chopped
2 garlic cloves, minced
2 pounds boneless beef chuck, trimmed
and cut into 1½-inch cubes
2 large tomatoes, peeled, seeded,
and chopped
1 large green pepper, seeded
and chopped
3 medium white potatoes, peeled
and diced
3 medium sweet potatoes, peeled
and diced

¼ teaspoon salt
½ teaspoon pepper
1 teaspoon honey
2 cups beef broth
1 medium pumpkin, about 12 pounds
(measured to fit your oven)
1 tablespoon unsalted butter, melted
1½ cups cooked corn kernels,
at room temperature
1 teaspoon chopped fresh marjoram,
or a pinch dried

1   Heat the oil in a large saucepot or Dutch oven. Add onion and cook 1 minute. Add garlic and cook until onion is soft, about 8 minutes. Transfer to a plate and set aside. Add meat to the saucepot and brown on all sides. Add tomatoes, green pepper, potatoes, salt, pepper, honey, broth, and reserved onions. Heat to boiling, reduce heat, cover, and simmer gently 1 hour.

2   Preheat oven to 350°. Cut the top off the pumpkin and scrape out all the seeds. Reserve top. Brush inside of pumpkin with melted butter and sprinkle with salt and pepper. Place pumpkin on ovenproof plate and set inside roasting pan. Fill pan with water just to lip of plate. Place top on a separate roasting pan. Ladle stew into pumpkin. Bake until pumpkin is just tender, about 1 hour. During last 5 minutes of baking time, stir in corn and marjoram. Carefully transfer pumpkin on plate to a serving platter. Ladle stew into bowls, including some of the pumpkin with each serving.

Seymour Lipkin

Multitalented Seymour Lipkin made his debut as a pianist with the New York Philharmonic under Charles Munch on Sunday afternoon, January 9, 1949. Ten years later, the pianist had become an assistant conductor under Leonard Bernstein.

"It was an exciting time," Seymour recalls. "I toured with Bernstein and the Philharmonic to Europe and Lebanon and Russia. I conducted and I played." He also ate. But in the Soviet Union he had problems. "The food was horrible. I remember some kind of cutlet Kiev we were served in Moscow. I stuck my knife in it and this awful yellow fat squirted out. Not butter. Fat," Seymour gushes.

It wasn't all bad, though. "The caviar was out of this world. We had huge amounts of it and were awed at the freedom with which it was served. Bernstein, of course, loved everything. He was always enthusiastic. Even about the food."

It was during Seymour Lipkin's tenure as assistant conductor with the Philharmonic that the orchestra recruited the chorus from New York's High School of Music and Art to perform Aaron Copland's *Second Hurricane* at a televised Young People's Concert. Being part of that chorus, I remember all our "Uncles"—Lenny, Seymour, Aaron—working with us for the concert and recording. But it was Uncle Seymour who picked about eight of us to come to his home once a week for the rest of the year to read through Bach cantatas with him.

There we were—high school juniors and seniors, black, white, not even at Juilliard or Mannes yet—singing every week with the assistant conductor of the New York Philharmonic. Why us? "Well," Seymour finally answers thirty years later, "you were available to come on a weekly basis, something most good singers who could read weren't able to do. And I love Bach cantatas. It gave me a chance, with all those young, musical voices, to do what I loved most." We loved it, too.

Seymour Lipkin also loves this recipe for chicken with vegetables, or Poule-au-Pot. "I found it in the *New York Times*, cut it out, and have used it ever since."

For Seymour Lipkin, we go back to a recording of Stravinsky's Concerto for Piano and Wind Orchestra made October 10, 1959, with Leonard Bernstein and the Philharmonic (Col. ML-6329). And for the chicken, Cole Porter's "I've Got You Under My Skin" sung by Thomas Hampson with the London Symphony and John McGlinn (EMI CDC 7 54203 2).

Poule-au-Pot

6 TO 8 SERVINGS

2 chickens, about 3 pounds each

5-6 large carrots, about 1 pound, cut into 2-inch lengths (about 2 cups)

5-6 white turnips, about 1 pound, cut into 2-inch lengths (about 2 cups)

³/₄ pound ripe tomatoes, cored and cut into ¹/₂-inch dice (about 2 cups)

1 pound green cabbage, cut into 1-inch cubes

2 garlic cloves, peeled

6 cups chicken or beef broth, fresh or canned

¹/₂ teaspoon salt

¹/₂ teaspoon pepper

2 cups broccoli flowerets, cut into bite-size pieces

1   Put chickens in large saucepot and add cold water to cover. Bring to boil. Drain, then chill chickens in cold running water. Drain and set aside.

2   Return chickens to saucepot and add carrots, turnips, tomatoes, cabbage, garlic, broth, salt, and pepper. Bring to a boil and simmer, uncovered, 30 minutes. Add broccoli and cook 5 minutes longer. Carve chickens and serve pieces in soup bowls with soup and vegetables spooned over.

Zdenek Macal

Zdenek Macal has made his way from Brno, Czechoslovakia, where he was born in 1936, to the podium of the Milwaukee Symphony, where he became music director in 1986. This is a conductor who has appeared with more than 150 orchestras around the world, from Berlin and Vienna to Atlanta and New York. It was in 1976 that the maestro first appeared with the New York Philharmonic, and for the occasion, he led the ensemble in music by Richard Strauss, Borodin, and Ravel.

But even though he's been at the helm of some of the mightiest music-making machines in the world, the conductor was still once a child. And, when it came to getting what he wanted, that little boy had to follow the beat of his parents' baton. "As a child," Zdenek Macal tells us, "I liked Ovocne Knedliky so much that I could eat it for my dinner, not just dessert. So, when I was on my best behavior, my mother and grandmother would serve it to me as a main course."

The conductor has continued getting his "just desserts" as an adult. "My wife Ginny surprises me from time to time and serves this at the dinner table."

What's so special about these dumplings? Maestro Macal describes them. "These are Czech fruit dumplings and the dish is an old Czech specialty that can be served as a dessert." But with butter, cottage cheese and eggs, sugar, fresh fruit such as apricots or cherries, and a topping of golden brown sugar-crusted bread crumbs, why wait so long?

Zdenek Macal received a glowing review recently for his recording of the Beethoven Ninth with the Milwaukee Symphony on the Koss Classics label. *The American Record Guide* wrote, "Unlike the recent crop of Ninths, [Macal's] is the genuine article, the complete aesthetic, emotional, spiritual, dramatic experience." Wait until that critic tastes these dumplings!

Along with the maestro's recording of the Beethoven Ninth with Milwaukee, we also recommend a touch of Czech music to keep these dumplings in check: Dvořák's Symphonic Variations, Op. 78, performed by the London Philharmonic with Zdenek Macal conducting (Angel CDB-62006).

Ovocne Knedliky
(Czech Fruit Dumplings)

SERVES 8

10 tablespoons unsalted butter,
    $^{1}/_{2}$ of it melted
1 cup drained cottage cheese or
    pot cheese, puréed
Pinch salt
2 large eggs, lightly beaten
2 cups all-purpose flour

$1^{1}/_{2}$ pounds fresh apricots, plums,
    or cherries, split in half and pitted
8-15 sugar cube dots (if using
    apricots or plums)
1 cup dry unflavored bread crumbs
3 tablespoons sugar

1 In a large mixing bowl, combine melted butter, cottage cheese, salt, eggs, and flour. Stir until dough holds together, shape into a ball, cover, and chill 30 minutes.

2 Place 1 sugar cube between halves of apricots or plums if using and place halves back together.

3 On a lightly floured board, roll dough out to $^{1}/_{2}$-inch thickness. Cut into 2-inch squares and fold around apricots or plums (if using cherries, cut into $^{3}/_{4}$-inch squares and fold around 2 halves).

4 Bring a large saucepot of salted water to a rolling boil. Add dumplings a few at a time, and cook apricots and plums 8 to 10 minutes, cherries 5 to 6. Remove with a slotted spoon and repeat until all are cooked.

5 In a large skillet over medium high, heat remaining 5 tablespoons butter. Stir in bread crumbs and sugar and cook, stirring, until golden brown, about 7 minutes. Place dumplings on a serving platter and sprinkle with bread crumbs. Serve immediately.

Kurt Masur

Kurt Masur came to the New York Philharmonic as its music director on September 11, 1991. And he did it with the kind of elegance that endeared him to critics, listeners, and musicians alike. Even the *New York Times* had good things to say—about him, about the performance, and about the orchestra.

This is a serious musicmaker with a gleam in his eye and a sense of humor in his heart. This is a conductor who doesn't need to carry a big stick. In fact, he doesn't even use a baton. He shapes his sounds with his hands, which may be one of the reasons the critics have begun using words like "sweet-toned," "rich," and "full" to describe the orchestra's playing.

Maestro Masur shares his skills with the Gewandhaus Orchestra of Leipzig, a position he's held since 1970. And, not to stop there, he's also a principal guest conductor of the London Philharmonic. He's held posts as director and chief conductor of Berlin's Komische Oper and the Dresden Philharmonic, and along with performing his duties as professor at the Leipzig Academy of Music, he's also received honorary degrees from the University of Michigan and the Cleveland Institute of Music.

The 1992–93 season is a busy one for the maestro. In addition to the New York Philharmonic's 150th Anniversary celebrations, Mr. Masur will also be celebrating the 250th anniversary of his Gewandhaus Orchestra.

With all those parties, celebrations, receptions, and performances one might wonder how and when Maestro Masur has time to cook. Well, for the most part, he doesn't. He's told us that his wife, Tomoko, is "a wonderful cook," and that she does most of the creating in the kitchen. But he's given us *his* favorite recipe for this book because it's something he makes himself. It's also something he loves to eat. It comes to us with the assurance that it's simple and delicious. It's also extremely healthy and, for a summer dish, cooling.

To welcome Kurt Masur to the New York Philharmonic and to accompany his Bulgarian Cucumber Soup, we suggest an overture by Franz von "Suppé" with the Philharmonic conducted by Leonard Bernstein (CBS MYK-37240) and Schumann's *Spring Symphony* with Mr. Masur leading the London Philharmonic (Teldec 46455-2).

Tarator
(Bulgarian Cucumber Soup)

MAKES 2½ CUPS

1 small cucumber (about 8 ounces),
peeled, seeded, and cut into
1-inch chunks
1-2 garlic cloves, peeled and minced
1 (16 ounce) container plain yogurt
¼ cup water

⅛ teaspoon salt
1 tablespoon chopped fresh dill
Salad oil (optional)
¼ cup chopped toasted almonds
(optional)

1   In a food processor, combine cucumber and garlic. Pulse until finely chopped. Add remaining ingredients except oil and almonds and pulse just until combined. Chill at least 1 hour. Before serving, add a drop of oil if desired and sprinkle with almonds. (If the weather is very hot you can add a couple of ice cubes.)

Zubin Mehta

If ever there were a chocoholic, it is Zubin Mehta. Despite the fact that everyone from Walter Cronkite to Werner Klemperer tells tales of Zubin's Little Bag of Spices, which he carries with him to properly heat up his food, give Zubin a chocolate cake or a box of chocolates, and bye-bye baggie. How do we know? We've seen him at the New York Philharmonic Radiothons.

Late at night, while he's sitting at the microphone with WQXR announcer Nimet, some Good Witch of the West Side of Manhattan delivers something in chocolate. And, from then on, the conversation turns dark, bittersweet, or milky. Lips are smacked and cakes are consumed faster than you can play the Minute Waltz.

"I'm not really fond of Western junk foods at all," Zubin recently divulged. He does like Indian street food, "bhel-puri and kulfi." (Not related in any way to the *Italian Street Song!*) But then again, his tastes aren't limited to Indian cooking. His favorite restaurants serve

French, Italian, and Chinese food (Le Cirque, Bellini, and Fu's in New York), what he calls "peasant" Italian (Le Cave di Maiano in Florence), or Central European (Casbah in Tel Aviv).

Bon Appétit magazine recently asked Zubin some questions about his favorite foods. One of his answers was particularly inspiring because it showed the conductor's international flair and imagination. Most of us, when planning a dinner, keep the entire menu in the tradition of one particular culture. We plan an Italian menu from antipasti to zabaglione. We create an all-French or all-American dinner right down to the place settings and candle color. Not so Zubin Mehta.

"I don't believe that courses on the menu have to necessarily be of the same ethnic variety," he says. He then goes on to create an evening of diversity, filled with his favorite courses:

SOUP—Senegalese

PASTA—Penne all'arrabbiata

MAIN COURSE—Parsee Dhansak (fried rice pilaf with deep-fried spicy meatballs served with Parsee-style lentils)

DESSERT—Danny Kaye's chocolate soufflé

Zubin Mehta also admits, "I don't believe in an ideal situation in which food has to be balanced as far as calories are concerned." And he adds, "I'm hopeless at making up menus." Zubin, that's true only if you're planning a meal for Weight Watchers. Otherwise, your menu has the same diversity that a good concert program cries for: a change of style and tempo blended with an ear to related keys and colors. Once again we see the balance between food and music.

For Zubin Mehta's culinary imagination, we award his menu a performance of the Berlioz *Symphonie fantastique*, performed by the New York Philharmonic under Zubin's direction (Lon. 400046-2). And, for those Little Bags of Spices Zubin reportedly carries with him: P.D.Q. Bach's oratorio *The Seasonings* with movements that include "Tarragon of virtue is full," "Bide thy thyme" (for soprano, alto, slide whistle, windbreaker, and tromboon—yes, tromboon!), "By the leeks of Babylon," "Open sesame seeds," and, the finale, "To curry favor, favor curry" in a performance by the Royal P.D.Q. Bach Festival Orchestra conducted by Jorge Mester (VBD-79223).

Breaded Shrimps in Green Paste

SERVES 4

1 cup fresh coriander leaves and
tender stems
1/2 cup fresh mint leaves
1/2 cup unsweetened grated coconut
1/4 cup fresh lemon juice
3 garlic cloves, peeled
8 fresh hot green chilies, stemmed

Salt to taste
1 tablespoon sugar
1 pound jumbo shrimps
Oil for shallow frying
2 large eggs, lightly beaten
3 cups bread crumbs

1 Combine the coriander, mint, coconut, lemon juice, garlic, chilies, salt, and sugar in a food processor, and process into a paste. Set aside.

2 Peel the shrimps, leaving the tails on, and butterfly them. To prevent the shrimps from curling during cooking, thread a toothpick along the length of each shrimp. Place shrimps in a dish, add the green paste, and coat them thoroughly.

3 Heat the oil in a large frying pan. Dip shrimps first in beaten eggs, then in bread crumbs, and slip them into the hot oil. Cook shrimps, turning, about 3 to 4 minutes altogether, until golden. Drain on paper towels before serving.

Seiji Ozawa

Seiji Ozawa's recipe came to us via a horn of plenty. *The WCRB Horn of Plenty*, to be specific. The music director of the Boston Symphony gave this recipe to a book that was put together by the staff of the Boston classical radio station WCRB. Laura Carlo, the guiding force behind this project, writes, "We at WCRB felt the need to do something [for the homeless]. Why not a team effort focusing on food-as-art and art-for-food for the hungry? Everyone told me it was impossible to do, but we put it together and brought in more than $50,000 for Project Bread," a nonprofit, nondenominational agency devoted to feeding the hungry in Massachusetts. Maestro Ozawa's recipe was one of about two hundred contributed by local listeners, radio staff members, and celebrities from actress Jane Alexander to Boston Pops conductor John Williams. This spiral book with advertising between sections even carried a section of blank music manuscript paper for "Cook's Notes."

　Seiji Ozawa's recipe is a nice balance of the conductor's Japanese-Chinese upbringing. It was prepared by the maestro's chef, Takeko Masamune, and given to us with the blessings of both Mr. Ozawa and the staff at WCRB as a reminder that without music we are all homeless. It is our obligation to feed those without food as well as those without art. That people can't live by bread alone becomes less a proverb and more a maxim each day.

Fundraising and the use of money to help others is a universal necessity. For this effort we offer the Boston Symphony's recording of Holst's *The Planets* conducted by Seiji Ozawa (Philips 416 456-2). And, as a tribute to its northern sister orchestra and its efforts in the community, the New York Philharmonic, brother oboist Harold Gomberg, and Leonard Bernstein offer William Schuman's *Evocation: To Thee Old Cause* (Col. MS-7392).

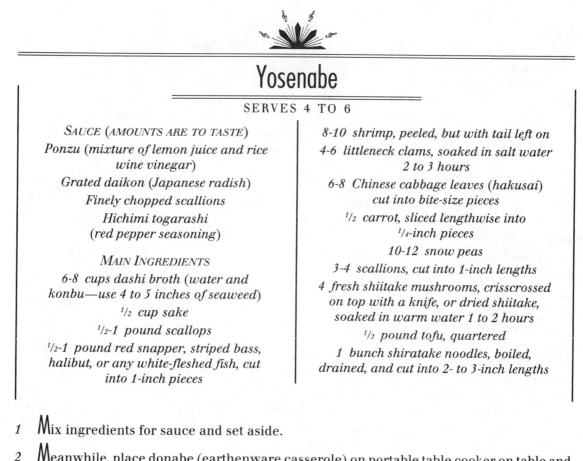

Yosenabe

SERVES 4 TO 6

SAUCE (AMOUNTS ARE TO TASTE)
Ponzu (mixture of lemon juice and rice wine vinegar)
Grated daikon (Japanese radish)
Finely chopped scallions
Hichimi togarashi (red pepper seasoning)

MAIN INGREDIENTS
6-8 cups dashi broth (water and konbu—use 4 to 5 inches of seaweed)
1/2 cup sake
1/2-1 pound scallops
1/2-1 pound red snapper, striped bass, halibut, or any white-fleshed fish, cut into 1-inch pieces

8-10 shrimp, peeled, but with tail left on
4-6 littleneck clams, soaked in salt water 2 to 3 hours
6-8 Chinese cabbage leaves (hakusai) cut into bite-size pieces
1/2 carrot, sliced lengthwise into 1/4-inch pieces
10-12 snow peas
3-4 scallions, cut into 1-inch lengths
4 fresh shiitake mushrooms, crisscrossed on top with a knife, or dried shiitake, soaked in warm water 1 to 2 hours
1/2 pound tofu, quartered
1 bunch shiratake noodles, boiled, drained, and cut into 2- to 3-inch lengths

1 Mix ingredients for sauce and set aside.

2 Meanwhile, place donabe (earthenware casserole) on portable table cooker on table and fill with dashi and sake. Bring to a boil. Arrange ingredients on a large platter and add half the fish and vegetables to the dashi. Simmer 12 to 15 minutes or until done. Serve cooked portions in individual bowls and let guests help themselves to Ponzu sauce. Now you are ready to cook remaining ingredients in the dashi broth for second helpings.

Halina Rodzinski

Was that a gun in the conductor's pocket or was he just glad to see them? Artur Rodzinski, musical director of the New York Philharmonic from 1943 to 1947, may be the only conductor in the history of the orchestra to have stood on the Philharmonic's podium packing a pistol. "He bought it when he was a teenager," Halina Rodzinski, the maestro's widow explains, "to kill the husband of a girl he was in love with. Of course, he never did that," she hastens to add. "I don't think it was ever even loaded. But he found that he always had good luck when he carried it around. So it got to be something like a superstition and he would never conduct without it.

"I remember one time that I forgot to pack it before a concert and the performance was delayed while I returned home to get it for him. He wouldn't walk out on the stage without it in his pocket. Not too many of the musicians knew he had it, but those who knew just laughed."

In addition to the distinction of being the only gun-toting conductor of the Philharmonic, Maestro Rodzinski was the orchestra's first official musical director. According to Howard Shanet in *Philharmonic, A History of New York's Orchestra*, "Damrosch has called himself Musical Director of the old Symphony Society, and Toscanini had been fleetingly referred to as General Musical Director of the Philharmonic-Symphony at certain moments during his last two seasons . . . but the Philharmonic had not used this title before." With the Rodzinski era the orchestra had, for the first time, a man who not only held a baton in his hand but who also held the reins of power over repertory, guest conductors, soloists, and all the "musical and artistic aspects" of the ensemble.

Virgil Thomson, in his role as writer and critic, said that Rodzinski "has done more for the orchestra . . . than any other conductor in our century has done." He became known as a builder of orchestras, an able administrator as well as musician.

Pocket pistol not withstanding, Artur Rodzinski got along famously with members of the Philharmonic. There were some rough spots early on when he attempted to fire several players he felt weren't worthy to wear the mantle of the renowned orchestra, but after that he was well liked and admired by the musicians. Shanet writes, "He had a tendency, which some members of the orchestra found appealing, to let his personal life touch theirs in little ways. When his son Richard was born, he celebrated the event with the Philharmonic by programming the *Toy Symphony*." He also helped Halina organize a club of the wives of the orchestra musicians. It was a time of spirited socializing and fraternity (and sorority) for the Philharmonic.

As for food, Mrs. Rodzinski remembers that he was not a fussy eater. "But he loved most of all the Polish dishes that he was used to from when he was small. And he loved my nut torte with chocolate." Loaded gun or unloaded gun, you might say this was a dessert that went over with a bang!

Our musical accompaniment for Artur and Halina Rodzinski opens with "You Can't Get a Man with a Gun," from *Annie Get Your Gun* in the original-cast recording (MCA 1626). And, to get an up-to-date sense of the conductor, we suggest his recording with the New York Philharmonic of Gershwin's *American in Paris*, one of the few discs available today of the maestro's work with the orchestra (CBS CS-8641).

Chocolate Nut Torte

SERVES 12

CAKE
1 pound walnuts
9 large eggs, separated and at room temperature
1 cup sugar
2 tablespoons fine cracker crumbs, plus additional for pan

GLAZE
¹/₄ cup water
2 tablespoons sugar
1 tea bag
1 tablespoon lemon
2 tablespoons rum

FILLING
4 ounces semisweet chocolate, finely chopped
1 stick unsalted butter
1 teaspoon vanilla
2 teaspoons sugar (optional)

TOPPING
3 ounces semisweet chocolate, finely chopped
4 tablespoons (¹/₂ stick) unsalted butter
¹/₄ cup heavy cream

1   Preheat oven to 350°. Grease three 9-inch cake pans and coat with cracker crumbs.

2   In a food processor or blender, grind nuts until very fine, working in batches of ½ cup at a time (try not to turn them into a paste—you want them as dry as possible).

3   In a large mixing bowl, combine egg yolks and sugar. Beat with an electric mixer until light and thick, about 3 to 4 minutes. Mix in nuts and cracker crumbs and set aside. In separate bowl, beat egg whites with electric beater until they form stiff peaks. Lighten the nut mixture with a quarter of the whites and then fold in remainder. Divide evenly among pans and bake 25 to 30 minutes or until cakes pull away from sides of pans. Let cool in pans and invert.

4   To make glaze, heat water until boiling and stir in sugar. Add tea bag and let sit 5 minutes. Stir in lemon and rum. Sprinkle evenly over cakes.

5   To make filling, in a double boiler or microwavable bowl, melt chocolate and butter together (microwave on high power 1 minute, stir, and repeat). Stir in vanilla and sugar. Spread filling over cakes, dividing evenly among the three. Place one on a serving platter filling side up. Repeat with remaining cakes.

6   To make topping, in a double boiler or microwavable bowl, melt chocolate and butter together (microwave on high power 1 minute, stir, and repeat). Stir in the cream and pour over cake, spreading evenly with a spatula. Let sit until firm.

Julius Rudel

onductor Julius Rudel first came before the New York Philharmonic at one of the summer Parks Concerts. The date was August 13, 1968, a busy time for the maestro, who was, under other circumstances, firmly planted across the Lincoln Center Plaza in the State Theater with his own New York City Opera. Although Julius has conducted orchestras throughout the world in strictly instrumental programs, he's best known—and loved—for his work with singers. So, it's fitting that part of his Philharmonic premiere program was devoted to vocal music: Carl Orff's *Carmina Burana.*

The driving rhythms and percussive passages of this work always conjure up feelings of passion among listeners. Audiences rarely understand the words. And good thing, too! The text, sung in kitchen and church Latin interspersed with early, gutter German and French, sings of passion. Passion for sex. Passion for wine. Passion for pleasure. Passion for love.

The tenor sings, in a high, eerie voice, the "Song of the Roasted Swan." The baritone follows him with the words, "I am the Abbot of Cucany, and my deliberation is among drinkers, and my desire to be in the school of Decius, and whoever seeks me early in the tavern, by evening he will go out bare. . . ." But a macho male chorus struts, "When we are in the tavern we do not mind what the place may be . . . some gamble, some drink . . . some of them are stripped . . . but they draw lots in Bacchus' honor."* In rapid succession they sing of all who drink, the mistress, master, soldier, cleric, man, woman, servant, invalid, exile, president, deacon, mother . . . "a thousand drink."

That's Orff in the Park with Julius.

Out of the park, Julius Rudel is a family man and a traveling conductor. When he steps off the podium, he enjoys his wine and his swan and his family and his schnitzel. This recipe comes to us from the Rudel family catalogue of favorite dishes.

---

* Translation from EMI recording.

The Rudel Wiener Schnitzel is properly accompanied by Lehár's lilting strains of *The Merry Widow* with Julius conducting the New York City Opera Orchestra and soloists who include Beverly Sills (Angel CDC-47585). And, after you've finished dinner, turn to the recording of Orff's *Carmina Burana* with Riccardo Muti and the Philharmonia Orchestra and Chorus—following the English translation carefully as you listen (EMI CDC 7 47100 2).

Wiener Schnitzel

SERVES 3 TO 4

2 tablespoons all-purpose flour
2 large eggs, lightly beaten
1/4 teaspoon salt
1/4 teaspoon white pepper
1 cup dry seasoned bread crumbs

1 pound veal scaloppine (preferably cut from the leg), pounded into paper-thin slices
1/3 cup olive oil
1 lemon, cut into wedges

1 Place flour on a plate. Beat eggs with salt and pepper and place in a shallow bowl. Place bread crumbs on a separate plate. Dip each piece of veal in flour, shake off excess, then dip in egg, and finally coat each piece with bread crumbs. Shake off excess.

2 Heat oil in a large skillet over high heat. Quickly cook the veal (in batches if necessary), turning once, about 1 to 2 minutes on each side or until golden brown. Serve immediately with lemon wedges.

Alexander Schneider

Music lovers, listeners as well as musicians, know Alexander Schneider as a conductor, violinist, chamber musician, and propagator of music among young, eager performers. Those who know him as "Sasha" know what a great host he is, how he loves good wine, good food and, yes, good women. And, if you're wondering if there's real life after eighty, just ask Sasha. His zest for life overwhelms age. It reaches into his music, his friends, and his food.

Alexander Schneider's New York String Orchestra, an ensemble built from young, outstanding instrumentalists who come together each year over the Christmas holiday to rehearse, learn, and perform, has given birth to musicians of the highest caliber. Sasha has a way with kids. He gives them more than his experience; he instills his enthusiasm in their souls, and they leave him with the resources to pursue their dreams.

It's fitting that this vigorous proponent of pride made his first appearance as a conductor of the New York Philharmonic leading a trio of young soloists, Yefim Bronfman, Shlomo Mintz, and Yo-Yo Ma. The year was 1978 and the program that Friday evening in May included the Beethoven Triple Concerto.

A visit to Alexander Schneider's home is a triple concerto in itself. Flowing wine, stimulating conversation, and tempting food turn a brief interview into a never-forgotten afternoon. Sasha can describe a meal with such mouth-watering detail that you feel full when he's done. But nail him down to a specific recipe, complete with numbers of table-spoons and cups and he's in over his head. "I pour, what measure?" he sputters, frustrated at the thought of being tied down to particulars.

But, with imagination and courage, the results are great. The most important thing to remember when reproducing any dish that comes from the mind of Alexander Schneider is: Measure only the ingredients. Liberally pour on the love. Always mix the food with good company, excellent wine, and the finest music. And listen to the music. Don't keep it in the background. Begin with Bach's Concerto No. 1 for Three Harpsichords, performed by the Marlboro Festival Orchestra with Sasha conducting pianists Rudolf Serkin, Mieczyslaw Horszowski, and Ruth Laredo (CBS MPT-39761), and continue with Mozart's Violin Concerto No. 4 played by Isaac Stern with the English Chamber Orchestra conducted by Alexander Schneider (CBS MYK-37808).

Shrimp with
Sour Cream Sauce

SERVES 2

*¹/₂ pound large shrimp, peeled
and deveined*
3 tablespoons sour cream
4 teaspoons sweet chutney

1 teaspoon Dijon mustard
2 teaspoons fresh lemon juice
2 teaspoons ketchup

1 Bring a medium saucepot of salted water to rolling boil. Throw in shrimp and cook 2 to 3 minutes or until just done (don't overcook—they easily start to resemble erasers). Drain and rinse with cold water. Chill.

2 In small bowl combine remaining ingredients and mix well. Serve as a dipping sauce for shrimp.

NOTE: These amounts are suggested—they can be changed to taste.

Gerard Schwarz

New York City's High School of Performing Arts is proud to list Gerard Schwarz among its alumni. It's fitting for this New York–bred musician, then, to have gone on to become a member of the New York Philharmonic. At the time, September 1973, Jerry was a terrifically talented trumpeter. Pierre Boulez was music director and he put the young horn player in the first-chair spot without missing a beat.

First stop: Lexington, Kentucky, September 6. A few days later the orchestra was in Greenville, South Carolina. And the next night found them moving a few miles to Rock Hill. Obviously, the Philharmonic was on the road. And Gerard Schwarz has been traveling ever since.

Jerry stayed with the orchestra as principal trumpeter for only a few years, because he had other aspirations. He wanted to conduct. And, once that dream came true, Jerry had little time for sitting still, even in the first chair of the Philharmonic's trumpet section.

Major ensembles in Los Angeles, Seattle, New York, New Jersey, and even the White Mountains have recordings with Maestro Schwarz. And, in Europe, he's visited various cities, staying awhile in England and Scotland to make his mark with their orchestras.

With all this traveling, you have to ask about a musician's family. How do people react to this kind of life? They react like musicians, because that's what they are. Gerard Schwarz may have left the New York Philharmonic as a trumpeter, but he still has ties. He married into the orchestra. His wife, Jody, a flutist, is a daughter of the late Sol Greitzer, principal violist of the Philharmonic until his retirement in the mid-1980s. And, since the entire Greitzer family is made up of professional musicians, the life of a mobile music director is nothing new.

In a typical summer week, Gerard Schwarz has one foot on the podium of Mostly Mozart in Avery Fisher Hall and the other on the podium of the Waterloo Festival Orchestra in New Jersey. As music director of both festivals, he must devote his undivided attention to each. Since they both take place at the same time, Jerry simply does what every good conductor does: he clones himself. And then, with help from family and staff, he does it all.

With this kind of rigorous schedule, Gerard Schwarz must make sure he's in top physical form. He tells us he does this by assiduously watching his diet and keeping the cholesterol out. That's why this Mostly Marvelous Banana Bread is one of his favorite breakfasts. It's healthful, light, and definitely delicious.

Jody and Jerry Schwarz recently collaborated on a wonderful recording of the complete incidental music by Richard Strauss to *Le Bourgeois Gentilhomme*. It's the first recording of the entire work and even includes the music Strauss chose to leave out of his suite. Jody produced the recording and Jerry conducted the New York Chamber Symphony and Chorus. Included in this work is an energetic and sumptuous movement called "The Dinner." Gerard Schwarz's Mostly Marvelous Banana Bread is fine for dinner as well as breakfast—and so is this music (Pro Arte 448).

Then, for old times' sake, listen to the Haydn and Hummel trumpet concertos with the Y Chamber Symphony of New York and Jerry splitting himself into conductor and soloist (Delos DCD-3001).

Mostly Marvelous
Banana Bread

MAKES 1 LOAF

2 cups whole wheat flour
1 teaspoon baking soda
Pinch salt
1 large egg, beaten
2 egg whites
1/4 cup canola oil

1/2 cup maple syrup
1/2 teaspoon vanilla
2 cups mashed banana (about 4)
1/2 cup (or more to taste) golden
or black raisins
1/2 cup walnuts, coarsely chopped

1 Preheat oven to 350°. Grease a 9 × 5 × 2" loaf pan.

2 In a large bowl, mix together flour, soda, and salt. Stir in remaining ingredients and mix well. Pour into pan and bake until toothpick inserted in center comes out clean (about 55 minutes for a metal pan, 60 to 65 minutes for glass). Cool and remove from pan.

Leonard Slatkin

There's no doubt that the Slatkin family is a musical family. Among the musical members, the father, Felix, was a well-known and well-recorded conductor. And Leonard has followed his father into the family business, inheriting a baton and podium of his own.

Currently the conductor of the St. Louis Symphony, Leonard Slatkin made his first appearance on the podium of the New York Philharmonic in January 1974. Byron Janis was the soloist for the series in Beethoven's Third Piano Concerto and the rest of the program was devoted to a Berlioz overture and the Symphony No. 5 of Prokofiev.

When Leonard Slatkin is not on the podium of a major symphony orchestra, he often can be found in the broadcast booth of the St. Louis Cardinals' baseball team. This conductor is one of many musicians who are batty for baseball. Music isn't the only passion of these musicians. Whether you say "bass" or "base" to Mr. Slatkin or Itzhak Perlman or Robert Merrill or Zubin Mehta, chances are they'll think of "first" or "second" before they'll think of "fiddle."

Leonard Slatkin is in the extraordinary position of occasionally doing a play-by-play for the Cardinals. "Baseball," he tells us, "is like Beethoven's Pastorale Symphony. There's even a thunderstorm in the middle to make it more realistic."

As to the conductor-sportscaster's taste in food, it seems to run toward the Orient. His favorite recipes are based on Chinese cuisine. But they have a certain midwestern sound. You'll be surprised at these Cantonese lettuceburgers. They're really outstanding.

To accompany Leonard Slatkin to the ballpark, we offer the entire recording of Richard Adler and Jerry Ross's *Damn Yankees,* with the original cast (RCA AYL1-3948E). And, to get us through the game, Leonard Bernstein hits a home run with the New York Philharmonic in Beethoven's Symphony No. 6 *Pastorale* (CBS MK-42222).

Cantonese Lettuceburgers

SERVES 6 TO 8

1 tablespoon soy sauce

1 tablespoon white wine

1 teaspoon sugar

1 large (8 ounce) pork chop, boned and
cut into fine julienne (¹/₈-inch strips)

1 tablespoon peanut oil

¹/₂ pound snow peas, trimmed and cut
into fine julienne (¹/₈-inch strips)

¹/₂ cup bamboo shoots, cut into fine
julienne (¹/₈-inch strips)

12-15 leaves of iceberg, red leaf, or
romaine lettuce, washed and dried

Fried rice

1   In a small bowl, combine soy sauce, wine, and sugar and stir well. Add pork and marinate 15 minutes.

2   Heat oil in a wok or large skillet over high heat. Add snow peas and cook, stirring, 1 minute. Add meat and marinade and cook, stirring, 2 minutes longer. Add bamboo shoots and cook 3 minutes, or until vegetables are cooked. Place in a serving bowl. Let guests serve themselves by placing some fried rice and meat mixture on a lettuce leaf and folding it like a crêpe. Eat with fingers.

Arturo Toscanini

"He was moderate and modest in his personal needs," Walfredo Toscanini recalls of his grandfather, Arturo. The legendary conductor, who died in 1957, was brought up in boarding schools, where he sold his meat ration coupons in order to buy music scores. That mentality managed to stay with Arturo Toscanini through his eminence and fortune as one of the most famous conductors the world has ever known.

Walfredo is the son of Walter Toscanini, one of the maestro's four children, the others being Wally, Giorgio (who died as a child of diphtheria), and Wanda, who married pianist Vladimir Horowitz.

Walfredo remembers sharing meals with his grandfather. "He didn't eat very much. We had lots of good, northern Italian food in the house. Sometimes meals would last three or four hours with six or seven courses. While we were all sitting there relishing every morsel, he'd eat a little soup, some bread, and a bit of veal.

"Even at large parties, and we had up to seventy people in the house for Christmas and New Year's, he ate sparingly. The settings were rather grand," Walfredo reminds us. "The house in Riverdale and the homes in Italy were imposing, but Grandfather's eating habits were almost spartan. He drank very little, just wine and brandy from what I remember.

"He loved soup. And it had to be good soup," Walfredo emphasizes. "Not something out of a can. Don't forget he was poor when he was growing up. So bread and soup were pretty much all he ate. Later it became his comfort food."

"They had a wonderful lady named Anna Saccomandi doing the cooking," Walfredo's wife, Elaine, adds. "Walfredo and I married in December 1958, and the maestro died the year before, so I just missed meeting him. But I know about Anna's recipes and reputation. She was a wonderful cook."

Anna was responsible for concocting one of the maestro's favorites, in fact. It was a simple rice soup with celery and parsley that called for one tablespoon of butter, three tablespoons of chopped celery, two tablespoons of uncooked rice, two cups of beef stock, and one tablespoon of chopped parsley.

Elaine tells us to heat the butter in a saucepan, add the celery, and cook until slightly softened. Add the rice and stir. Add one cup of the stock, cover, and cook until the rice is done. Then add the remaining stock, reheat, add the parsley, and serve with good, crusty bread. This recipe is for one serving and makes a lovely, comforting, easy lunch on a quiet day at home.

Elaine Troostwyk Toscanini's Panettone Milanese is different from most other recipes. "I tried so many ways to prepare this specialty. And I finally found the secret ingredient. Candied orange peel! It really makes the difference."

To honor Elaine's discovery of the Secret Ingredient for this Panettone, we suggest Arturo Toscanini's recording of Cimarosa's *Il matrimonio segreto* (The Secret Marriage), recorded on November 14, 1943 (Vic. LSC 2448). And we can't resist setting Toscanini's favorite rice, celery, and parsley soup to the maestro's recording of the Good Friday music from Wagner's opera "Parsley-fal" (VIC-1278).

Panettone

MAKES 1 LOAF

*³/₄ cup milk, heated to about
100 to 110 degrees*
3 (¹/₄ ounce) packages active dry yeast
¹/₃ cup sugar
5 large egg yolks, lightly beaten
1 teaspoon vanilla extract
1 teaspoon grated lemon zest
¹/₂ teaspoon salt
3-3¹/₄ cups all-purpose flour

6 tablespoons unsalted butter, melted
¹/₄ cup diced candied citron
¹/₃ cup diced candied orange peel
*¹/₃ cup golden raisins, plumped in
hot water, drained, and dried*
*¹/₃ cup dark raisins, plumped in
hot water, drained, and dried*
Melted butter for glaze

1 Place warm milk in a large bowl and stir in yeast and ¹/₂ teaspoon of the sugar. Let sit until yeast bubbles, about 5 minutes. Stir in egg yolks, vanilla, lemon zest, salt, and the remaining sugar. Add 1¹/₂ cups of flour, ¹/₂ cup at a time, beating well to incorporate each addition. Add remaining flour, ¹/₂ cup at a time, alternating with the melted butter. Before adding the last of the flour, stir in the candied fruits and raisins. Knead until smooth and no longer sticky, about 6 to 10 minutes. Place dough in a large greased bowl, cover with a clean kitchen towel, and let rise in a warm place until doubled, about 2 to 3 hours.

2 Grease a 2-quart soufflé dish. Punch dough down. Roll into a ball and place in prepared dish. Make a brown paper collar (23 × 5″). Butter inside of collar and wrap around outside of the dish. Tie a cotton string around middle of dish to hold paper together. Cover and let rise until dough comes to top of paper (1 to 2 hours).

3 Preheat oven to 400°. Brush top with melted butter and bake 10 minutes. Turn heat down to 350° and bake 30 to 40 minutes more, until a cake tester inserted in middle comes out clean. Cool on a rack 10 minutes before removing from pan.

Hugh Wolff

With so many conductors using their podiums as stepping stones to cross continents and oceans, Hugh Wolff stands out as an enigma. He's achieved the kind of recognition in his early years that others would give their batons to have in old age. But while they fight for seats on the next plane out, Hugh has delivered himself into the arms of just two orchestras, one wife, and two small children. "I'm awfully busy guest conducting here and there," he explains. "Right now I want to make my mark on one or two ensembles. There's plenty of time to spread myself thin later."

Hugh Wolff has certainly made his mark on the New Jersey Symphony. And now he's moved on to take the reins of the St. Paul Chamber Orchestra. "It's awfully cold up there," the conductor confides. "But the people are wonderfully warm, the musicmaking allows me to be creative, and it's a great cultural community."

Perhaps one of the reasons Hugh Wolff has a tendency to settle down more than some other conductors is his family background. "My father was in the Foreign Office. So we moved around quite a bit. We lived in London and Paris and traveled a lot from there.

"My mother is Italian and she's the cook in the family," he adds, getting around to food. "I learned a lot from watching her when I was growing up and even today I'll call her and ask for a recipe. My wife is a Japanese-food freak, so when we eat out we go to Japanese restaurants fairly often. But when I'm traveling I generally eat in the hotels. And, if I've been on the road a lot, I like to go out, buy something fresh in a store and bring it back to the room."

What happens on the day of a concert? "I have a big pasta lunch somewhere around three and I make sure I don't eat anything just before the performance. Afterward, I have a sandwich or something simple."

One of the few places in the world that tempts Hugh Wolff out of his hotel and into parties and receptions is Asia. "I was the assistant conductor with Rostropovich on a tour to Japan, Taiwan, and Korea and the food was so lavish that we could barely believe it. They're exceptionally gracious hosts, very generous, and they really go all out to give you their best.

"The snake market in Taiwan is not to be missed," the conductor adds with a twisted, serpentine grin. "You can see them drink snake blood. I just watched," he assures us.

While he may not drink snake blood, Hugh Wolff does indulge in a passion for coffee. "I drink it before a concert and it hasn't affected my tempos yet!"

For the all-American side of this young and much sought-after conductor, we suggest his recording of music by Aaron Copland with the St. Paul Chamber Orchestra (Teldec 229463142). And, for a gift from Hugh Wolff to accompany you through the holiday season, sample Christmas music, from traditional carols to contemporary popular songs, performed by Thomas Hampson and the St. Paul contingent (Teldec 273135-2).

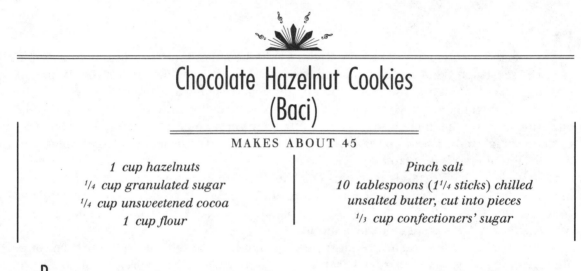

Chocolate Hazelnut Cookies (Baci)

MAKES ABOUT 45

1 cup hazelnuts	Pinch salt
1/4 cup granulated sugar	10 tablespoons (1 1/4 sticks) chilled
1/4 cup unsweetened cocoa	unsalted butter, cut into pieces
1 cup flour	1/3 cup confectioners' sugar

1   Preheat oven to 350°. Place hazelnuts on a baking sheet and toast for 10 minutes. Remove and place in a clean kitchen towel. Rub together to remove skins. Raise heat to 400°.

2   Place nuts and granulated sugar in a food processor and process until almost a paste. In a small bowl, combine cocoa, flour, and salt. Add to nuts along with the butter and pulse until a ball forms on top of blade. Form into 1-inch balls and place on ungreased cookie sheets about 1 inch apart. Bake 10 to 12 minutes or until slightly cracked on top. Let cool on sheet about 5 minutes and then remove to cooling rack. When completely cool, sift confectioners' sugar over cookies.

New York
Philharmonic
Family

Lisa Batchelder

The assistant director of public affairs at Lincoln Center, Lisa Batchelder, has several connections with the New York Philharmonic. And they aren't necessarily public. For one, Lisa has studied with Philharmonic violinist Oscar Ravina since 1985. "I've taken a hiatus here and there to have two children. But I consider him my dear friend and mentor."

And then there are the Radiothons. "They really put on a good spread." And Lisa's not talking about music now. She's describing the nonstop orgy of food put out for the hundreds of volunteers, celebrities, musicians, and guests who help raise funds for the Philharmonic at this annual event. "I've sampled lots of food at Lincoln Center but nobody does it like the Radiothons."

Does Lisa cook for her children? "Well, they're still pretty young. But they eat pretty much what we eat. Since my husband and I are both very busy, we eat a lot of fast food. But our fast food is pasta," she admits with a grin of pride. "I love to cook. It's my way of relaxing and having fun."

To accompany Lisa's Swordfish Quintet, we suggest a name change for the Schubert Trout Quintet (A fish by any other name may smell as sweet?) with the Cleveland Quartet and Alfred Brendel (Philips 400078-2). And for Lisa's passion for the kitchen, "I Can Cook, Too" from *On the Town* by Bernstein, Comden, and Green (RCA CK 2038).

Swordfish Quintet

SERVES 2

2 swordfish steaks, each about ¹/₂″ thick
¹/₄ cup key lime juice (fresh or bottled)
¹/₂ tablespoon ground cumin

¹/₂ tablespoon ground ginger
1 fresh avocado, cut into slices

1   Place swordfish in a small glass or stainless steel dish and pour lime juice over. Marinate in refrigerator 1 hour, turning once, or at room temperature for 30 minutes, again turning once.

2   Light the grill or preheat the broiler and broiling pan. Pat swordfish dry. Combine spices and sprinkle over fish. Grill swordfish over medium high heat about 3 to 4 minutes on each side, turning once (alternatively, broil 3 to 4 inches from source of heat for 4 to 5 minutes on each side). Garnish with avocado slices and serve with extra lime juice if desired.

Kimberly Brockman and Bonnie Draina

Kim Brockman and Bonnie Draina both work for the New York Philharmonic. Although they're both singers, neither has performed with the orchestra. But their role backstage is what gets the orchestra on stage and keeps it there. Bonnie and Kim are two of the fundraisers for the New York Philharmonic. "The big thing," Bonnie tells us, "is that we've had reduced aid from corporations and the government and we need more individual help." The two of them are part of the staff that makes sure the Philharmonic gets that help.

Of course, there are some special perks that come with their jobs. According to Kim, "Working for the New York Philharmonic helps me keep in touch with what's going on in music. Just being on the Lincoln Center Plaza is exciting." And Bonnie adds, "One of the greatest things about our office is that it's right on the third tier and I can go out and watch the rehearsals. I listened to Kathleen Battle the other day. Her voice is just like a brook." With a bit of a sigh, the fundraiser and aspiring singer admits, "I'd like to try to apply what she does to my own technique."

Along with the musical and artistic extras that come with working for the New York Philharmonic, there's the food. Occasionally, when a patron can't make a preconcert dinner in the hall, Bonnie and Kim get to sample the food, all of which is supplied by Restaurant Associates. "The lamb chops are great!"

Where there's cake and bread, even *beer* bread, the music has to be George Gershwin's "Let 'Em Eat Cake," written in 1933 but newly orchestrated by Russell Warner and performed by soloists with the Orchestra of St. Luke's and the New York Choral Artists (CBS2-M2K-4522).

Kim's Kjorski Cake

SERVES 8 TO 10

CAKE

4 large eggs at room temperature
1 cup sugar
¹/₂ teaspoon vanilla extract
1¹/₄ cups unbleached flour
³/₄ teaspoon baking powder
Pinch salt
²/₃ cup melted butter or margarine

FILLING

1 stick (¹/₂ cup) unsalted butter or margarine, softened
1 cup sifted confectioners' sugar
¹/₄ teaspoon vanilla extract
3 tablespoons strong coffee
Confectioners' sugar for garnish

1 Preheat oven to 350°. Grease two 9-inch cake pans. Line bottoms with wax paper.

2 In a large bowl or the bowl of a heavy-duty mixer, combine eggs and sugar. Beat on high with electric hand-held or heavy-duty mixer until thick and pale yellow, about 5 minutes. Beat in vanilla. In a small bowl, combine flour, baking powder, and salt, and mix well. Beat in half the flour mixture, then half the melted butter. Repeat with the remaining flour and remaining butter, beating until well combined. Pour into prepared pans, dividing evenly. Give each pan a hard rap on the countertop to release large air bubbles and bake 25 minutes (or until cake tester inserted in middle comes out clean). Cool in pans. When cool, run a knife around edge and invert. Peel off wax paper and prepare icing.

3 With electric beater, cream butter and sugar together until light and fluffy, about 2 to 3 minutes. Beat in vanilla and coffee. Spread filling on top of one cake. Place other cake on top and sprinkle with confectioners' sugar.

Bonnie's Beer Bread

MAKES 1 LOAF

3 tablespoons dark brown sugar,
packed
1 (12 ounce) bottle of beer

3 cups self-rising flour
2 tablespoons unsalted butter, melted

1   Preheat oven to 375°. Grease and flour a 9 × 5 × 3″ loaf pan.

2   In a small mixing bowl, combine sugar and beer. Stir well and set aside. Place flour in a large mixing bowl. Make a well in center of flour and pour beer gradually into well. Using a whisk, start stirring together the flour and beer, whisking to prevent lumps. When batter is well combined and smooth, pour into prepared pan. Bake in lower third of oven 40 minutes. Brush with melted butter and bake 10 minutes more or until golden brown. Remove from pan and cool on a wire rack.

Henry Fogel

Henry Fogel is to the New York Philharmonic what Santa Claus is to Christmas and the Bunny is to Easter. He pops up once a year for three days, hands out presents, puns, and premiums for a price and then disappears for another 362 days. Henry Fogel is the "Radiothon Man." But it wasn't always like that.

No. Once upon a time, Henry had a real job with the New York Philharmonic. He was the orchestra's manager. He also was the orchestra's unofficial but outspoken fundraiser. Because it was Henry who invented the Radiothon.

The rest of us didn't know Henry. We met him back in the bowels of Avery Fisher Hall, where the very first Radiothon was run, and we thought he was quite mad. "Who is that person, running from microphone to microphone with that money?" "Where did that money he's trying to match come from?" "Where did *he* come from?" "What makes *him* such an expert?"

Hundreds of Radiothons for dozens of orchestras later, we no longer question Henry. He *is* the expert. He wrote the book on these strange but successful events. He's like a madman when he gets into it, but he gets the job done. The New York Philharmonic's coffers speak clearly: Henry Fogel has brought the orchestra more than five million dollars in fifteen years. He's also left the Philharmonic and gone on to manage the National Symphony in Washington, D.C., and the Chicago Symphony. In fact, he now has the exalted title in Chicago of executive vice president and executive director. Not bad for a madman!

And . . . he cooks. Being a good Jewish boy from the Upper West Side of Manhattan, he cooks Chinese. But watch out. After you try Henry Fogel's recipe, you may find him on your doorstep trying to auction off your dirty dishes. For the Philharmonic, of course!

In the spirit of Henry the Punster, we offer the following musical suggestions to accompany his Hunam Lamb: "All We Like Sheep," from Handel's *Messiah* with the Westminster Choir and New York Philharmonic (complete recording, made December 31, 1956—ML-5023/4); Bach's "Sheep May Safely Graze (VOX MCD 10012); Lehár's "Lamb" of Smiles (2-Ara. 8055 9055) and Wnag Guo Tong playing "Strong and Loyal Su Wu" on the Er Hu (HK 6340073)!

Hunam Lamb

SERVES 8

3 pounds boneless leg of lamb, cut into
1-inch pieces
$^{1}/_{4}$ cup peanut oil
12 cloves garlic, minced
12 hot dried chili peppers
1 (1 inch) cube ginger, thinly sliced
4 scallions, cut into 2-inch lengths

$^{1}/_{2}$ pound yellow rock sugar or
$^{1}/_{4}$ cup brown sugar
2 tablespoons chili paste with garlic
$^{1}/_{4}$ cup dark soy sauce
2 teaspoons salt
1 (12 ounce) can beer

1 Bring a large saucepot of water to boil. Add lamb, simmer 3 minutes. Drain well. Preheat oven to 350°.

2 In a wok or large skillet, heat oil over high heat. Add garlic and cook about 10 seconds, stirring. Add chili peppers and ginger and continue cooking, stirring constantly, about 2 minutes. Add scallions and lamb and cook 1 to 2 minutes longer. Add rock sugar, chili paste, soy sauce, and salt. Stir and cook 1 minute longer.

3 Stir in beer and transfer to an ovenproof 2½-quart casserole. Cook uncovered 1 hour.

Serve with rice and Chinese vegetables. This is quite spicy—to cut the heat use only 6 peppers and 1 tablespoon of chili paste.

NOTE: Rock sugar can be found in Chinese grocery stores.

Neal Gilliatt

Neal Gilliatt, advertising executive and member of the boards of a variety of organizations from the Institutes for Religion and Health to the New York Philharmonic, was born on Christmas Eve. Perhaps that legacy has instilled in him the graciousness and glow of giving. He also receives. "I think that being a member of the board of the Philharmonic and the executive committee speaks for my interest in music," he says with modesty.

Neal and his wife, Mary, were married in 1943 and, at that time, Neal's sister "gave us one of those golden oak filecard boxes filled with my favorite recipes, written in her own handwriting.

"This recipe for Butter Chews has been with me since I was a child. It actually originated with my sister, who lived her life in a small town in Indiana. She was a home economics graduate, an innovative cook, and always told us how she loved to doctor up a lot of recipes to her own taste."

These Butter Chews come with more than a pedigree. They come with a tried-and-tasted guarantee from Neal Gilliatt: "Mary and our two sons and their friends have enjoyed Butter Chews for some fifty years. And they still do."

While chopping the nuts for the Gilliatt family's Butter Chews, we suggest the New York Philharmonic's recording of Tchaikovsky's *Nutcracker Suite* (CBS MYK-37238).

Butter Chews

MAKES 24

1½ sticks unsalted butter
(¾ cup) softened
3 tablespoons granulated sugar
1½ cups unbleached flour
3 large eggs, separated and at
room temperature

1 cup coarsely chopped pecans
1¼ cups dark brown sugar, packed
¾ cup shredded, sweetened coconut

1   Preheat oven to 375°. Grease a 9 × 13″ baking pan.

2   In a large mixing bowl, cream together by hand or with an electric mixer the butter, granulated sugar, and flour. Spread evenly over bottom of prepared pan and bake 15 minutes. Remove and turn oven down to 350°.

3   In another bowl, combine egg yolks, nuts, brown sugar, and coconut until well mixed. In a separate bowl, with electric mixer, beat egg whites to stiff peaks. Lighten the nut mixture with one quarter of the whites and then fold in remainder. Spread over partially cooked crust and bake 25 minutes or until set. Let cool and cut into squares.

Karen LeFrak

I t's time to break a stereotype. So many people, looking at the women who give their time and energy to orchestras and opera companies around the country, assume them to be wealthy matrons who want a social place to do their good deeds. The assumption is made that because they're well dressed and rather spiffy-looking they have nothing better to do with their time or their minds, so they make themselves look good by devoting their energies to a charitable organization.

Now, take a look at one of these women, Karen LeFrak. "I became interested in working with the New York Philharmonic in 1973 because a friend knew of my involvement with music and she thought I might want to join the orchestra's Junior Committee." Karen was teaching music to nursery-school children at the time. But she was also getting her master's degree in music history.

"While I was studying for my master's, I went to work in the Philharmonic's archives and Barbara Hawes, the director of the archives, hired me because I was doing my thesis on the role of commissioning and the New York Philharmonic."

But her involvement didn't stop there. "The Volunteer Council wanted me to get more involved," Karen explains. And she went on to become vice president, executive vice president, and, finally, president of the Council. She also became a director of the Philharmonic Society.

"The Council is a musical and social group. Social in the sense that I got to meet a lot of women with spectacular ideas and energy. I am proud to be part of them and, in the earlier years, they helped me feel secure in this big city."

Now Karen has two children "with wonderful ears" who love opera. Who cooks for the "ears"? "Well, we have a wonderful housekeeper who does the cooking, but we do it together," Karen emphasizes. "When I first got married, I didn't know anything about cooking. In fact, this Bride's Cake was one of the first things I made when I got married. It's perfect for the newlywed who can't cook. It's foolproof.

"I got the recipe from an old friend. We used to share recipes and ingredients. We taught each other cooking techniques, starting with things like layered salads—you know, where you take a can of green peas and put them in a glass bowl and then put something red on top of that and keep adding until you reach the top," Karen says with a laugh.

    Being part of the New York Philharmonic's Volunteer Council is something very special, not only for the good it does the orchestra, but for the vitality and interest of the individuals who are its members. The volunteers work in every part of the organization, from writing and public relations to operating the gift shop and pouring coffee during rehearsal breaks. In honor of this very special organization, we suggest Bach's *Coffee Cantata*, with Ann Monoyios, Stephen Oosting, and John Ostendorf singing with another New York–based ensemble, the Amor Artis Baroque Orchestra, under the direction of Johannes Somary (Vox Cum Laude MCD-10046). And for the Bride's Cake, Bach's Cantata No. 202, the *Wedding Cantata,* performed by Kathleen Battle with the Ravinia Festival Ensemble and James Levine (RCA ARK1-2788).

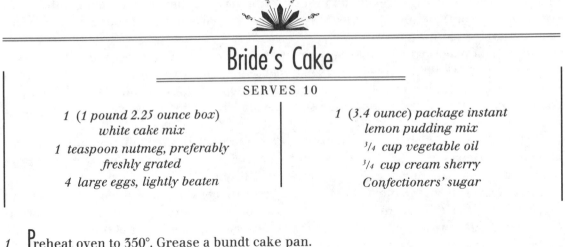

Bride's Cake

SERVES 10

1 (1 pound 2.25 ounce box) white cake mix	*1 (3.4 ounce) package instant lemon pudding mix*
1 teaspoon nutmeg, preferably freshly grated	*³/₄ cup vegetable oil*
4 large eggs, lightly beaten	*³/₄ cup cream sherry*
	Confectioners' sugar

1   Preheat oven to 350°. Grease a bundt cake pan.

2   In a large bowl, combine cake mix and nutmeg. With hand-held electric mixer add eggs and beat until smooth. Beat in pudding mix, oil, and sherry. Beat until mixed well and pour into bundt pan. Bake 45 minutes or until cake tester inserted in middle comes out clean. Remove and cool in pan 10 minutes. Invert onto serving platter. Let cool completely. Refrigerate at least 1 day before serving, as flavor improves overnight. Sprinkle lightly with confectioners' sugar before serving.

Nathan Leventhal

Nathan Leventhal, president of Lincoln Center, likes to experiment. Much of the work at the Center itself is experimental, even the programs we take for granted today: Mostly Mozart, the Great Performers' series, Live from Lincoln Center. These all had a first time, a time when no one knew how they'd turn out.

Just recently Lincoln Center added a jazz department to its organization. Nat Leventhal wanted to mix this musical format with the more established constituents—the Philharmonic, Metropolitan Opera, New York City Ballet, New York City Opera—for several good reasons. "It will bring us a new audience"—a big part of Nat's thinking. "And jazz is an important part of our culture and should be part of one of the most important centers for culture in the world. We're trendsetters here," he adds with pride.

Nathan Leventhal also enjoys mixing and experimenting with recipes. His "low-cholesterol, high-caloric dark chocolate marble sheet cake" is "based on a combination of public domain stuff like cake mix boxes and my own experimentation." Nat says he got the idea of using powdered cocoa instead of hard chocolate from Dr. Kenneth Cooper (who is not the harpsichordist).

Nat stresses that this is not a cake for someone on a weight reduction diet. "But it is useful for someone who wants to control cholesterol." He says, "By substituting margarine for butter, egg substitute for egg, 1 percent milk for 4 percent milk, and the lowest-fat vegetable oil you can find, you get a delicious low-cholesterol cake."

As President of Lincoln Center, he adds a disclaimer to the recipe: "Chef has no medical credentials."

When contemplating this cake, we suggest the musical comedy score for *She Loves Me*, especially the song "Ice Cream," with Barbara Cook (Polydor 831968-2). And, for the low-cholesterol fans, a wonderful anthology, *The American Musical Theater*, volume 1 (1898–1933), which includes original-cast performances of such heartfelt songs as "Deep in My Heart, Dear," "I Want to Be Happy," and "Life Is a Funny Proposition, After All" (Smithsonian Collection RD 036-1).

Nathan Leventhal's Low-Cholesterol, High-Caloric Dark Chocolate Marble Sheet Cake

MAKES ONE 9 × 13″ CAKE

1 (1 pound 2.25 ounce) box marble cake mix
³/₄ cup egg substitute
1¹/₄ cups water
¹/₃ cup canola oil

FROSTING
1 stick (8 tablespoons) unsalted margarine, softened
1 pound sifted confectioners' sugar
1¹/₂ teaspoons vanilla extract
¹/₂ cup 1 percent milk
1 cup unsweetened cocoa

1 Preheat oven to 350°. Grease and flour a 9 × 13″ baking pan. In a large mixing bowl with hand-held electric mixer, blend cake mix, egg substitute, water, and oil. Beat on medium for 2 minutes. Follow package directions for marbling and bake 28 to 30 minutes. Remove to a rack and cool in pan.

2 In a large mixing bowl, using an electric beater, cream margarine. Add half the sugar, the vanilla, and half the milk. Gradually add cocoa, beating constantly. Add remaining sugar and remaining milk and beat until smooth.

3 When cake has completely cooled, remove from pan and frost sides and top.

NOTE: This can be made using 3 eggs instead of the egg substitute, butter instead of margarine, and whole milk instead of 1 percent, but it will no longer be low-cholesterol.

Joe McKaughan

Joe McKaughan is so much a part of the Lincoln Center family that the institution wouldn't be the same without him. He began at the center in 1970 as a publicity assistant and, twelve years later, became vice president of public affairs. Not bad for a boy from Griffin, Georgia, who has managed to retain the charm of his Southern accent and the enthusiasm of the country child.

Joe has also made his mark on Lincoln Center and each of its constituents. He looks back to the Center's twentieth anniversary celebration. "In those days, I had a lot to say about the food we ordered for parties and receptions and I had a ball with that one! I was able to help plan the menus and select the caterers"—something Joe McKaughan loves to do because he loves to cook and to eat.

That twentieth anniversary party was quite a bash. It began in the lobby of the Vivian Beaumont Theater. Tables had been set in an open square with chefs in the center shucking clams and oysters for the rest of us to gulp down with our drinks. Suddenly, out of nowhere, an army of about a hundred bagpipers made an entrance and piped us out to the Plaza for a showing of slides on enormous screens draped across the front of the Metropolitan Opera House.

From there, the crowd was divided in two sections with one group heading to the New York State Theater and the other entering Avery Fisher Hall for dinner on the grand promenades. Champagne and wine flowed, the table settings were elegant, and the food abundant. But that wasn't the end of the evening. Not by a long shot!

We had a choice into the wee hours of the morning: dancing at the Beaumont or cabaret at Juilliard. And, in both places, more wine and more food, including crêpes and omelets made to order by chefs just waiting to serve us. I didn't make it much past two A.M. but I heard that 'round about four in the morning a few couples wound up dancing in the Reflecting Pool under Henry Moore's massive sculpture.

Joe McKaughan had a hand or two in the planning of that evening. Especially the food. Now he has a hand in another project. This one, however, is personal. "We have an informal club that got started in 1989. It's a very exclusive club," he assures us. "There are only four of us. We call it the Square Table and we get together on a monthly basis."

The Square Table's four members are press agents in the arts and they've built themselves a very special institution. "Each month we select the best restaurant we can find, take turns with the bill, and just pig out!" What's their favorite so far? "There's a new place in the St. Regis Hotel called Restaurant Lespinasse. It's absolutely divine and I think it has the best French food in the world." No wonder he's a press agent!

Along with planning parties and eating, Joe McKaughan loves to cook. He took this recipe for Southern Peanut-Butter Pie from a cookbook called *Old Timey Recipes,* a collection from Bluefield, West Virginia. Thinning it's not, but it's unusual and delicious. The pie goes well with "Tea for Two" (or four at a square table) in the arrangement of the Vincent Youmans classic by Dmitri Shostakovich, called "Tahiti Trot" and played by the London Brass (Teldec 243 713-2). For the peanuts themselves: "How You Gonna Keep 'Em Down on the Farm?" sung by Michael Feinstein (EMI CDC 7 49768 2).

Southern Peanut-Butter Pie

SERVES 8 TO 10

3 large eggs
1 cup dark corn syrup
¹/₂ cup sugar
¹/₂ cup creamy peanut butter

¹/₂ teaspoon vanilla extract
1 cup salted peanuts, shelled
1 unbaked 9-inch pie crust, chilled
(*see page 53*)

1   Preheat oven to 400°.

2   In the large bowl of an electric mixer, beat eggs. Beat in corn syrup, sugar, peanut butter, and vanilla. Continue beating 3 minutes or until smooth. Stir in the peanuts and pour into pie shell. Bake 15 minutes and turn oven down to 350°. Bake 30 to 35 minutes or until middle is completely set. Let cool on rack.

Carlos Moseley

Carlos Moseley answers to almost any title—press director, managing director, president, or chairman of the board. He held all those positions with the New York Philharmonic between 1955 and 1978. But one of the most cherished is pianist.

It was in 1959, when Carlos was associate director, that he made his keyboard debut with the orchestra in a Bach triple concerto. With him were David Keiser, the Philharmonic's president, and Leonard Bernstein, who doubled as pianist and conductor of the all-Bach program. Carlos didn't stop there.

His titles with the orchestra grew and, in 1975, he tripled again, this time in a Mozart concerto with Rudolf Firkusny and Erich Leinsdorf. "That Mozart Triple Concerto was more than I'd bargained for," Carlos drawls. "And by that time I'd played with more than twenty-five different orchestras."

Now chairman emeritus of the Philharmonic, our real-life "Poo-Bah the Grand" spends much of his time in his beloved South Carolina, "But I still come to New York about once a month," he assures us. And he still does quite a bit of traveling—Philharmonic-related traveling.

"I was in France recently, visiting a thirteenth-century château. But I also went to Paris to visit Pierre Boulez. We had some really great meals in the Périgord region."

While with the orchestra, of course, there were many, many trips. "Let's see," he muses, "we visited Europe, the Far East and Japan, the Soviet Union. And there were many great state occasions. I can't tell you how many heads of state, there were so many. In India Mrs. Gandhi gave us a dinner. In Russia, back in 1959, we lived on vodka and caviar because we couldn't get enough nourishment from anything else.

"We had a forty-minute ovation in Poland," Carlos beams. "Finally Bernstein dismissed the orchestra from the stage and sat himself at the piano to play encores."

Continuing the travelogue, he remembers that in South America "we were on every radio station and in every newspaper in the country. People would line up for four or five days and sleep on the street to wait for the box office to open so they could get their tickets to hear us."

Those were exciting times, on and off stage. These days Carlos Moseley still gets plenty of excitement out of life. "I'm a trustee for a bunch of foundations—and," he adds emphatically, "I'm still very much affiliated with the New York Philharmonic."

The triple concertos of Bach and Mozart featuring Carlos Moseley aren't available but, if you can still find it, there's a gem of a performance of a Mozart triple with Gold and Fizdale and Bernstein (doubling as conductor and pianist) with the New York Philharmonic (Col M-32173).

Baked Crab in Seashells

SERVES 8 AS AN APPETIZER

1 pound lump crab meat	1 small onion, chopped (about $1/2$ cup)
3 cups fresh bread crumbs	1 tablespoon chopped Italian parsley
(about 12 slices bread)	$1/4$ teaspoon cayenne pepper (or to taste)
$1/2$ cup milk	$1/2$ teaspoon salt
$3/4$ cup mayonnaise	2 tablespoons unsalted butter, melted
1 teaspoon Worcestershire sauce	Paprika for garnish
4 hard-cooked eggs, peeled and chopped	

1 Preheat oven to 375°. Grease 8 seashells or 8 ovenproof 1-cup dishes.

2 Flake crab and remove any shell or cartilage. Place in a large mixing bowl. In a small bowl, mix 2 cups of the bread crumbs with the milk and soak until milk is absorbed. Add to crab with next 7 ingredients. Mix well and fill seashells. Place on a baking sheet. In a small bowl, combine melted butter and remaining bread crumbs and mix well. Sprinkle crab with crumbs and bake 15 minutes or until hot. Sprinkle with paprika if desired.

Neil Parker

"I've gone to lots of parties and receptions given by the New York Philharmonic over the years," Neil Parker informs us, "but one of the most spectacular was the chocolate orgy that followed Zubin Mehta's final concert in the spring of 1991." If Neil says this, it must be true. After all, he has been the publicity manager of the Philharmonic since 1984. And he's certainly seen his share of orgies—er, parties. But, by all reports this was really something.

Jean Crystal was the chairman of the event. And she had three of the best restaurants in New York—Arcadia, Aureole, and Le Régence—create desserts and submit the recipes to the Philharmonic. Then Nestlé's created three of their own and the six were prepared for the party by Great Performances, the caterers. Nestlé's even donated the chocolate to the Philharmonic for the occasion.

Another Philharmonic event that Neil remembers was a special picnic he shared under the stars at a Parks Concert. And, returning to the Radiothons, he recalls with great pleasure slicing a luscious cake prepared and decorated for the fundraiser by William Greenberg Jr. Desserts, the sumptuous New York bakery.

Neil's contribution to our book is based on a recipe he got from his grandmother, who loved brewing a steaming pot of this concoction on cold winter days. In fact, he tells us that just making Grandma's Pea Soup is a perfect activity on an icy afternoon. The warmth and aroma permeate the house and make you hungry for a good, hearty dinner—if you can wait that long.

A huge hunk of peasant bread with butter goes on the plate next to this soup. And on the stereo: Rossini's "Oh! the Green Peas" performed by Bruno Canino (Camerata CMT 1038).

Grandma's Pea Soup

SERVES 6 TO 8

1 pound dried split green peas,
rinsed and drained

2 quarts water

1 large onion chopped (about 1 cup)

4 ribs celery, chopped (about 1½ cups)

1 pound (2 strips) flanken (beef short
ribs), cut into 1-inch strips

1 pound carrots, peeled and cut into
1-inch chunks

1 bay leaf

1 sprig fresh thyme or ½ teaspoon dried

2 teaspoons salt

½ teaspoon pepper

1 In a large saucepot or Dutch oven, combine peas and water. Bring to a boil over high heat. Lower heat to simmer and add onion, celery, and flanken. Simmer, covered, for one hour, stirring once. Skim off scum. Add carrots, bay leaf, thyme, salt, and pepper. Simmer, covered, 2 hours longer, stirring every half hour.

Pauline Plimpton

The Plimpton family is a cooking family. It's also a celebrated family. Pauline's son is George Plimpton, the author. Her husband, Francis, held an ambassadorial rank and represented the United States at the UN from 1961 to 1965. Her brother is Amyas Ames, former chairman of the board of the New York Philharmonic and Lincoln Center. And Pauline, a founding member of the Philharmonic Council, loves to cook. In fact, she presented me with a little purple booklet of old family recipes she's collected over the years.

And there have been many years. Pauline Plimpton recently celebrated her ninetieth birthday. The event was marked at a Philharmonic Council luncheon.

It was difficult to choose one recipe from among the many Pauline has compiled but we finally decided on the bran muffins because they're easy, delicious, and, unless the powers that be change their collective minds again, healthful. Bran has had its ups and downs over the last ten or fifteen years. But when it's been up, it's received superstar status among health and gourmet foods and is generally considered a must for any serious baker and eater.

Bran Muffins make a lovely breakfast, especially if you're one of those "Oh! How I Hate to Get Up in the Morning" types and need a musical accompaniment provided by Michael Feinstein (EMI CDC 7 49768 2). And, even kids like them so you can put them in the hamper for "The Teddy Bear's Picnic," sung by the King's Singers (EMI CDC 7 47870 2).

Bran Muffins

MAKES 12 MUFFINS

¹/₄ cup unsalted butter, softened
¹/₄ cup sugar
1 large egg
¹/₄ cup molasses
1¹/₂ cups unbleached flour

1¹/₂ cups unprocessed bran
1 tablespoon baking powder
¹/₂ teaspoon salt
1¹/₂ cups milk
¹/₂ cup raisins

1 Preheat oven to 400°. Grease 12 standard (2¹/₂ inch) muffin cups.

2 In a large mixing bowl, cream together butter and sugar with a hand-held electric beater until very fluffy, about 2 minutes. Beat in egg and molasses. In a small bowl, mix together flour, bran, baking powder, and salt. Add to butter mixture, stir in milk, and mix until just combined. Stir in raisins and spoon into tins. Bake 15 minutes or until a toothpick inserted in muffin comes out clean.

Stephen and Elaine Stamas

"If only my father were alive now," sighs Elaine Stamas, whose father, a doctor, came to this country from Greece to practice medicine and found music along the way. Elaine thinks of him when she talks about her husband, Stephen Stamas, the chairman of the New York Philharmonic, because she knows how proud and happy their lives would make him.

"Steve was vice president of public affairs, in charge of corporate giving at Exxon, when he became involved with the Philharmonic," she recalls. "He really helped them get 'Live from Lincoln Center' started in the mid-1970s. He was on a committee at the Philharmonic and, after a while, they offered him the position of president of the board. It was a terribly busy time for us, but that was an offer we just couldn't refuse. I guess we had to rationalize our way around it, but Steve accepted it and we've been having a wonderful time ever since."

The Stamases entertain musicians, travel with the orchestra, and attend just about every concert. No wonder her father would be *qvelling*! Or the Greek equivalent thereof.

"Both Zubin Mehta and Kurt Masur came to our house for dinner after one of the Parks Concerts," Elaine tells us. "I served all kinds of Greek dishes including moussaka, spanokopita and tarama (smoked carp roe with olive oil and bread). Masur loved it. Zubin took out his bag of spices and mashed them into the moussaka. But he didn't do that to the cake!"

That was a German chocolate cherry cake. But since both Steve and Elaine are of Greek origin, by way of Massachusetts, we offer a mixed musical bill. For the Greeks and the phyllo that follows, we suggest Ravel's *Five Popular Greek Folk Songs* sung by Dietrich Fischer-Dieskau (Orfeo S-061831). And for the German chocolate, Beethoven's Symphony No. 9 performed by the New York Philharmonic with Martina Arroyo, Regina Sarfaty, Nicholas Di Virgilio, Norman Scott, and the Juilliard Chorus, singing the "Ode to Joy," conducted by Leonard Bernstein (2-CBS M2S-794).

Chicken Breasts in Phyllo

SERVES 4

10 tablespoons unsalted butter

2 whole skinless and boneless chicken breasts, cut in half

1 medium onion, finely minced

1/2 pound mushrooms, finely minced

2 tablespoons chopped Italian parsley

1 tablespoon flour

1/3 cup vermouth or dry white wine

1/4 teaspoon salt

1/4 teaspoon pepper

8 sheets phyllo dough

1 cup plain dry bread crumbs

1/4 pound feta cheese

1 In a large skillet over high heat, melt 2 tablespoons of the butter. Add chicken and brown, about 2 minutes on each side. Remove to plate. Add onion and cook until softened, about 4 minutes. Add mushrooms and cook 5 minutes longer. Stir in parsley and flour and cook, stirring, about 1 minute. Add vermouth and bring to a boil. Stir in the salt and pepper. Remove mixture to a bowl and set aside. In a small saucepot, melt remaining butter.

2 Preheat oven to 350°.

3 Lay 1 sheet of phyllo on work surface and brush with melted butter. Sprinkle with bread crumbs and lay a second sheet over crumbs. Brush with more melted butter and sprinkle with more crumbs. Place a chicken breast on the phyllo. Put one fourth of the mushroom mixture and one fourth of the feta cheese over the chicken. Fold up sides of dough to form an envelope. Repeat with remaining breasts. Brush phyllo rolls well with melted butter and place seam-side-down on a baking sheet with sides. Bake 35 minutes or until golden brown.

NOTE: This recipe freezes very well and is great for dinner parties.

Alice Tully

The temptation to call Alice Tully "Miss Hall" is, at times, overwhelming. After all, not many people have had the honor of meeting this generous, music-loving philanthropist, and all they know of her is her name and the fact that a theater at Lincoln Center is named for her. But Alice Tully is too human to be made of marble. And the story of how she came to have a theater named for her is filled with warmth and emotion.

Alice Tully has, herself, been a singer. A mezzo-soprano who performed in all the great concert theaters of a slightly earlier New York, from Aeolian Hall to Town Hall, she has a great understanding of the voice and what it takes to make a career.

"Alice and I have been dear, devoted friends for more than thirty years. The 'Tully' is Irish, you know," tenor Robert White informs us. "Alice gives some of the most wonderful musicales in her home with absolutely fabulous food and spectacular concerts."

Even in these musicales, Miss Tully shows compassion and care. The guests are served champagne and something light and elegant to start. Then the invited artists perform. And, when the musicians have put down their instruments, everyone is invited to sit down to a sumptuous supper.

"I often invite the Curtis String Quartet to join me," Alice Tully tells us. "And then I serve something hearty afterward. Perhaps the best rack of lamb in the city."

Alice Tully lived in Paris all through the 1920s and '30s, so this type of evening, combining the musical and culinary arts, is nothing new for her. Besides, music has always been her passion. And she's had the family background that's allowed her to support her passion and make it flourish for the rest of us. Her grandfather, Amory Houghton, founded Corning Glass. An uncle gave us Steuben. She even has a second cousin of note: Katharine Hepburn.

But it was a first cousin, Arthur Houghton, who first approached Alice Tully and told her of the future plans for Lincoln Center. "We were at lunch in a restaurant that is now La Caravelle when he spoke to me about the need for a chamber music hall at the Center." That luncheon discussion turned into Alice Tully Hall.

Miss Tully has inspired so many musicians that it would be impossible to name them all. She supported the Musica Aeterna concerts at the Metropolitan Museum for some twenty years. She has been the backbone of both vocal and instrumental chamber music at Lincoln

Center since her hall opened in the late 1960s. And it was Alice Tully who, at dinner in her home one night, suggested that tenor Robert White look at the repertoire of John McCormack, a repertoire Robert has been singing ever since. "At that dinner," Robert recounts with emotion, "Alice said that one of her favorite McCormack songs was 'Mavis' and I immediately stood up from the table and sang it to her." Robert remembers, "Tears welled up in her eyes because she told me it brought back her childhood."

Robert White has since recorded *Memories—Tribute to John McCormack* (RCA AGL1-5400). And "Mavis" is sung on *I Hear You Calling Me*, a recording featuring the tenor with pianist Samuel Sanders (RCA AGK1-4895).

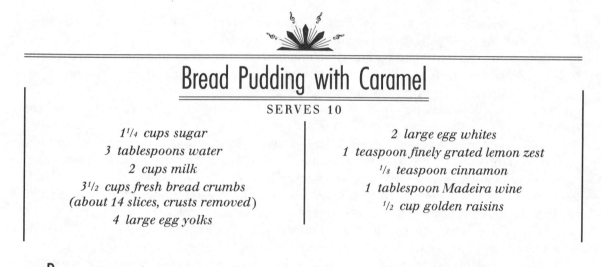

Bread Pudding with Caramel

SERVES 10

1¹/₄ cups sugar
3 tablespoons water
2 cups milk
3¹/₂ cups fresh bread crumbs
(about 14 slices, crusts removed)
4 large egg yolks

2 large egg whites
1 teaspoon finely grated lemon zest
¹/₈ teaspoon cinnamon
1 tablespoon Madeira wine
¹/₂ cup golden raisins

1   Preheat oven to 350°. Grease a 2-quart casserole or round baking pan.

2   In small, heavy saucepot, combine ³/₄ cup of the sugar and the water. Bring to a boil over medium high heat without stirring. Brush down sides of pot from time to time with additional water and cook until sugar is golden, about 7 to 8 minutes, swirling the pot occasionally to stir. Pour immediately into prepared dish. Set aside.

3   In a medium saucepot over high heat, bring milk to a boil. Place bread crumbs in a large bowl and pour milk over. Let stand and mash to form a purée.

4   In a small bowl, whisk together egg yolks and whites, remaining sugar, lemon zest, cinnamon, Madeira, and raisins. Stir into bread mixture and pour into prepared dish. Place in a large baking pan and fill pan with hot water. Bake 60 to 70 minutes, or until a knife inserted in center comes out clean. Remove from water bath and cool about 30 minutes. Invert onto serving plate.

Albert K. Webster

Albert K. Webster, better known as Nick, spent some twenty-eight years in a close association with the New York Philharmonic, and until recently he was the ensemble's managing director. But this particular recipe, which is contributed by Nick and his wife, Sally, dates from his early days with the Philharmonic, when Nick was a fledgling assistant manager.

"One of Nick's very first assignments," Sally tells us, "was to move the orchestra's offices from the Steinway Building on West Fifty-seventh Street to the brand new Philharmonic Hall at Lincoln Center."

Sally and Nick made many friends in the Philharmonic during this period, and one couple in particular, Marge and Jimmy Chambers, stand out as being particularly close. "Jimmy was the Philharmonic's legendary principal horn," Sally reminds us. The Chamberses had come to New York from Philadelphia years before and they'd brought with them the Philadelphia Orchestra Cheesecake recipe, a treasured secret.

"Fortunately for us and the New York Philharmonic family, Marge hadn't been forced to take a blood oath and we were ultimately honored with the recipe," says Sally.

"Marge and Jimmy were fabulous storytellers," she continues, "and many incredible tales accompanied the serving of this cheesecake. We were told never to open the oven door while baking. We were given strict counsel not to make any big noises, not to slam doors, and even to get the kids out of the house so they wouldn't jump up and down and shake the floor. The most important instruction," Sally remembers, "was to be sure to invite good friends and family to share this divine dessert."

Marge and Jimmy Chambers have passed away, but their recipe has been immortalized by the Websters. Sally serves it to us "with particular pleasure and love. Our family calls it a great cheesecake. But when you know its origins it becomes even more extraordinary."

In honor of the immortal Jimmy Chambers, one of the world's greatest horn players, we suggest you listen to his recording of the Corelli Sonata in F (Award 33-704). But be sure to listen *after* the cake is out of the oven. Bake this one in silence.

Chambers/Philadelphia Cheesecake

SERVES 10

CRUST

13 double graham crackers or
1³/₄ cups graham cracker crumbs
¹/₂ cup sugar
¹/₂ cup unsalted butter, melted

FILLING

4 tablespoons unsalted butter, softened
2 (8 ounce) packages cream cheese, softened
1 pint sour cream
4 large eggs, separated and at room temperature
1 cup granulated sugar
2 tablespoons cake flour
2 teaspoons vanilla extract

1 Preheat oven to 350°.

2 Finely crush graham crackers and add sugar and melted butter. Stir to combine and press into an 8- or 9-inch springform pan. Press crumbs evenly over bottom and up sides, saving a few teaspoons for top of cake.

3 In a large mixing bowl or the bowl of a heavy-duty electric mixer, cream butter with electric beater. Beat in cream cheese and sour cream and beat well to blend. Beat in egg yolks, sugar, flour, and vanilla. In a separate large bowl, beat egg whites until stiff peaks form. Lighten the cream cheese mixture with a quarter of the whites and then carefully fold in the remainder, mixing well. Pour into prepared pan and sprinkle with remaining crumbs. Bake 1 hour and remove from oven to a cooling rack. Let cool completely and chill.

Reva Wurtzburger

"This recipe for a Cornflake Ring came with my husband," Reva Wurtzburger tells us. "It was part of *his* dowry."

Reva has been sharing her humor with the New York Philharmonic Council since 1980. In fact, she's a past council president. Humor aside, Reva is very serious about both music and food. In fact, she's helped to write and organize three cookbooks "from soup to nuts."

"This is really good, even at a grown-up dinner party," Reva says. She's right. Dressed with ice cream and berries, it's quite suitable for any occasion. Let your guests taste it first. Then, when they're pestering you for the recipe, surprise them with the ingredients. They'll be amazed.

You'll also be amazed, and more than amused, when you match the Wurtzburger Ring with Anna Russell's analysis of Wagner's *Ring* on the newly reissued *Anna Russell Album* (Sony MDK 47252). Wagner will never be the same.

Cornflake Ring

SERVES 8

8-10 tablespoons unsalted butter
1¼ cups packed dark brown sugar
1 (7 ounce) box cornflakes
(about 7 cups)

Vanilla ice cream
Strawberries or raspberries or
fruit sauce

1   Grease an 8-cup ring mold. In a large saucepot, melt butter over medium high heat. Add sugar and stir until dissolved, about 5 minutes. Add cornflakes and stir quickly to coat. Pack them into the ring mold and let sit until cool. When ready to serve, place serving plate over mold and quickly invert. Place ice cream in middle and pass fruit or fruit sauce on the side.

Adele Young

Adele Young, a member of the New York Philharmonic Council, divides her passions among baking and cooking, music, and her family. And she manages to bring them all together in the happiest of ways. "Henryk Szeryng, the violinist, came to our home to play a concert," Adele tells us, recalling an evening of chamber music and dinner. "My daughter, who was ten years old at the time, was sitting in the back row of the chamber orchestra I had assembled for the event. A few years later when she was attending Juilliard, she changed her instrument to viola and, at the age of twenty, she became the youngest female in history to join the New York Philharmonic."

While her daughter, Rebecca, fiddles in the viola section of the orchestra, Adele devotes her time to working for the New York Philharmonic as a volunteer. In fact, she's been in charge of recordings for the Radiothon since 1987 and, if you're lucky enough to participate in this annual event and partake of the magnificent meals served to the volunteers, you'll probably see Adele behind a table or two dishing up lunches and dinners.

When she's not serving at the Philharmonic, this busy lady spends a great deal of her time cooking. In fact, she had been interested in writing a cookbook for the Philharmonic for some time, so she was anxious to be part of this one. Of the recipes she sent for us to sample, we chose this Tomato Cheese Log because it's so unusual and so delicious. It may sound peculiar, but try it! You'll like it.

The music to accompany this appetizer begins with a tribute to Henryk Szeryng: Brahms's Sonata No. 1 for Violin and Piano with Mr. Szeryng and Arthur Rubinstein. And, since this log is such a tasty surprise, we suggest Haydn's *Surprise Symphony*, No. 94, with Leonard Bernstein and the New York Philharmonic (Columbia MQ-32101).

Tomato Cheese Log

MAKES 2½ CUPS

1 (14 ounce) can whole tomatoes, drained and seeded (1 cup)

1 (8 ounce) package cream cheese, softened

1 stick (½ cup) butter, softened

½ cup chopped onion

2 cloves garlic, minced

1 teaspoon salt

½ teaspoon cayenne pepper

2 cups (16 ounces) finely chopped walnuts

1 tomato, seeded and chopped

Assorted crackers

1 In the bowl of an electric mixer, combine all ingredients except walnuts and chopped tomato. Beat until smooth, about 2 minutes. Spoon onto a large sheet of wax paper and roll into a log. Chill in freezer for 1 hour or until firm. Unwrap, cover with chopped walnuts, and garnish with chopped fresh tomato. Serve with crackers or place in a lettuce-lined bowl and serve as a dip.

WQXR

WQXR and the New York Philharmonic have had a long, healthy, and happy relationship. It began in 1936 when the radio station broadcast its first signal (as W2XR), spinning 78 rpm discs, one after another, to the surprise and delight of all those hearing, for the first time, a complete, uninterrupted recorded symphony wafting over the airwaves. What a shock it must have been to listen to a recording of a Beethoven symphony, performed by the New York Philharmonic, played all the way through without those frustrating pauses to change the record. How clever it was of this radio station to have more than one turntable, more than one recording, and to segue from one to the next and the next after that.

We've all come a long way since those early radio days. We've heard years of live, simulcast, and tape-delayed New York Philharmonic broadcasts. We've visited with music directors, managers, concertmasters, and last-chair members. We've publicized and promoted, raised funds and musical consciousnesses, opened ears to new sounds, bade farewell to the past, and prepared for the future.

All of the people in this chapter have been associated with WQXR and its Philharmonic patronage. All have contributed time, talent, and testimony. And all love food as well as music.

Warren and Ellen Bodow

Warren Bodow came to WQXR in 1978 as sales manager. He stepped into the office of president and general manager in 1983 after the untimely death of Walter Neiman.

Three hundred and sixty-four days a year, Warren works to raise the financial and artistic standing of WQXR. But on the final day of the New York Philharmonic–WQXR Radiothon, The Boss puts ledgers and records aside, picks up his pen, and proceeds to thank the audience, the orchestra, and all the participants—in rhyme. It's the one time Warren appears on the air and he makes the most of it.

Throughout the Radiothons, which began in 1977, Warren and his wife Ellen have been seen socializing with the volunteers and volunteering themselves to answer phones and take donations. At least one of those donations buys a jar of one of Ellen's specialties.

"Every September since 1973, my cousin Helen Freidus and I have gotten together to make Spiced Plum Jam from our grandmother's recipe," she recounts. "The jam is excellent on toast and can be used as a delicious condiment for veal or chicken cutlets."

Ellen Bodow contributes this creation to the Radiothon. "One of our friends likes this jam so much that she has begun a new tradition of 'purchasing' a jar every year with her check to the New York Philharmonic–WQXR Radiothon."

I suggest that you make plenty of Ellen's jam. It goes with just about anything from fish to beef. And try this: Around Thanksgiving and Christmas, cook up some fresh cranberries, following the directions on the package or using your own favorite recipe. Cut down on the sugar a little (I use about three quarters the amount called for) and, after the cranberries have popped, stir in about ½ cup of Ellen's plum jam. Allow to simmer about five minutes more, then cool. The combination of plums, ginger, spices, and tart cranberries is unbeatable. Your turkey will thank you!

In recognition of all the wonderful "jam sessions" this recipe brings us, we suggest a recording of the orchestra performing Gershwin's "Embraceable You" with Cleo Laine and conductor Zubin Mehta (CBS MK 42516).

Grandma Freeman's Spiced Plum Jam

MAKES 8 OR 9 8-OUNCE JARS

5 cups pitted Italian blue prune plums
(about 2¼ pounds whole)
½ cup water
7½ cups (about 3¼ pounds) sugar
1¼ teaspoons cinnamon
1¼ teaspoons ground cloves
⅛ teaspoon ground ginger

1¼ pouches liquid pectin
2 tablespoons chopped crystallized ginger
16 whole cloves
8 or 9 8-ounce jelly jars, sterilized and kept hot
Melted paraffin

1 Chop plums coarsely and place in a 4-quart saucepot. Add water and bring to a boil. Cover and simmer 5 minutes, stirring occasionally.

2 Measure out 4½ cups of prepared plums using mostly solids and place in an 8-quart saucepot. Add sugar and mix well. Bring mixture to a full rolling boil over high heat and stir constantly while boiling 1 full minute. Remove from heat and stir in cinnamon, ground cloves, and ginger. Stir in 1¼ pouches of the liquid pectin. Stir for 5 minutes, making sure pectin dissolves. Stir in crystallized ginger.

3 Place 2 cloves in each jelly jar and ladle jam into jars, leaving ¼-inch space at top. Wipe rims and inner edges of jars with a damp cloth. Seal by ladling melted paraffin over jam surface. Let cool a few minutes and ladle another layer of paraffin over tops. Make sure jam is completely covered with paraffin. Cool and cover with caps or foil. Store in a cool, dry place.

NOTE: *This recipe can be doubled but not tripled.*

Irwin Brodsky

If you've stopped by to visit any of the recent New York Philharmonic–WQXR Radiothons, you've seen Irv Brodsky. This tall, calm, bespectacled engineer is one of several staff members who stand for hours at a time, spinning records, tapes, and compact discs, adjusting music and talk levels and still finding time to laugh and respond to the on-air conversation around the radio table in Avery Fisher Hall.

An avid chef and cookbook connoisseur, Irv is equally happy spinning spoons at the stove and creating healthful recipes for himself and his wife. Healthful is great, but we need some wine, some good wine, to accompany this inspired recipe. And, with the wine, music: "O vin en vigne" ("O wine on the vine, sweet little wine on the vine and—oops—and sweet little wine on the vine. O wine in the grape, sweet little wine in the grape. Grapi, Grapa, grape on the grape and—oops—and sweet little wine on the vine." This tipsy little four-part madrigal was written in 1570 by Orlandus Lassus and it's sung for us by the King's Singers (EMI CDC 7 49158 2). Oops!

Shrimp and Pasta Adriatica

SERVES 4

1 pound fettuccine

2 tablespoons unsalted butter

½ pound medium shrimp, peeled and deveined

1 clove garlic, minced

2 tablespoons olive oil

5 plum tomatoes, peeled and coarsely chopped (or substitute 2 cups canned drained, chopped plum tomatoes)

¼ cup calamata olives, pitted and chopped

¼-½ teaspoon red pepper flakes

½ cup feta cheese (preferably Bulgarian), cut in ¼-inch dice

¼ cup chopped Italian parsley

9 basil leaves, torn into small pieces

¼ teaspoon salt

½ teaspoon pepper

1 Bring a large saucepot of salted water to a boil. Cook fettuccine al dente according to package directions.

2 Meanwhile, in a large skillet over medium high, heat butter. Add shrimp and cook, stirring just until pink, about 2 minutes. Add garlic and cook 1 minute longer. Remove shrimp from skillet and keep warm.

3 Heat olive oil in a skillet and add tomatoes, olives, and red pepper flakes. Cook, stirring, over high heat about 3 to 4 minutes. Add shrimp and feta and cook 1 to 2 minutes longer. Stir in parsley, basil, salt, and pepper. Place hot drained pasta in serving dish and spoon sauce over. Serve immediately.

Stephanie Feuer

"I came to WQXR to work on publicity after several years as nighttime disc jockey in a nonclassical radio station in New Hampshire." Now there's a switch. But, in some ways, it's the perfect setup for Stephanie Feuer's pumpkin cheesecake recipe, since that was a switch, too.

"This recipe is really a happy accident," Stephanie admits. "One Thanksgiving I was supposed to bring a cheesecake to my family's dinner. I was also asked to bake a pumpkin pie for a friend's gathering the day after the holiday. Or was it the other way around?" Stephanie muses, still a little confused.

"Well, I decided to make them both when I got home from my overnight shift at WGIR-FM up in Manchester. I guess I was a little more tired than I realized and somehow I managed to mix the two recipes. Together."

Stephanie's confusion brings gratification to us. This unusual combination is great!

The music for this spirited and piquant concoction has got to be Saint-Saens's "Danse macabre," in a classic recording featuring the New York Philharmonic under Dimitri Mitropoulos with violinist John Corigliano. It was recorded on November 27, 1950, and first issued on 78 rpm. Columbia later reissued it as a 10″ LP (ML-2170). And there's a current recording with Bernstein and the Philharmonic (CBS MYK-37769).

Pumpkin Cheesecake

MAKES TWO 9-INCH PIES

2 (8 ounce) packages cream cheese,
softened
1¼ cups sugar
4 large eggs
1 (16 ounce) can pumpkin purée
1 teaspoon ground ginger

½ teaspoon nutmeg, preferably
freshly ground
1 teaspoon cinnamon
1 tablespoon cognac
2 prepared pie crusts, either graham
or conventional

1 Preheat oven to 350°.

2 In a blender or with an electric mixer, beat together cream cheese and sugar until well combined. Add remaining ingredients except pie crusts and blend or beat until fully mixed. Pour into prepared crusts and bake 60 minutes or until fully set (cake tester will not come out completely clean). Remove to racks and cool to room temperature. Chill.

David Marx

Another WQXR engineer turns over his turntable, rolls up his sleeves, and bites the challah! Dave Marx often does the engineering work on programs such as "McGraw-Hill's Young Artists' Showcase" with Bob Sherman and "The Vocal Scene" with George Jellinek.

Dave has all sorts of background information that goes with Aunt Sophie's Challah. "Actually, Aunt Sophie is my grandmother," he explains, confusing us before we even get started, "but I call her Aunt Sophie because that's what everyone else calls her." Oh!

David's strongest musical memory of Aunt Grandma is "when she sat down at the Knabe in the living room for a thumping rendition of 'Under the Double Eagle,' just about the only song she ever played." We wonder, is that related to "Would You Rather Be a Colonel with an Eagle on Your Shoulder or a Private with a Chicken on Your Knee?"? (CDC 7 497682)

But chow about the challah, Dave? "This recipe makes one very large loaf," he chollers, "suitable for *large* family gatherings, small weddings and bar/bat mitzvahs, with plenty left over for Sunday Morning French Toast.

"Cut the challah into thick (3/4-inch) slices. Dip the slices into a batter that's made of 1 egg, 1 cup milk, grated orange rind and dark rum, to taste. This stuff," Dave grins, "is like a good eggnog, so what could be bad?" Continuing, Dave instructs us to soak the bread in the batter "so the center of the bread gets moistened, and then fry the slices in a buttered skillet, turning (the bread, not the skillet) until the French Toast is golden brown on both sides."

For those interested in the chistoric implications of challah, Dave tells us that the traditional Rosh Hashanah challah is round, not braided. Raisins and almonds are generally consigned to the Jewish New Year, "but why not add them all year round? It's easy enough to do, but the entire recipe does take some practice. Rehearse a few times," says the engineer, egging us on. "That's how they get to Avery Fisher Hall . . ."

While you're getting the bread hook for Dave, put on the recording of the traditional "Raisins and Almonds" (VAN. 73004). If you use lots of rum in the French Toast batter, listen to *The Buddy "Chally" Story* (Epic EK-35412). Where's the hook?

Aunt Sophia's Challah

MAKES 1 VERY LARGE LOAF
OR 2 SMALLER LOAVES

¹/₄ cup warm water (about 100 degrees)
*2 packages active dry yeast or 1 ounce
(¹/₂ package) compressed yeast*
2 cups boiling water
*5 tablespoons unsalted butter or
margarine, cut into small pieces*
1 tablespoon salt
¹/₂ cup sugar

2 large eggs
8 cups sifted, unbleached flour
1¹/₂ cups golden raisins
*1 to 2 tablespoons unsalted butter or
margarine for coating dough*
*Whole almonds, unsalted and dry
roasted, for decoration*

1 Combine warm water and yeast. Let prove 5 minutes or until yeast bubbles. In a large bowl or heavy-duty mixer, combine boiling water, butter, salt, and sugar. Mix until butter has melted and is well combined. Add 1 egg, yeast, flour, and raisins. If mixing by hand, add the flour a few cups at a time. If mixing by machine, add all the flour at once but cover the mixer with a cloth or the machine's splash guard, because 8 cups of flour can really fly! When combined, knead 5 minutes on a lightly floured board, or use a dough hook and knead 5 minutes on low. Add more flour if required (though this should be a bit sticky). Smear the dough with butter or margarine and place in a bowl. Cover with a towel and let rise in a warm place for 1 hour or until doubled.

2 Grease and flour a large cookie sheet. Turn dough out onto a lightly floured board. Divide into 4 pieces. Roll 3 of the pieces into 14-inch long (about 1¹/₂-inch wide) rolls. Place on cookie sheet and braid, pinching ends together. Divide remaining dough into two pieces and roll into two 14-inch ropes. Pinch ends together and twist together to form a spiral. Make a slight lengthwise crease with your hand in the top of the larger braid and lay the spiral down the length of the braid. Pinch ends of sections together. Cover and let rise 15 minutes. Preheat oven to 400°.

3 Lightly beat the remaining egg and brush loaf completely. Place almonds decoratively over entire loaf. Place loaf in oven and immediately reduce heat to 350°. Bake 40 to 50 minutes or until nice and brown. Cool on a wire rack.

NOTE: Bake smaller loaves 10 minutes less. To freeze dough, follow all directions up until glazing the loaf. Thaw, covered, before baking, and then glaze with the egg.

Muriel Neiman

"Walter had very catholic tastes when it came to food," remembered Muriel Neiman of her husband. "He liked simple food, you might say 'undressed' food, food that had no gravy or sauce."

Fortunately for WQXR, the New York listening area, and arts organizations in and around the city, Walter Neiman's ideas about music and culture were much more expansive. "Walter was the one who first got the idea to give free air time to the great arts organizations of the city to help them raise funds," Muriel reminded us with pride. "He felt that the station had an obligation to support the arts. The New York Philharmonic Radiothon grew from that idea. And that affiliation with business and the arts was very important to him. He felt he was making a contribution that way.

"Walter and I met when he was just an administrative assistant to [Elliott] Sanger. I was living in an apartment on West Tenth Street in Manhattan and my roommate invited him to an open house we were throwing. I opened the door when he arrived and he looked at me and said, 'You're the one.' I thought he was crazy." Not too crazy. They were married one year later, "almost to the exact day!"

Walter Neiman came to WQXR in 1953 and took on the job of program director after Eleanor Sanger left. He went on to become vice president in charge of operations and, in 1973, he became president. His untimely death in 1983 was a shock to everyone and caused tremendous sadness in the arts community and at WQXR, where he was well loved.

We spoke with his widow, Muriel, just three months before her death from cancer in March 1992, nearly nine years to the day after Walter's passing. But her words, her love, and her memories remain.

"Walter didn't like to combine business with his family life," Muriel recalled. Yet he managed to make friends among the 'QXR staff and members of a variety of arts organizations, people who missed him sorely when he died. Perhaps it was because he didn't look at people as business. Maybe that was his secret. "We did have people up to our house for small dinner parties. In fact, I served this Curried Fruit recipe fairly often because it was something we both loved and it went with so many things.

"This isn't a dessert or a jam," she added. "I use this as a side dish with chicken or turkey or a roast. It's a terrific accompaniment." The musical accompaniment for Muriel Neiman's Curried Fruit begins with the Brahms Double Concerto, simply because Walter loved Romantic symphonic music. This is the recording with the New York Philharmonic, Isaac Stern, and Leonard Rose conducted by Bruno Walter (Odys. Y-34621). And, we draw the curry in the recipe and the *New York Times*'s ownership of WQXR together with a work called *New York Times—August 30, 1964* by Harold Farberman, sung by mezzo-soprano Corrine Curry (Ser. 12011). And, in tribute to the memory of the Neimans—a beloved and loving couple who met and married under the most romantic of circumstances, we offer "Some Enchanted Evening" sung by Mary Martin and Ezio Pinza on the original cast recording of *South Pacific* (Columbia CK 32604).

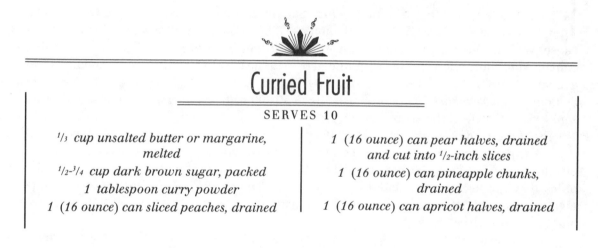

Curried Fruit

SERVES 10

¹/₃ cup unsalted butter or margarine, melted

¹/₂-³/₄ cup dark brown sugar, packed

1 tablespoon curry powder

1 (16 ounce) can sliced peaches, drained

1 (16 ounce) can pear halves, drained and cut into ¹/₂-inch slices

1 (16 ounce) can pineapple chunks, drained

1 (16 ounce) can apricot halves, drained

1 Preheat oven to 325°.

2 In a small bowl, combine butter, brown sugar, and curry powder. Place fruit in a 2-quart baking dish. Pour butter mixture over fruit and bake uncovered 35 to 40 minutes. Serve hot or at room temperature.

This is excellent with chicken, lamb, or pot roast.

Eleanor Sanger

It is fairly safe to say that without Eleanor Sanger and her husband, Elliott, there would never have been a New York Philharmonic–WQXR Radiothon. We make this claim because, without the Sangers, there probably would not have been a WQXR. It was Elliott Sanger who, with John V. L. Hogan, founded the classical station in 1936 and brought it from a small laboratory with a turntable spinning 78-rpm discs in Long Island City to the Radio Stations of the *New York Times* broadcasting at 50,000 watts and spinning compact discs on sophisticated, state of the art machinery.

But Elliott did not work alone. His wife, Eleanor, began by helping him with the mail. "It was an experimental station in the beginning and we got a lot of listener mail. I opened envelopes and did things around the office," she remembers. She did so much around the office that she became the station's program director in 1943. And she stayed for some eighteen years. "I did some consulting after that for about two years, but it was time for me to leave the work force."

That doesn't mean she stopped working or consulting. Elliott died in 1989, well into his nineties. And Eleanor still leads an active life, painting, reading (various members of her family write for the *New York Times*), advising, and socializing with her many friends.

The Sanger home, overlooking Central Park, is filled with beautiful pieces of art, its walls lined with an eclectic collection of books. The dining room is warm and inviting. And Eleanor's recipes are simple and delicious. The music we suggest for Eleanor Sanger's Summer Dessert is the "Summer" movement of Vivaldi's *Four Seasons* with Itzhak Perlman, Zubin Mehta, and the Israel Philharmonic (DG 419214-1 GH), and *Les Nuits d'été*, the song cycle by Berlioz, sung by Elly Ameling with Robert Shaw and the Atlanta Symphony (Telarc DG-10084).

Summer Dessert

MAKES 6 SERVINGS

2 (11 ounce) cans mandarin oranges,
drained

1 (20 ounce) can pineapple chunks,
drained

1 cup sour cream

2 cups miniature marshmallows

2 tablespoons orange liqueur

¹/₃ cup shredded coconut

1 In a large mixing bowl, combine all ingredients except coconut. Mix well and place in a serving dish. Chill at least 30 minutes or up to 4 hours. Half an hour before serving, sprinkle with coconut.

Herb and Laurie Squire

Herb and Laurie Squire are engineers with an ear for the classics. Herb has been chief engineer at WQXR since 1985, and Laurie coordinates the timings of the performances at the Metropolitan Opera for the company's worldwide Saturday afternoon radio broadcasts.

Having spent their earlier radio years at WOR in New York, where they worked with Bob and Ray, the famous radio team, the Squires suggest a recording of "Rum and Coca-Cola" while you stir up their recipe for Rum Balls. Their rum balls are infamous at a variety of radio stations with very different formats, from talk and country to classical.

As for music, after you've had your fill of "Rum and Coca Cola," try "The Rumble" (say it slowly and you'll get it) from Bernstein's *West Side Story* in the recording conducted by the composer with the Israel Philharmonic (DG 415 253-2). Then, turn to Christine Lavin's performance of "Ballad of a [Rum] Ballgame" (Philo CD-1107).

Rum Balls

MAKES ABOUT 40

4 *cups vanilla wafers*	2 *tablespoons light corn syrup*
1 *cup walnuts*	2 *tablespoons rum*
2 *tablespoons unsweetened cocoa*	2 *tablespoons water*
1 *cup sifted confectioners' sugar*	*Cocoa for coating*

1   Place wafers in a food processor and pulse until coarsely chopped. Add walnuts and process until wafers are crumbs and walnuts are coarsely chopped. Add all remaining ingredients except cocoa for coating and pulse until well combined. With your hands, form into 1-inch balls and roll in cocoa to coat.

Dancers

Gerald Arpino

It was the New York Philharmonic's Spring Ball, better known as "An Evening in Vienna," and it took place at Lincoln Center's Damrosch Park. The presentation included wine, dinner, and dancing for everyone, and Zubin Mehta conducted the "band" for the dancers' pleasure. Among those dancers were students from the Joffrey Ballet School and they made that Philharmonic Spring Ball on May 15, 1985, an event to remember.

Most everything the Joffrey Ballet touches is memorable. Take Robert Joffrey's holiday parties. "Christmas at Joffrey's was a tradition. There was a huge Victorian tree, lots of friends, tons of food, and wonderful wines." Gerald Arpino, artistic director of the Joffrey Ballet, isn't talking about Christmas on stage. He's remembering Christmases-past at the home of Robert Joffrey, the founder of the company, who died in 1988.

ROBERT JOFFREY

"Every door and window had a huge wreath. Garlands hung from the banisters and the tree was magnificent. It was featured in *House and Garden*, you know." And then Gerald Arpino remembers the guests. "John Ashbery, the Lauders, Tom Tryon, Willa Kim, dancers, artists. They were all there. And the presents! They were mounded around the tree, from all over the world."

The food was like something out of a storybook, too. "We had the traditional honey-glazed ham," Jerry remembers, with a slightly glazed expression. "Roast turkeys with stuffing. Cranberry sauce that glistened. A marvelous green salad. Oh, and big bowls of shrimp.

There was so much and so many people that Christmas went right into New Year's.

"Bob's favorite was beluga caviar. We had it by the spoonful with buckets of iced champagne. And there was always a special cake from Greenberg's."

It wasn't always that way for the Joffrey Ballet and its directors. "In the beginning it was hot dogs and hamburgers. We traveled in a station wagon. And I remember lots of times when we danced over the kitchens of Baptist churches." Gerald Arpino admits those were good times, too. "Black-eyed peas, fried chicken, cornbread. The aromas would float up through the stage while we danced."

These days the Joffrey dances at City Center in New York City. There's no kitchen beneath the stage, but Gerald Arpino's recipe for Shrimp with Capers and Tomatoes does bring to mind one of his balletic creations, "Sea Shadow." This pas de deux, inspired by the romantic Ondine fable, is set to the slow movement of Ravel's Concerto in G for Piano and Orchestra. Sample the recording with Philippe Entremont performing with the Cleveland Orchestra and conductor Pierre Boulez (Sony Classical SBK 46338).

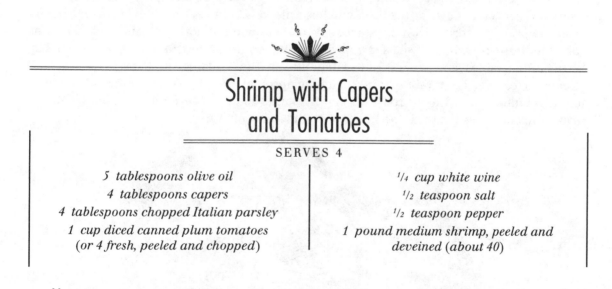

Shrimp with Capers and Tomatoes

SERVES 4

5 tablespoons olive oil	1/4 cup white wine
4 tablespoons capers	1/2 teaspoon salt
4 tablespoons chopped Italian parsley	1/2 teaspoon pepper
1 cup diced canned plum tomatoes (or 4 fresh, peeled and chopped)	1 pound medium shrimp, peeled and deveined (about 40)

1   Heat 4 tablespoons of oil in a large skillet over medium high heat. Stir in capers and parsley, and cook, crushing the capers with the back of the spoon. Add tomatoes and wine and simmer 5 minutes or until sauce has thickened. Add salt and pepper.

2   Meanwhile, heat remaining tablespoon of oil in another large skillet over high heat. Add shrimp and cook, stirring, until just barely done, about 2 to 3 minutes. Add the caper mixture to shrimp and continue cooking, stirring, 1 to 2 minutes more.

Serve over orzo or rice.

Jacques d'Amboise

When we think of the New York Philharmonic and at least its last two homes at Carnegie Hall and Lincoln Center, we think of the orchestra on the stage, the conductor on the podium, and a soloist or two in front of an audience of people lined up in long, sedate rows fanning out from the stage.

In the late 1960s and early '70s, however, this whole concept got turned upside down by a series of concerts known as the Promenades. This New York version of the historic London Proms kept the performers on the stage, but that was about it. Philharmonic Hall, as it was called in those days, had its seats stripped from the entire orchestra level and replaced by large, round tables and chairs, like a banquet at the Waldorf. Ribbons, balloons, and streamers festooned the walls, ceilings, and the apron of the stage, turning the entire house into a gigantic party. And André Kostelanetz, the director of those entertaining evenings, made it his business to match the music with the atmosphere.

And so the stage was set in June 1968 for Jacques d'Amboise, leading male dancer with Balanchine's New York City Ballet, to make his debut with the New York Philharmonic. With him on the nights of June 4 and 5 was prima ballerina Melissa Hayden. And, on a stage that normally seated 106 musicians, they managed to dance the Tchaikovsky Suite for packed, happy houses.

Jacques is one of those rare ebullient and optimistic people whose very presence is capable of creating energy and enthusiasm in others. He began dancing with the New York City Ballet when he was barely out of his childhood and became one of the world's leading dancers in his teens, drawing gasps of admiration from audiences with his seemingly effortless leaps and elegant, handsome partnering of beautiful Balanchine ballerinas from Diana Adams and Allegra Kent to Suzanne Farrell and Violette Verdy.

Jacques, now the head of the National Dance Institute, where he brings the love of dance to thousands of schoolchildren around the world, was at a recent dinner party where he was asked whether he missed his career as a dancer. "That was a different life," he answered with a bit of impatience. But doesn't he miss it at all? Does he ever feel nostalgic when he sees his movies or films? "I feel as if I'm watching someone else. There's so much to do now . . ." And with that he was off on a million ideas he would put into action.

Jacques' eating habits have definitely changed over the years. When he was a young ballet star, taking class all day and dancing almost every night, he ate as if he were hollow. Bottles of wine, scotch, fruit juice, whole steaks, boxes of pasta disappeared with enormous gusto and flourish. It wasn't fast eating. It was merely awesome in its quantity. And he never seemed to gain an ounce. "Those days are gone and now I'm a different person," he tells us again. "Now I watch what I eat. I'm careful about fatty foods and meats. I love salads and vegetables."

Again a memory comes to mind. Jacques, in the late nineteen fifties or early sixties, in his kitchen whipping up a salad for five. It's in a bowl that looks like a bathtub. His arms, sleeves rolled up, hands presumably washed, are the servers—tossing lettuce, endive, peppers, cukes, and tomatoes into the air as if the veggies were sugar plum fairies. His wife, Carolyn, hovering. Children, a set of twins and two older sons, somewhere, but not eating so late. Wine open on the table. Conversation, laughter, and food flying through the electric atmosphere. Music was almost unnecessary. Jacques created a song of his own by his very presence. But if he's not in your kitchen at the moment, the musical accompaniment has to be something of great joy, passion, and strength: Stravinsky's *Firebird* with Boulez and the New York Philharmonic (CBS MK-42396) and something with elegance and humor: Mahler's Symphony No. 1 with Bernstein and the Philharmonic, recorded in 1966 (Col. MS-7019).

Diane's Lima Bean Soup, by the way, came to Jacques by way of Diane Boatwright, who has been part of the d'Amboise household since 1963. "My grandmother used to make this soup when I was a child growing up in a little town in North Carolina," Diane tells us. "When I made it for Jacques, he liked it so much that I had to sit down and write out the recipe for him. It was hard to do because my grandmother and I never thought about the amounts of each ingredient. But I finally figured it out and got it down on paper." For Diane's Southern grandma: "Four Southern Hymns" by Virgil Thomson, sung by the Gregg Smith Singers (Vox Box SVBX 5353).

Diane's Lima Bean Soup

MAKES 12 CUPS

4 cups baby lima beans, washed, picked over, and soaked overnight

3 celery ribs, cut into 2-inch chunks

1 large onion, chopped (about 1 cup)

9 cups chicken stock (preferably homemade) or (if you have it)

4 cups ham-hock stock and 5 cups chicken stock

1 ham hock (if you don't happen to have the ham-hock stock)

Salt and pepper to taste

1 In an 8- to 10-quart stockpot combine all the ingredients except the salt and pepper over high heat. Bring to a boil, cover, reduce to a simmer, and cook 1 hour. Uncover and cook 1½ hours longer, or until beans are tender. Remove 2 cups of the beans and purée in a food processor or blender. Return to soup and stir well. If too thick, add a bit more stock. Season with salt and pepper.

Arthur Mitchell

ARTHUR MITCHELL AND SUZANNE FARRELL IN
SLAUGHTER ON TENTH AVENUE

When Arthur Mitchell made his debut with the New York Philharmonic in 1966, he'd already been getting standing ovations across the Lincoln Center Plaza at the New York City Ballet for some time. But this dancer's Philharmonic debut was an historic event. That July the orchestra was celebrating the Heritage and Legacy of Igor Stravinsky. And the evening of the fifteenth was dedicated to an all-Stravinsky dance program. The stage was lit up by stars of the magnitude of Aaron Copland, Elliott Carter, John Cage, Lukas Foss, Jaime Laredo, and Suzanne Farrell.

Can you imagine the excitement of having on one program Mitchell and Farrell dancing *Ragtime*, Aaron Copland narrating *L'Histoire du soldat*, and the very first performance of the danced version of *Elegy*, with choreography by George Balanchine?

Of course, it was 1966 and audiences may have taken all that talent for granted, just as today we're blasé about tomorrow's super heros of the stage. Looking back on that evening, though, is enough to make you wish you'd been there so you might remember it today.

Since his days dancing Balanchine, Arthur Mitchell has gone on to found his own company and school: the Dance Theatre of Harlem. An effervescent man with tremendous charisma and charm, Arthur Mitchell has a strength that makes things happen. *Good* things. And, like most great dancers, he also loves great food.

"This recipe for Sweet Potato Pie," the dancer-teacher-choreographer tells us, "is my favorite. It's from my mother's kitchen." To date, we know of no one who's done a study of how many pliés and jetés it takes to dance off sweet potato pie, but eating this delicacy certainly hasn't hurt Arthur Mitchell's form over the years.

To be on the safe side, while baking the pie, tap your toes to Stravinsky's *Ragtime for 11 Instruments* in a recording with the Bolshoi Theatre Soloists (Melodiya MFCD-891). Stay with Stravinsky and move on to the *Pulcinella Suite* with the New York Philharmonic and Leonard Bernstein (CBS MY-44709) while eating.

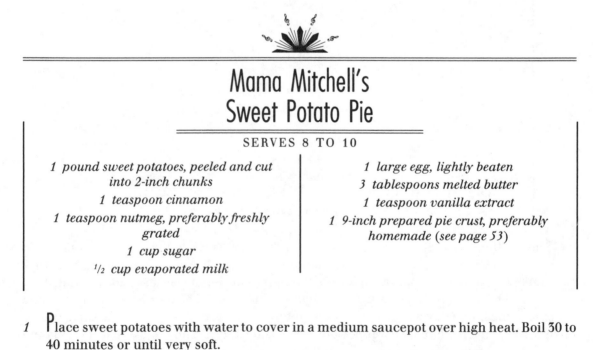

Mama Mitchell's
Sweet Potato Pie

SERVES 8 TO 10

1 pound sweet potatoes, peeled and cut into 2-inch chunks

1 teaspoon cinnamon

1 teaspoon nutmeg, preferably freshly grated

1 cup sugar

1/2 cup evaporated milk

1 large egg, lightly beaten

3 tablespoons melted butter

1 teaspoon vanilla extract

1 9-inch prepared pie crust, preferably homemade (see page 53)

1   Place sweet potatoes with water to cover in a medium saucepot over high heat. Boil 30 to 40 minutes or until very soft.

2   Preheat oven to 400°.

3   Drain potatoes well, peel, and return to pot. Add all ingredients except pie crust and mash well, making sure there are no lumps. Transfer to pie crust and bake 30 to 35 minutes or until completely set. Let cool.

Martine van Hamel

Martine van Hamel made her New York Philharmonic debut at a spring Promenade concert conducted by André Kostelanetz. But the prima ballerina from American Ballet Theatre appeared as both choreographer and dancer that night in May 1977. The evening was dubbed "Promenade a la Danse," and Martine chose works by Fauré, Foote, and Debussy to set the scene in Avery Fisher Hall for her divertissement with Clark Tippet and Kristine Elliott.

Was her mind on anything but her feet that night? "I don't really taste what I eat before à performance," Martine van Hamel tells us. "I'm thinking of what I'm going to dance too much to notice what's on my plate. I just make sure that I have some protein and some carbohydrate, maybe some fish and rice, but not too much. And I eat it around four o'clock if I have an eight o'clock curtain."

The ABT ballerina, who danced with the company for twenty years starting in 1970, is careful of what she eats. "But not too careful. I mean I just try not to eat too much or too little. Isn't that the way it is for everyone?" Not really, Martine. I've never been concerned about eating too little, but then I'm not a dancer.

"I lose a couple of pounds with each performance," Martine continues, "but that's really water weight. And it depends on what I'm dancing. I'm sure I lose more if I do a full-length ballet than I do if I just dance an excerpt." Still, it's very hard, physical work. The great dancers make it look easy, but they're up there sweating and they need energy food to give them endurance.

Since leaving ABT in 1990, Martine van Hamel has been concentrating more on her own company, the New Amsterdam Ballet. "The group is based in New York and it has anywhere from four to twelve people. I say it's based in New York, but it's really a touring company. I'm doing a lot of freelance work myself, both dancing and choreography, so I don't spend as much time with them as I'd like to."

The skate recipe we have from Martine came to her from a friend who was staying at her house. "He's a composer and a wonderful cook. I used to buy skate once in a while, but I never really knew what to do with it. Then I watched him, because what he made was so delicious. This recipe is my version of what he showed me."

We need some "skating" music to accompany Martine van Hamel's Skate with Capers and Lemon Butter Sauce. Emil Waldteufel wrote some just for us: "The 'Skater's' Waltz," performed by the Monte Carlo Opera Orchestra conducted by Willi Boskovsky (Angel S-37208).

Skate with Capers and
Lemon Butter Sauce

SERVES 2

¹/₂ cup white wine	*¹/₄ teaspoon grated lemon zest*
4 cups water	*¹/₂ lemon, peeled and coarsely chopped*
¹/₂ cup chopped onion	*1 tablespoon capers*
1 rib celery, coarsely chopped	*2 tablespoons chopped Italian parsley*
3-4 parsley stems	*Pinch salt*
1 pound skinned skate wings	*¹/₄ teaspoon pepper*
¹/₂ stick (4 tablespoons) unsalted butter	

1 In a large deep skillet or saucepot, combine first 5 ingredients. Bring to a boil over high heat, cover, lower heat to a simmer, and cook 15 minutes. Add skate and cook 6 to 7 minutes or until almost cooked. Remove with a slotted spatula to a broiling pan.

2 Preheat broiler.

3 In a small saucepot over medium heat, melt butter. Stir in zest, chopped lemon, capers, chopped parsley, salt, and pepper. Cook over low heat 1 to 2 minutes or until flavors are blended. Keep warm.

4 Place skate in broiler, 2 to 3 inches from source of heat. Broil 5 to 6 minutes or until lightly browned. Remove to a serving platter and pour butter sauce over.

Instrumentalists

STRINGS AND OTHER THINGS

Nancy Allen

The archives of the New York Philharmonic tell us that Nancy Allen made her debut as a solo artist with the orchestra at an all-contemporary Rug Concert conducted by Pierre Boulez in 1977. The program featured three works, including one called *Love in the Asylum.* But even with a tantalizing title like that, the harpist has trouble remembering the specific event. "I was just a student at Juilliard at the time," she tells us. Even more surprising, she divulges, "That must have been my second real orchestral job.

"When I was just a teenager, Claude Monteux, the son of Pierre Monteux, knew my playing. He was the conductor of the Hudson Valley Philharmonic and I was still in high school. But he asked me to play just about every harp concerto there was! It was pretty overwhelming," she adds.

"I did most of my playing with the New York Philharmonic when I was just a student at Juilliard. Jimmy Chambers, the orchestra's personnel manager and one of the greatest horn players ever, was giving a course at Juilliard. It was a repertory class that everyone was dying to get into. There were no strings." The harpist means, *no strings.* No violins, cellos, violas, double basses. "That meant your part was really exposed," she explains. "And Jimmy Chambers had all these wonderful insights from all the great conductors he'd worked with. It was great.

"Anyway, he was the one who brought me into the Philharmonic to perform. Boulez was the music director and he was doing a lot of pieces that called for two harps or solo harp. And there I was, finishing my bachelor's degree and playing with this great orchestra." There's a slight pause and then she adds, "He must have asked me because he knew I could count.

"One of the first things I did with the Philharmonic was the Bicentennial tour with Leonard Bernstein. We went all over Europe and the United States for seven weeks. I was sort of adopted by the percussion section. Walter Rosenberger and Buster Bailey chaperoned me. Don't forget, I was a student with what seemed like an enormous stipend for food. So every meal was like a dream. After all, in New York I had been living on wheatina and oatmeal.

ON TOUR

"One of the funniest things that happened on that tour took place at the Amsterdam Hilton. We flew there after a week of playing in Florida. The day after we arrived, there was a big reception in the hotel. I never was sure if it was put on for the orchestra, if it was open to everyone, or it was for someone else entirely. But we all showed up.

"They had these incredible displays of fruits and vegetables piled high on all the tables. Just for show, you know? Well, we all loaded up our plates with the regular food. But, as we were leaving, everyone started taking the display bananas and apples and oranges and stuffing them in their pockets. The head waiter kept screaming about his displays."

Musing on this sophisticated musical ensemble, the harpist adds, "They were really a lot of fun."

Also a lot of fun: Nancy Allen's *Celebration for Harp* with music by Loeillet, Bach, Scarlatti, Prokofiev, and Respighi (Angel CDM-69070), and to match the warm glow of Nancy's recipe for Carrot Soup, George Rochberg's *Slow Fires of Autumn, for Flute and Harp* with Carol Wincenc (CRI S-436).

Carrot Soup

SERVES 8

2 pounds organic carrots, peeled and
cut into ½-inch dice (about 6 cups)
4 cups chicken stock or canned
chicken broth
1 teaspoon salt
1 tablespoon unsalted butter
1 medium onion, chopped
1-2 garlic cloves, minced

½ cup unsalted chopped cashews
1 cup plain yogurt
1½ cups milk
1 teaspoon pepper
¼ teaspoon nutmeg, preferably freshly
grated (optional)
Chopped cashews for garnish

1   In a large saucepot over high heat, combine the carrots, broth, and salt. Bring to a boil, cover, lower heat to simmer, and cook 15 minutes or until carrots are very soft. Remove from heat.

2   Meanwhile, heat butter in a medium skillet over medium high heat. Add onion, garlic, and cashews and cook, stirring, until onion is translucent, about 4 to 5 minutes. Add to carrot mixture and purée in batches in a blender or food processor until smooth.

3   Return to saucepot and stir in yogurt, milk, pepper, and nutmeg. Reheat gently over medium heat just until hot, about 5 to 6 minutes. Garnish with cashews and serve with fresh bread.

Buster and Barbara Bailey

Elden (Buster) Bailey was a member of the New York Philharmonic from 1949 until his recent retirement. He's a percussionist and his wife, Barbara, is a percussionist! With all that blasting going on in the Bailey household, it's a wonder anything ever gets baked. "Although Buster grew up in Maine," Barbara booms, "I am a product of the Pennsylvania Dutch country, certainly an area where good food is important, especially baked goods."

Barbara has been a member of the percussion and timpani section of the Bergen (New Jersey) Philharmonic since 1955. But the Bailey household has some diverting outside interests. "Buster is crazy about the circus. It's his major hobby and has provided not only entertainment but many friendships as well."

Whether or not his association with the circus and circus people has ever allowed Barbara an opportunity to throw one of her delectable pies at her husband, we don't know. But we sincerely hope she didn't waste one of her Fairy Pies on this clown trick. It's too good to spend all on one face!

"This recipe," Barbara reports, "was often used as a dessert for summer celebrations, birthdays, and all sorts of parties." It was a hard choice deciding between this recipe and the one she uses for her famous pecan pies, sold as premiums at the Philharmonic's annual Radiothons. But Barbara finally settled on this Fairy Pie because the other one comes from a cookbook. "After forty-plus years of marriage it's a little difficult to identify the origins of many of my recipes, but I'm certain about this one. The Fairy Pie was my mother's recipe and it's a real family favorite."

In honor of Barbara's mother, Sarah Raudenbush, "a Pennsylvania Dutch lady," we suggest the score of *Plain and Fancy* (Capitol S-603), and for this luscious Fairy Pie, we recommend the incidental music to *A Midsummer Night's Dream*, by Mendelssohn, played by the Philadelphia Orchestra with Judith Blegen and Frederica von Stade, conducted by Eugene Ormandy (RCA RCD1-2084).

Fairy Pie

SERVES 8 TO 10

2 sticks (¹/₂ pound) unsalted butter, softened

1 cup sugar

4 large eggs, separated and at room temperature

¹/₂ cup plus 2 tablespoons sifted unbleached flour

1 teaspoon baking powder

¹/₄ cup milk

Pinch salt

1 teaspoon vanilla extract

¹/₂ cup chopped nuts of your choice (optional)

1 cup heavy cream

2 cups fresh or canned sliced peaches or strawberries

1 Preheat oven to 350°. Grease and flour two 9-inch cake pans.

2 In a large mixing bowl, cream the butter and ¹/₂ cup of the sugar with an electric hand mixer until light colored and fluffy, about 3 minutes. Add the egg yolks and beat well. In a small bowl, mix together the flour and baking powder and add half to the butter mixture. Add half the milk and beat well. Repeat with remainder of flour and then remainder of milk. Divide equally between prepared pans.

3 In another mixing bowl, combine the egg whites, pinch of salt, and vanilla. Beat on high speed to stiff peaks. Gradually beat in the remaining sugar, beating until stiff peaks form again. Spread meringue on cake batter, dividing equally between pans. Sprinkle each with chopped nuts if desired (the Baileys never do). Bake 20 to 25 minutes or until meringue is lightly browned and set. Cool in pans.

4 Shortly before serving, remove cake from pans. In a large mixing bowl, beat cream with electric mixer on high until stiff. Invert one cake layer (meringue side down) and cover with half the whipped cream. Cover with half the fresh or drained canned fruit. Place the other layer on top, meringue side up, and cover with remaining cream. Decorate with remaining fruit. Serve immediately.

Julius Baker

Julius Baker joined the New York Philharmonic as principal flutist in 1965 and he remembers that it was the same year he appeared as the soloist in the Nielsen Flute Concerto with Leonard Bernstein in Philharmonic Hall.

Over his years with the orchestra, Julie, as he's called by his many friends, traveled extensively throughout the United States and abroad. But one of his strangest memories comes from Korea.

"You know the Chungs," he asks rhetorically, referring to the talented family that's turned out violinist Kyung-Wha Chung, pianist-conductor Myung-Whun Chung, and cellist Myung-Wha Chung. "Well, they have a flutist, too. She was my pupil. Oh, and the mother was into food. She was a big dealer of mushrooms! Well, anyway," Julie gets back on track, "we were playing in Korea and, one night after a concert, there was this big party for us. I got in line for the food, but my pupil saw me there, pulled me out of the line, and handed me a plate piled with things I'd never seen before. It all was so good that I ate much too much. My wife will tell you. We had to call the house doctor that night." He adds with a laugh, "It was worth it."

Since leaving the Philharmonic, not to retire but to do more solo work, Julius Baker has taken on even more traveling. He talks more about the food, though, than the music. "Have lunch in Iceland," he recommends as if it were up the block. "Their herring is spectacular."

And what about the people? "They're big on bakeries but they can afford it. They're tall and blond and thin. They can afford to eat cheesecake." Julie has a second thought. "Actually their flutists are small for Vikings."

Julius Baker's wife, Ruth, tells us that her method of making short ribs, often prepared with enough beef to feed several bassoon-size Vikings, comes from a recipe she saw about thirty years ago in *Family Circle* magazine. "We've served it often and our guests have included many of the musicians of the New York Philharmonic during the years that we lived in the city." Julius Baker listens to his wife's explanation of the recipe and adds, "They didn't call her Mrs. Baker for nothing."

The musical accompaniment we suggest for the Bakers' Sweet and Spicy Short Ribs begins with Julius Baker's recording of Telemann's "Sweet" in A minor with the Solisti di Zagreb (Vanguard HM-17). After several glasses of good red wine, move on to Placido Domingo's performance of "Beef My Love" (DG 413415-2).*

---

*Credit (or blame) must be given to the great jazz pianist George Shearing for this musical suggestion. The author had nothing to do with it!

Sweet and Spicy Short Ribs

SERVES 6 GENEROUSLY

4 pounds beef short ribs	1 tablespoon sugar
1 cup ketchup	1 tablespoon dry mustard
1 cup water	1 teaspoon salt
1 tablespoon vinegar	$^1/_4$ teaspoon pepper
1 tablespoon Worcestershire sauce	1 bay leaf
1 tablespoon prepared horseradish	2 medium onions, sliced

1 In a large saucepot over medium high heat, combine all ingredients except onions. Bring to a boil, cover, and reduce heat to a simmer. Cook 2 hours or until beef is tender. Cool, then chill at least 1$^1/_4$ hours (this can be done the night before).

2 Preheat oven to 350°.

3 Skim off all fat and remove loose bones and bay leaf. Place meat in a 6-cup baking dish, pour sauce over, and top with sliced onions. Cover and bake 30 minutes. Remove cover and baste onions with sauce. Recover and bake 40 to 45 minutes longer, or until onions are very tender.

Gabriel Banat

Gabriel Banat joined the violin section of the New York Philharmonic in 1970, the year after Leonard Bernstein's departure and the year before Pierre Boulez began his directorship. 1970 was the year of George Szell. But the violinist remembers, "My first real duty with the Philharmonic was a tour with Bernstein." Some duty!

And there was a special tour for Gaby that brought him home to Budapest after an absence of forty-three years. "I was very nervous about going back. I didn't know how I'd react to the city, even though we only had a twenty-two-hour stopover there. I mean it had been forty-three years!" But his confrontation with the city went so well that he decided to go back two years later for what he called "a food and wine" trip.

"We had a wonderful time. I'd never had a chance to go out to the provinces. We traveled to Debrecen for the sausages and to Eger, where the Hungarian wine comes from. It's a good, sturdy "bull's blood" wine.

"We ate mostly at restaurants," he recalls. "We had lots of paprika chicken and palacsinta. Of course, you can get really good Hungarian food in New York—if you're really lucky—but some of it is too much like home cooking, too bland. I liked India for the food," he says, switching countries again.

"It's spicy and I love spicy food, but I can't take it as spicy as Zubin [Mehta]. Not that spicy." And moving on, "Brussels has perhaps better food than Paris. Belgian food is more succulent. The asparagus and strawberries are marvelous.

"Then, Italy is Italy," he announces on his culinary travelogue. "I'm crazy about pasta. Turkey was disappointing [the country, not the bird]. In Spain we go out a lot."

The Banats live part of the year in Spain. "The problems we have there are what beach to go to and what restaurant to eat in.

"Where we live it's Catalan cooking. They have this chicken with langostinos [crayfish]. In the nineteenth century, when it originated, there was more lobster than chicken. Chicken was rare in those days. Now the lobster has thinned out and fishermen have to spend a lot for fuel. So it's the opposite. They do chickens—two dozen at a time—on the spit with herbs and stuffed with lemon." Gaby moves on, like a menu. "There's rice with it, too. Escalivada, a wonderful appetizer: scorched green pepper and eggplant and onions. Scorched separately and cooled in paper bags. It's served with olive oil. Fresh, healthy, delicious . . ." he trails off.

You see, Gabriel Banat likes food. Almost as much as he likes music. And travel. Since Transylvania smacks of Romania and Gaby is Hungarian, we split the difference and offer works from both countries: Bartok's *Concerto for Orchestra* with the New York Philharmonic and Leonard Bernstein (CBS MK-44707), and a classic recording of Enescu's *Romanian Rhapsody No. 1*, recorded in 1946 by the New York Philharmonic under the direction of Artur Rodzinski (Columbia ML-2057 . . . in the 10″ LP!).

Transylvanian Stuffed Peppers

SERVES 6 NORMAL PEOPLE
OR 2 TRANSYLVANIANS

1 pound ground round beef
1 large onion, chopped
1 garlic clove, minced (optional)
$^{1}/_{2}$ teaspoon salt
$^{1}/_{2}$ teaspoon pepper
$^{1}/_{2}$ teaspoon dried thyme
$^{1}/_{2}$ teaspoon dried basil
$^{1}/_{4}$ teaspoon freshly grated nutmeg
$^{1}/_{4}$ cup raisins
1 cup cooked rice
$^{1}/_{4}$ cup pine nuts
6 medium red peppers, cored and seeded

SAUCE
1 (28 ounce) can peeled plum tomatoes
1 (28 ounce) can crushed tomatoes
1 (16 ounce) can tomato sauce
$^{1}/_{2}$ teaspoon salt
$^{3}/_{4}$ teaspoon pepper
2 tablespoons red wine vinegar
1 tablespoon sugar
1 bay leaf

1   In a large skillet over medium high heat, brown meat, stirring to break up lumps, about 5 minutes. Add onion and garlic (if using) and continue cooking until meat is browned completely and onion is translucent, about 5 minutes longer. Stir in salt, pepper, thyme, basil, nutmeg, raisins, rice, and pine nuts. Cut a thin slice off bottom of peppers if they don't stand up, and fill them with the mixture, dividing evenly. Place peppers upright in a 5 to 6 quart saucepot.

2   Meanwhile, combine all ingredients for sauce in a large mixing bowl and pour carefully around peppers (there should be just enough sauce to cover). Bring to a boil over high heat, cover, and lower heat to a simmer. Cook 1 hour or until peppers are tender.

Lorin Bernsohn

Brooklyn-born cellist Lorin Bernsohn joined the New York Philharmonic in the spring of 1958. And, although he's given recitals and played chamber music with the orchestra at a variety of events over the years, Larry's life is not wrapped entirely around his cello. It can't be, because this multitalented musician has too many other things going on in his life.

For one thing, when Larry isn't sweeping his bow across the cello, he's sweeping a brush across a canvas. And because so much of his time is spent around conductors and other musicians, many of his paintings and drawings depict performers. Then there are portraits of an even more important subject, his family: Alison, Luke, and Amanda.

Lorin Bernsohn met his wife, Alison Jarvis, right in Philharmonic Hall. Now a practicing therapist, Alison was a tour guide at the time and it was fairly obvious that the cellist was interested in more than the Metropolitan Opera when he came around the tour desk every day. Friendship blooms at the Philharmonic. So does romance.

"In the early days, especially, we had lots of gatherings in our homes for chamber music and dinners," Larry tells us. "Brogan Nigrine, the wife of my good friend Henry and a real 'bonne vivante,' hosted many of these Sunday evening buffets. Alison will tell you. Brogan is the one who gave us the recipe for 'Adlai's Dish,' because she served it at some of those parties. I lost the written recipe a long time ago, but found it again recently in *Marblehead Cooks*, a fundraising cookbook for the Tower School in Marblehead, Massachusetts."

Neither Lorin nor Alison is sure where they read it, but they both tell us that this Shrimp and Artichoke Casserole is reputed to have been one of Adlai Stevenson's favorites. Thus the title, "Adlai's Dish." Did Adlai ever attend any of those Sunday night suppers at the homes of the Philharmonic friends? No, but his spirit was there.

"Henry Nigrine is retired now," says Larry, "but many of us in the orchestra still get together for food and music. Maybe more food than music. But Brogan is one of the great hostesses."

In honor of Adlai's casserole, we recommend a rare recording of Aaron Copland's *Lincoln Portrait, for Speaker and Orchestra*, featuring Adlai Stevenson (COL. MS-6684). And in honor of Lorin Bernsohn's painting talent, Mussorgsky's *Pictures at an Exhibition* performed by the New York Philharmonic with Zubin Mehta (MK-35165).

Shrimp and Artichoke Casserole
("Adlai's Dish")

SERVES 4

6 tablespoons unsalted butter
1/2 pound mushrooms, sliced thin
(about 2 1/2 cups)
1 (10 ounce) package frozen
artichoke hearts, thawed
1 pound medium shrimp, peeled,
deveined, and cooked
4 tablespoons all-purpose flour
3/4 cup milk

3/4 cup cream
1/4 teaspoon salt
1/4 teaspoon pepper
1/4 cup dry sherry
1 tablespoon Worcestershire sauce
1/4 cup freshly grated Parmesan cheese
Dash paprika
Chopped parsley

1 Preheat oven to 350°. Grease a 2 1/2-quart casserole dish.

2 Heat 2 tablespoons butter in a large skillet over medium high heat. Add mushrooms and cook, stirring until browned and cooked, about 3 to 4 minutes. Set aside.

3 Spread thawed artichokes evenly over bottom of casserole. Cover with shrimp and top with cooked mushrooms. Set aside while preparing cream sauce.

4 Melt remaining 4 tablespoons of butter in a small heavy saucepot over medium high heat. Whisk in flour and cook 3 minutes, whisking constantly. Whisk in milk, cream, salt, pepper, sherry, and Worcestershire and cook, stirring, until thick, about 6 minutes. Pour sauce over shrimp in casserole and sprinkle with Parmesan and paprika. Bake 20 to 30 minutes or until heated through and garnish with chopped parsley.

NOTE: You can substitute 3 to 4 split chicken breasts for the shrimp.

Canadian Brass

Canadian Brass has a special arrangement with the New York Philharmonic. The members of Canadian Brass, Frederic Mills, Ronald Romm, David Ohanian, Eugene Watts, and Charles Daellenbach, team up with the principal brass players from major orchestras, including the New York Philharmonic, for recordings and concerts.

This is more than a marketing ploy. It's a way for these talented musicians to present repertoire they ordinarily wouldn't be able to handle without the extra forces.

We know the five members of the ensemble are clever. But it helps to have more than a quintet when you set out to tackle a Gabrieli canzona with double echo, or *Finlandia* by Sibelius. In fact, Canadian Brass has joined forces with ten principal players from the New York Philharmonic and the Boston Symphony for an all-brass recording of Beethoven's Fifth! This means there are more crazy, zany people on stage with brass instruments in their hands, and that kind of thing can lead to mass hysteria, in the audience as well as on stage.

Although they generally prefer vegetarian dishes to meat, all five members have been known to eat their own weight at receptions and on tour. Tuba player Charles Daellenbach remembers a trip to China. "We were in the middle of that vast country, in Wu Han, in another terrible hotel. To our surprise we had a really fabulous meal. It was so good," he remembers, "that we called for the chef to come out to meet us so we could thank him in person.

"This man appeared before us with tears in his eyes. He was so touched that we liked what he'd done because during the Cultural Revolution he'd been paraded through the streets wearing one of those dunce caps for his decadence in cooking food in an unnecessary way." What had the chef prepared? "Mostly vegetables and, to tell the truth, a lot of cabbage. But it was Chinese cabbage and he had a way of making it that was out of this world."

Trumpeter Ronald Romm has a way with bananas that turns the simple fruit into a decadent dessert or brunch dish. And the musical accompaniment for this sweet confection comes from a Canadian Brass recording of "Sweet Georgia Brown" (CBS MK-42367). After you've finished the bananas, wash them down with a Fifth of Beethoven with Canadian Brass and principal brass players from the New York Philharmonic and the Boston Symphony (Philips Classics 426487-2).

Baked Bananas

SERVES 4

4 large ripe bananas, peeled
Juice of 2 large oranges, freshly squeezed
(about $^3/_4$ cup)

3 tablespoons sweet sherry

1   Preheat oven to 375°.

2   Cut bananas in half lengthwise. Place in a 9-inch-square glass baking dish. Pour orange juice and sherry over bananas and bake 30 minutes or until soft and lightly brown.

Sol and Shirley Greitzer

"My husband was trained in the old school when men sat at the table and women stood in the kitchen," Shirley Greitzer remembers of her late husband, Sol. "And lucky he was that I liked to cook!"

Sol Greitzer first joined the New York Philharmonic in 1954. "He was inside last stand viola back then," says Shirley. "Then auditions were held for outside fourth stand and he got that. Then, some years later, he auditioned for inside second stand. Got that one, too. And, finally, he auditioned for first chair and he became principal violist. I want you to know, he didn't have any inside track with any conductor, either. Each time he moved up there was a different music director, Mitropoulos, Bernstein, and Boulez.

"He did a lot of solo work with the orchestra, too," Shirley Greitzer says proudly. "He played the Walton Viola Concerto twice, with Barenboim and Bernstein. And he did *Harold in Italy* three times, with Levine, Davis, and Boulez."

The Greitzer family is a musical family. Shirley is a pianist, and their three daughters are all performing musicians: Debbie, the oldest, plays bassoon. Pamela, the youngest, is a cellist. Jody plays flute. And two of them have married musicians. "Debbie met Jerry, a trumpeter, when they were each principal players in the Jerusalem Symphony," Shirley tells us. "And Jody is married to a conductor who used to play trumpet with the Philharmonic. His name is Gerard Schwarz," she adds with another swell of pride.

Shirley remembers one of Sol's tours with the Philharmonic. "Jody was just six weeks old when he went off to Russia. He was gone for ten weeks!" That tour was in the earlier days. Once the children were grown up, Shirley traveled with her husband.

"In 1970 we went to Japan. That was the first tour for me and it was just wonderful. We spent a week in Osaka, three or four days in Kyoto, and about a week in Tokyo. We even had some time in Nagoya. We took a train ride up into the mountains there and saw the largest primate zoo in the world. Then we came back down in a boat, through the rapids." So much for any sign of a dull life!

Shirley tells us that the food in Japan was fantastic. "We ate mostly sushi and sashimi. But it was better than anything you could get here. You learn a lot when you travel," she adds thoughtfully. "I found that you had to learn something of the language. One line in particular.

I'll never forget it in Japanese. *'Ote arei wa doko desuka?'* " Translation? "Why it's the most important thing you can know. 'Where is the bathroom?' "

The last time I heard Sol and Shirley Greitzer perform together, they did a program of works by Fritz Kreisler arranged for viola and piano. They went on to record these pieces and an album was going to be released, but Sol died and, so far, the recording has not been made available. To remember their performances together, let's go back to a collection of recordings made by Fritz Kreisler himself (Pearl 233). And, to continue the Philharmonic-Greitzer-Schwarz connection, Bernstein's *Arias and Barcarolles* with Jane Bunnell, Dale Duesing, and the Seattle Symphony conducted by Gerard Schwarz (Delos DE 3078).

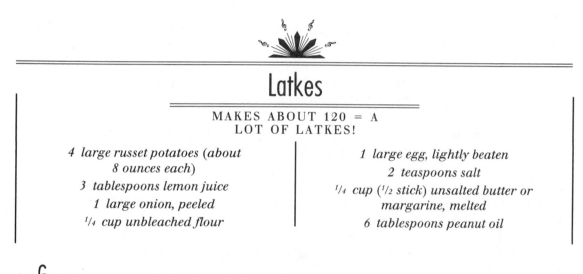

Latkes

MAKES ABOUT 120 = A
LOT OF LATKES!

4 large russet potatoes (about
8 ounces each)

3 tablespoons lemon juice

1 large onion, peeled

¹/₄ cup unbleached flour

1 large egg, lightly beaten

2 teaspoons salt

¹/₄ cup (¹/₂ stick) unsalted butter or
margarine, melted

6 tablespoons peanut oil

1 Grate the potatoes by hand on the large holes of a grater (you should have about 6 cups). Place in a large bowl, cover with water, and add the lemon juice. Meanwhile, grate the onion on the same side of the grater and place in a large mixing bowl. Add the flour and mix well. Drain the potatoes in a colander set in the sink and squeeze out as much excess water as possible. Add potatoes to onion mixture along with the egg, salt, and melted butter and mix well.

2 Heat the oil in an electric frying pan set at 400° or place a heavy skillet over high heat. Drop the pancakes by teaspoonfuls into the hot oil. Cook about 2 minutes on each side or until well browned. Remove to paper towels and serve at once with sour cream or applesauce.

These are best served as soon as they are cooked. If you would like to do them for a big party, they can be prepared the day before and reheated in a 400 oven for about 7 minutes.

Lynn Harrell

Someday someone should do a study of musicians who come from musical families. If they do, they might want to start with Lynn Harrell. The cellist, who made his New York Philharmonic debut in 1961 at a Young People's Concert, is the son of Mack Harrell, one of the great baritones of his day. And the father-son, singer–string player relationship may account for the cellist's ability to "sing" phrases on his instrument.

When Lynn was just eighteen, conductor George Szell invited him to join the ranks of the Cleveland Orchestra. Two years later, Mr. Szell appointed him principal cellist. He stayed in that chair until 1971, feeling that those years were the "foundation of my musical education."

Then, Lynn Harrell stretched his parameters (and his legs), left the Clevelanders, and embarked on the life of a soloist and chamber musician, with considerable time devoted to teaching. He and his family stretch themselves between homes in Los Angeles and Scotland. But Lynn's food smacks more of America than Europe. Some of his favorite recipes revolve around fruit, such as fresh blueberries, bananas, and strawberries. But there's always a touch of cream, iced, whipped, or soured.

Since the cellist obviously has a sweet tooth, our musical accompaniment begins with his recording of the Bach Unaccompanied "Sweets" (2-Lon. 414163-1 LH2). Then, for music so lush you must serve it after dinner and listen, uninterrupted, there's the Brahms Double Concerto with Pinchas Zukerman, Lynn Harrell, and the New York Philharmonic conducted by Leonard Bernstein (CBS 35894).

Fresh Blueberry Pie

SERVES 8 TO 10

1 prebaked 8-inch graham cracker crust
2 pints fresh blueberries, washed and
        picked over
1 (8 ounce) jar currant jelly

1 cup sour cream
1 large strawberry

1   Place blueberries in crust. In a small saucepot, heat jelly over high heat until fully melted (or microwave on high power 2 minutes, stirring twice). Pour over berries. Spread sour cream over top and refrigerate 1 hour or until serving time. Place the strawberry in the middle and serve.

This is great for a Fourth of July dessert.

Stephen Kates

Stephen Kates's debut with the New York Philharmonic was a good news–bad news situation. The good news was that Steve had won a spot on a Young People's Concert with Leonard Bernstein and the Philharmonic. The bad news was that the concert was scheduled for November 23, 1963, the day after President John F. Kennedy was assassinated. The cellist remembers, "We had a rehearsal Friday morning and everything was fine. Then the president was shot and the world was canceled."

The concert finally took place the following Saturday. And quite a concert it was. Stephen Kates was one soloist in the Bartók Rhapsody No. 1 with conductor Zdeněk Košler on the first half. And then he was asked by Leonard Bernstein to play first chair cello with the orchestra in a performance of the *William Tell* Overture. "What an honor," Steve recounts. You see, his father, David, had been a fixture in the Philharmonic's viola section for years. "I grew up calling all these guys by their first names because they were my father's friends. It was Harold, not Mr. Gomberg, the oboist. And it was John, not Mr. Corigliano, the concertmaster. It was like coming into the Yankees' locker room, with all the players knowing you as a kid. And suddenly it was your turn at bat."

Stephen Kates, a New Yorker from the tips of his toes to the pegs of his cello, attended the High School of Music and Art. He remembers a revered orchestra teacher, Isadore Russ, screaming at him one day. "He yelled at me, 'Just because your dad plays in the Philharmonic doesn't mean you can do that!' " And there he was, Dad in the viola section, John and Harold and all the dinner companions in their first chairs, and grown-up Stephen as the soloist. "I didn't call Bernstein Lenny. That I can tell you!"

There have been awards, rewards, and unpostponed concerts since that debut in 1963. Now the summers see Stephen Kates in Santa Barbara, California, teaching, performing, and cooking. That's where he created his Margarita Chicken. "We ran out of bread crumbs one night but there were plenty of tortilla chips. It was California and out there, tortilla chips are like bread," he explains. "So I invented this chicken that's a real Southwestern treat."

The obvious musical accompaniments to Margarita Chicken are Aaron Copland's *El Salon Mexico* with the New York Philharmonic and Leonard Bernstein (CBS MYK-37257), and Haydn's Symphony No. 83 ("The Hen") performed by the Orchestra of the Age of Enlightenment conducted by Sigiswald Kuijken (Virgin Classics VC 7 90793-2).

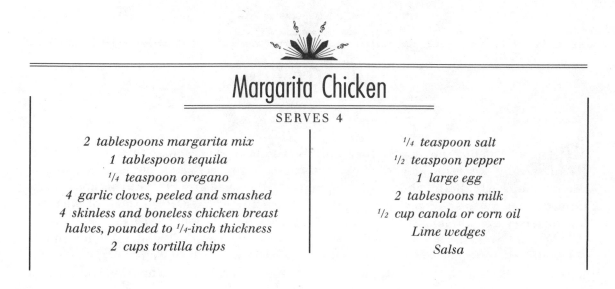

Margarita Chicken

SERVES 4

2 tablespoons margarita mix
1 tablespoon tequila
¹/₄ teaspoon oregano
4 garlic cloves, peeled and smashed
4 skinless and boneless chicken breast halves, pounded to ¹/₄-inch thickness
2 cups tortilla chips

¹/₄ teaspoon salt
¹/₂ teaspoon pepper
1 large egg
2 tablespoons milk
¹/₂ cup canola or corn oil
Lime wedges
Salsa

1 In a medium-size glass or stainless steel bowl combine margarita mix, tequila, oregano, and garlic. Add chicken and marinate at room temperature 30 minutes, or 1 hour in refrigerator.

2 Meanwhile combine tortilla chips, salt, and pepper in a blender and pulse to crumbs. Pour out onto plate. Beat together egg and milk in a small bowl.

3 Heat oil in a large heavy skillet over medium high heat. Dip chicken pieces in egg mixture and coat with tortilla crumbs. Transfer to hot oil and cook until golden brown, about 3 minutes on each side. Drain on paper towels and serve at once with lime wedges and salsa.

Ani Kavafian

"My debut with the New York Philharmonic was quite an experience," recalls violinist Ani Kavafian. "It was the first time I was performing with Erich Leinsdorf and he thought I was too young to be playing the Beethoven Concerto. He asked me to come to his house to go through some sonatas with him and I think we were both surprised. He liked my playing and I thought he was really fantastic at the piano." To sum it up, Ani adds, "We had a great time!"

So Ani Kavafian made her first appearance with the New York Philharmonic, and in celebration of the event, "we had a party at our house." She quickly tells us that she didn't do the cooking that time around. "I was too taken up with performing to do that. But I do cook for crowds. I have a method."

The violinist launches into a description of a party she's preparing to throw for a mere one hundred at the end of the week. "I have a schedule I follow for each day until the party. There's chopping and preparation, freezing what I can and just getting everything ready in advance."

Like most of us, the violinist has a few other things to do at the same time. "I have rehearsals all week, so I have to plot out my time carefully to be sure everything gets done. But we're pretty lucky. This party will be indoors and out, so some of the food can be prepared for the grill and that's easy."

What's the menu for the masses? Ani describes part of the feast. "I have a recipe for a huge pasta dish with pesto and sun-dried tomatoes. I do that inside. Then we're having sausages. Since I don't have time to make them myself from scratch, I'm having the butcher prepare them and we'll grill those outside on the fire." Ani's Armenian heritage shows itself here and there in the meal, especially at dessert when she presents her special baklava.

When Ani Kavafian is away from home, "We have our favorite restaurants in every town. I love San Francisco. And, believe it or not, one of the best places in the country is Detroit! I never would have guessed that, but we keep having marvelous meals in that city. When I'm home I stick pretty close to where we live in North Salem [New York]. You can find us in Auberge Maxime and, of course, the Box Tree Inn."

Ani's sister, Ida, keeps things very much in the family for our musical accompaniment:

Sarasate's *Navarra* for two violins, with Ani and Ida Kavafian (Elektra/Nonesuch 79117-1). And if you eat too much, play *Bach*lava's Cantata 82, "Ich habe genug" ["I've had enough"] (Novalis 150028-2).

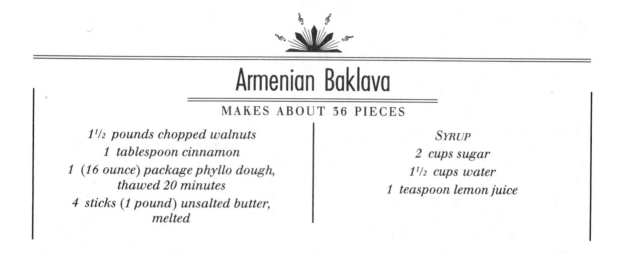

Armenian Baklava

MAKES ABOUT 36 PIECES

1¹/₂ pounds chopped walnuts
1 tablespoon cinnamon
1 (16 ounce) package phyllo dough,
    thawed 20 minutes
4 sticks (1 pound) unsalted butter,
    melted

SYRUP
2 cups sugar
1¹/₂ cups water
1 teaspoon lemon juice

1   Preheat oven to 350°. In a medium mixing bowl, combine the walnuts and cinnamon and mix well.

2   Cut a sheet of wax paper the size of a 13 × 9″ baking pan. Unwrap the phyllo dough and lay wax paper over it. Using the wax paper as a pattern, cut dough to size of pan. As you work, keep dough covered with a clean damp towel to prevent it from drying out. Brush pan bottom and sides with melted butter. Separate 5 sheets of dough and carefully lay one at a time on bottom of pan. Brush the top sheet with butter. Add 5 more sheets and brush with butter. Sprinkle with half the nuts and add 5 more sheets. Brush with butter and lay down 5 more sheets. Brush with butter again and sprinkle with remaining nuts. Arrange remaining phyllo pieces in layers on top. Cut dough in pan diagonally in both directions about every 1¹/₂ inches, forming diamonds. Pour some of the melted butter over the whole pan and bake 15 minutes. Heat remaining butter while baking (in microwave or on top of stove) and pour over baklava (it should sizzle). Bake an additional 20 minutes or until lightly golden. Remove pan to a cooling rack. Let sit 15 minutes.

3   Combine sugar and water in a small saucepot over medium high heat. Bring to a boil, cook just until sugar is dissolved, and add lemon juice. Let cool to lukewarm and pour over baklava.

Roland Kohloff

"**Y**ou're in this big cow pasture and, as my son Steven would say, it's okay," says Roland Kohloff. The principal timpanist of the New York Philharmonic is recalling his first solo appearance with the orchestra. "It was a couple of years after I joined the Philharmonic in 1972. We were in the parks, Henry Lewis was the conductor and I was playing the Concerto for Percussion Soloists and Orchestra by William Kraft.

"There have been some indoor solo performances, too," Roland reminds us. "I did a work by Donatoni with Boulez and a piece called *Déjà Vu* by Michael Colgrass. Leinsdorf conducted that one and Colgrass was awarded a Pulitzer Prize for the piece the same year."

Roland Kohloff, his wife, Janet, and their children, Jami and Steven, came to New York from San Francisco in 1972 because Roland had been asked to take up the position of principal timpanist with the Philharmonic. "I had the same title in San Francisco with the Symphony and the Opera," Roland says. Janet was a tour guide at Lincoln Center for a short time but she soon found her way to more agile and animated activities. In fact, Janet pursued a more athletic life through yoga and ice skating.

The Kohloffs' daughter, Jami, a pianist in her school years, combined the professions of her father and mother and became a music therapist. "She lives in Napa, California, now," Janet tells us, "and she's gone back to school to become an exercise physiologist.

"You should see where they live. They grow their own vegetables in their garden and they have a vineyard. They make their own wine and bottle it for friends."

Jami Kohloff Grassi has also looked into cooking. She learned the basic techniques from her mother, but now she bakes her own bread and makes her own pasta. Meanwhile, back in New York, her father is working harder than ever.

"On Tuesdays I have a morning rehearsal with the Philharmonic. Then I teach at Juilliard all afternoon and, in the evening, there's an orchestra concert." That's not exactly enough time to get back to Westchester for dinner. "I order out. There's a little Greek diner on West Fifty-eighth called Circle West. Sometimes I go there. Other times I have them deliver it to me in Avery Fisher Hall."

Where does a musician eat when he has takeout? "Well, my preference would be the board room on the sixth floor. Why not go right to the top?" Then again, preference is not reality. With a concert just a couple of hours away, the quality of the food is more important than the ambience. Roland would probably appreciate "It Don't Mean a Thing" sung by Elly Ameling with pianist Louis van Dijk (Philips 412 433-2). For the Cornish Game Hens, glazed as they are, there's the "Ballet of the Unhatched Chicks" from Mussorgsky's *Pictures at an Exhibition* played by pianist John Browning (Delos DCD-1008).

Glazed Cornish Game Hens

MAKES 2 TO 4 SERVINGS

2 tablespoons honey

1¹/₂ teaspoons fresh rosemary, chopped, or ¹/₂ teaspoon dried

2 tablespoons white wine or apple juice

2 teaspoons Dijon mustard

¹/₄ teaspoon salt

¹/₂ teaspoon pepper

2 Cornish game hens, split in half

Orange slices or chopped parsley for garnish

Preheat oven to 350°. Mix first 6 ingredients in a small bowl. Place game hens, skin side up, on rack set in baking pan. Brush with glaze and bake 15 minutes. Brush again and bake 15 minutes longer. Brush once more and bake 10 minutes longer, or until hens are cooked (a knife inserted into the joint will release clear juices—if juice is pink, cook 5 minutes longer and test again). Place hens on a serving platter, pour remaining glaze over them, and garnish with orange slices or parsley.

Joel Krosnick

Joel Krosnick took up the cello because there was an opening for the position in his family. You see, his father, a professional pediatrician, was an amateur violinist. Joel's mother, whose professional name was Estelle Crossman, was a professional pianist who studied with Alexander Siloti, a pupil of Franz Liszt. And the Krosnick household, holding forth in New Haven, was filled with a variety of Yale music students and teachers. By the time Joel reached the musically ripe old age of eight, the one instrument that seemed to be missing was the cello. So the youngster went off to study with William D'Amato, a cellist with the New Haven Symphony. When he was older, he worked with Claus Adam, and Joel eventually replaced his teacher in the Juilliard String Quartet.

The Quartet joined with the New York Philharmonic for a historic concert on March 7, 1985, when Erich Leinsdorf led a performance of Schoenberg's Concerto for String Quartet and Orchestra. That was some meeting of musical minds—the Philharmonic, the Juilliard String Quartet, and Leinsdorf!

Joel Krosnick's musical mind evidently caught more than a passion for the cello and chamber music from his family. He caught the spirit of diversity. Don't forget, his father divided his time between the doctor's office and the music stand, and in his spare time he developed a colossal collection of records. Joel has a collection of his own—he's gone in for contemporary American paintings. But his interests don't stop there. He, like so many other musicians today, is an avid sports fan. And his greatest passion is for Chinese food, the eating and cooking of it. In fact, Joel has become a gourmet cook and specializes in Mandarin and Szechuan dishes.

The modern Krosnick household is brimming with activity. Joel's wife, Dinah, is a teacher who specializes in children with behavior problems. And she has an interesting family background, too. She's the daughter of Michael Straight, onetime editor of the *New Republic* and a ghostwriter for members of the Roosevelt cabinet. His name may be familiar also as author of *After Long Silence*, his controversial memoir.

If you speak with Joel Krosnick, he'll be happy to talk about music. But just mention either sports or Chinese food and the cello comes down a peg or two. Perhaps the family's greatest claim to fame is the fact that their first child, Gwendolyn Anya, was born on Bach's birthday in 1986. Joshua came along two years later. At this writing, they haven't yet decided on instruments for the children.

Joel's recipe for Red-Cooked Chicken Wings is one of his favorites. They make great finger food for a party and they'd make a fine dinner for children as well as adults. For an Italian translation of these red-cooked wings, listen to Servais's Grand Fantasies on Rossini's (Rossi, get it?) *Barber of Seville* and Donizetti's *Daughter of the Regiment*, played by Joel Krosnick (Orion 7290). And for the wings themselves, it's Mendelssohn's "On Wings of Song" performed by Isaac Stern with Frank Brief (Col. M-31425).

Red-Cooked Chicken Wings

MAKES 10 WINGS

10 chicken wings (2 pounds)
1 ounce fresh ginger, peeled and chopped (¹/₄ cup)
5 star anise or ¹/₂ teaspoon Five Spice Powder

1 bunch scallions (about 6) cut into 2-inch lengths (white and green)
1 cup low sodium soy sauce
¹/₂ cup white wine, sake, or dry sherry

1   Preheat oven to 375°.

2   Place 5 wings in a 2¹/₂-cup casserole or Dutch oven. Cover with half the ginger, all the anise, and half the scallions. Cover with remaining chicken, ginger, and scallions and pour soy sauce and wine over. Cover with foil or lid and cook 45 minutes. Uncover and stir to place top wings on bottom. Re-cover and bake 45 minutes more.

Hanna Lachert

Many people who attend an orchestra concert never get a chance to know the people who make up the ensemble. They see, and hear, only an anonymous bunch—fiddle players, flutists, bass players—just men and women holding instruments and making music that is sometimes pleasing and sometimes not.

Those who go to hear the same orchestra on a regular basis, however, begin to see individuals, friends. They come to think of the ensemble as *their* orchestra. They look for a cellist when she changes her chair. They miss a horn player when he's not scheduled to play.

Best of all, many major orchestras—including the New York Philharmonic—feature members of the ensemble as soloists or chamber players. And then we get to know them for their individual sounds and talents.

That was the case during a series of four concerts that started on November 8, 1979. Zubin Mehta was conducting and the program included works by Vivaldi, Henri Tomasi, Mozart, and Richard Strauss that featured one or more members of the Philharmonic. Violinist Hanna Lachert joined with three of her colleagues for a performance of the Vivaldi Concerto for Four Violins. The audience at those concerts got an insight into the quality of Hanna's musicianship. What they didn't learn about was her Polish legacy and heritage. And they certainly weren't able to sample her Bigos, a Polish hunters' dish.

The New York Philharmonic violinist is, understandably, proud of this dish. "One day the great Henryk Szeryng, after helping himself to another portion of my bigos, announced, 'Hanna, your recipe is even better than Nela's [Mrs. Arthur Rubinstein].' " She adds, "To this day, I am impressed by that compliment!"

Hanna's secret ingredient is the plum jam. And, since Ellen Bodow, the wife of WQXR president Warren Bodow, has given us a marvelous recipe for plum jam (see page 217), we suggest you use it for this dish. Hanna also warns that when you make Bigos, "your entire house will smell of cabbage." But it's worth it.

"This is a very popular dish, especially during the fall and winter," the violinist says. "It's a 'cold weather' dish. Originally it was served at dawn to hunters, together with a glass of vodka to give them a good, warm start for the day of hunting.

"Since it would be associated with the life of 'Szlachta,' or well-to-do gentry and aristocrats," Hanna tells us, "the music which they were hearing in the evening after the hunt would most likely be played on the piano by the ladies."

The violinist even gives us some idea of the composers they might have played: "Maria Szymanowska, Michael Cleophas Oginski, and, later on, Paderewski." But she confesses that her favorite is Chopin. We fill in the details for this century, or what's left of it: Chopin's Mazurkas, played by Martha Argerich (DG 413425-4GW).

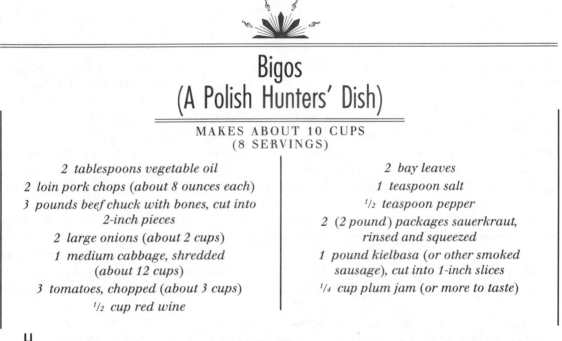

Bigos
(A Polish Hunters' Dish)

MAKES ABOUT 10 CUPS
(8 SERVINGS)

2 tablespoons vegetable oil

2 loin pork chops (about 8 ounces each)

3 pounds beef chuck with bones, cut into 2-inch pieces

2 large onions (about 2 cups)

1 medium cabbage, shredded (about 12 cups)

3 tomatoes, chopped (about 3 cups)

$^1/_2$ cup red wine

2 bay leaves

1 teaspoon salt

$^1/_2$ teaspoon pepper

2 (2 pound) packages sauerkraut, rinsed and squeezed

1 pound kielbasa (or other smoked sausage), cut into 1-inch slices

$^1/_4$ cup plum jam (or more to taste)

Heat oil in an 8-quart saucepot or Dutch oven, over high heat. Add pork chops and brown well, about 3 to 4 minutes on each side. Remove to a plate and add beef. Brown on all sides (in batches if necessary), about 10 minutes more. Remove to same plate. Add onions and cabbage and cook, stirring, about 5 minutes or until cabbage is wilted. Add tomatoes, red wine, bay leaves, salt, pepper, and sauerkraut. Stir well. Stir in kielbasa and return pork and beef to pot. Cover and simmer 4 to 5 hours, stirring occasionally. Let cool and refrigerate overnight. The next day bring to a boil over high heat, cover, lower heat to a simmer, and cook 3 hours. Uncover and cook 1 hour longer. Let cool and refrigerate overnight once more. The third day, reheat over medium high heat and stir in jam and more salt and pepper if needed.

Gary Levinson

There's a pair of Levinsons in the Philharmonic. Eugene is the orchestra's principal bass player. Gary is in the first violin section. And they're not only related, they're father and son. "My father joined the orchestra around 1986," Gary tells us. "I was already in New York because I'd come to the city in 1984 to study with Dorothy DeLay at Juilliard."

The Levinsons are originally from Russia. Gary began playing the violin when he was five and went on to study at the Leningrad Music School. When the family came to this country, they settled in Minnesota, where Eugene joined the Minneapolis Symphony.

"I was still working on my bachelor's degree," Gary says, "with just a couple of months left to graduation, when I found I'd gotten the orchestra job. In fact, when I played for my graduation jury at Juilliard, they told me that I'd gotten a full scholarship for my master's. So, there I was with the opportunity to get a higher degree from Juilliard—free—and a job in one of the greatest orchestras in the world. I spent all my time after that running between the two buildings at Lincoln Center. If I wasn't at the Philharmonic, I was at Juilliard. It was very hard work, but I'd grown up thinking I'd be a great soloist and, as I got more and more involved with orchestral playing, I realized I loved *that* dream even more."

Gary entered the Philharmonic just about two years after his father, in 1988. Now he's finished his time at Juilliard and his life has calmed down a bit. But there have been some hectic moments.

Gary recalls one of them vividly. "We were moving into our new apartment in the Flatiron district of Manhattan. We were hungry and tired and I couldn't think of anything to make for dinner. So I looked around and came up with this version of lasagna. Since we'd just come to the neighborhood, I called it 'Flatiron Lasagna.'"

"I do most of the cooking in the house. I guess I've just always cooked. I don't really remember learning except that I really got into it when I came to New York to go to Juilliard. I was alone and if I wanted to eat I had to cook."

To accompany Gary Levinson's Flatiron Lasagna: Beethoven's Symphony No. 4 in B-flatiron Major, performed by the New York Philharmonic and Leonard Bernstein (CBS MK-4221).

Flatiron Lasagna

SERVES 8 TO 10

3 tablespoons olive oil

4 garlic cloves, minced

1 large onion, finely chopped

2 (28 ounce) cans stewed tomatoes

1/2 cup small green olives, finely chopped

3 dashes Tabasco

1/2 teaspoon basil

1/2 teaspoon oregano

3 tablespoons lemon juice

1 medium eggplant, coarsely chopped

1/2 cup sherry or white wine

1 pound lasagna noodles

1 pint ricotta cheese

1 pound fresh mozzarella cheese, thinly sliced

1/2 pound Parmesan cheese, freshly grated

1/2 pound Fontina cheese, torn into pieces

1 In a large saucepot, heat 1 tablespoon olive oil over medium high heat. Add the onion and half the garlic and cook, stirring, until golden, about 6 minutes. Add tomatoes, olives, Tabasco, basil, oregano, and lemon juice. Bring to a boil, lower heat to a simmer, and cook uncovered while preparing remaining ingredients.

2 In a large skillet, heat the remaining olive oil over medium high heat. Add remaining garlic and eggplant and stir to coat with oil. Cook 5 minutes and add sherry or wine. Cover and cook until liquid is almost gone, about 8 minutes.

3 Bring a large saucepot of salted water to a rolling boil and cook lasagna noodles al dente according to package directions. Drain well.

4 Preheat oven to 350°. Ladle about ¾ cup of sauce on bottom of a 9 × 13″ baking pan. Line bottom with noodles and begin layering some of the eggplant, then the cheeses, using a third of the ricotta, mozzarella, Parmesan, and Fontina. Coat with more sauce and noodles and repeat two more times, ending with a layer of noodles, sauce, and additional Parmesan. Bake 40 minutes, or until bubbling and heated through (stick a knife into the middle and feel blade—if the blade feels hot it is done).

Cho-Liang Lin

Here's a lesson in fate and why it's a good idea to keep your windows open. Cho-Liang Lin was five years old when he heard the sound of a violin wafting from the window of a neighbor's home in Taiwan. He was so excited by what he heard that he talked his parents into buying him a little instrument of his own. Two years later, he gave his first public performance.

Things continued to move fast for the youngster. When he was twelve, he was sent to study at the Sydney Conservatorium in Australia. Itzhak Perlman was there giving a master class. Little Jimmy Lin got that gleam in his eye all over again and next thing anyone knew, he was in New York, enrolled at Juilliard, and studying with Itzhak's teacher, Dorothy DeLay.

That takes us to 1975. Ten years after his graduation, Cho-Liang Lin returned to Juilliard as a member of its faculty. And, in 1987, he joined the United States as a citizen.

The violinist had a gala time at his debut with the New York Philharmonic. He first appeared with the orchestra on New Year's Eve, 1981. Zubin Mehta was conducting and, among all the polkas, waltzes, and marches that ushered out the old year, was the Mendelssohn E minor Violin Concerto—played by Jimmy Lin.

The violinist recently returned to Taiwan, with a stop or two in Japan, for a special tour of concerts with the NHK Symphony and the Japan Philharmonic. You'd think with those travels still fresh, Jimmy would have given us a regional recipe from his homeland. But this scrumptious shrimp with mustard sauce testifies to the international turn this violinist's life has taken. And we won't complain.

To commemorate Cho-Liang Lin's debut with the New York Philharmonic back in 1981, we suggest the violinist's recording of the Mendelssohn Concerto, this time with the Philharmonia Orchestra and Michael Tilson Thomas (CBS MK-39007) and, for some international flavoring, Stravinsky's *Suite Italienne* with Jimmy and pianist André-Michel Schub (CBS MK-42101).

Shrimp with Mustard Sauce

SERVES 8

2 tablespoons unsalted butter

32 shrimp (about 2 pounds medium size), shelled and deveined

1 tablespoon chopped shallots

5 tablespoons dry white wine

1 cup heavy cream

1 tablespoon Dijon-style mustard

$^1/_8$ teaspoon salt

$^1/_4$ teaspoon pepper

Parsley for garnish

1 Melt butter in a large saucepan over medium high heat. Add shrimp and cook, stirring, until just done, about 3 to 4 minutes. Remove with a slotted spoon to a warm dish. Add shallots to skillet. Cook stirring about 3 minutes, or until soft. Add wine and cook 2 minutes. Add cream and cook 5 minutes longer. Stir in mustard, salt, and pepper, and return shrimp to skillet to warm through. Place shrimp on serving dish and cover with sauce. Garnish with parsley.

Newton and Maria Mansfield

Like Lorin and Alison Bernsohn, Newton and Maria Mansfield met at Lincoln Center while Maria was a tour guide and Newton was a member of the orchestra. And, as they say in the movies, they're still there! You'll find Newton in the first violin section of the orchestra. And Maria, during the day, is still taking visitors through the various halls of the Center with the same eager enthusiasm she had more than twenty years ago.

Actually, Newton made his "official" debut with the orchestra as a featured soloist and chamber player at the same concert as his friend from the cello section, Larry Bernsohn. Newton's wife, Maria, a bubbly blond actress with an Italian accent that doesn't quit, is a little like a European Gracie Allen, hysterically funny and oh, so clever. Never mind what the story is. She manages to make it spellbinding. Maybe that's how she's lasted all these years giving the same tour to all those people.

She's even received a special award from Lincoln Center for the great public relations role she's played over the years. And they hadn't even tasted her cooking! You can imagine, with a personality and wit that can charm the coldest kisser into a grin, Maria manages to throw some pretty impressive parties. And, since Newton has participated in so many aspects of the Philharmonic, from player to players' committee, they certainly have the friends to invite.

Maria's Mandel Cookies might be the next thing to be passed out on a guided tour of Lincoln Center. Meanwhile, you have the recipe and, to give you a sense of this very special couple, we go back to the original-cast recording of Leonard Bernstein's *West Side Story* to hear "Maria" sung by Larry Kert (Col. CK-32603).

Maria's Mandel Cookies
(Mandelbrot)

MAKES 5 DOZEN

2 large eggs
1 teaspoon vanilla or almond extract
³/₄ cup sugar
¹/₂ cup olive oil
2 cups unbleached flour

1 teaspoon baking soda
Pinch salt
1 cup ground nuts (preferably almonds)
2 teaspoons grated lemon or orange zest

1 In a large mixing bowl, combine eggs, vanilla or almond extract, sugar, and oil, and mix well. In a separate small bowl, mix together flour, soda, and salt. Add to the egg mixture and stir just until well mixed. Stir in nuts and zest and refrigerate for 2 hours.

2 Preheat oven to 350°. Grease a cookie sheet. Divide dough into 3 parts and form 3 two-inch-wide loaves. Bake 30 minutes or until golden brown. While still warm, cut into ¹/₂-inch-wide slices.

Midori

Eleven-year-old Midori burst into the music world on New Year's Eve, 1982, looking like a doll and sounding like an angel. Zubin Mehta had heard the little violinist and had been so impressed that he invited her to appear for the New York Philharmonic's New Year's Eve gala as a surprise guest. The audience was bowled over by her musicianship, tone, and charm and rose to give her a thunderous ovation.

From her polished shoes and tiny socks to her chiseled face, Midori was an international sensation within moments of her first notes and even her approaching adulthood didn't threaten her celebrity. This was no shooting star, to burn brightly and then fizzle. The violinist's career has grown with the girl—young woman, that is.

From the White House to the "Tonight" show, from the Musikverein in Vienna to the Philharmonic in Berlin, Midori's music-making has taken center stage. And it was the New York Philharmonic that brought her to the world in the first place.

You can imagine, with this kind of career blossoming and flourishing, that Midori has little time to spend in the kitchen. "I cook on the fly," she admits, conjuring up a picture of the violinist borrowing the galley of an SST on her way to Paris.

Surprisingly, Midori's recipes rarely give us an insight into her ethnic background, which is Japanese. Goat Cheese with Sun-Dried Tomatoes, risotto alla Milanese, and strawberry-lemon Bavarian cream shortbread, her three favorites, aren't found on any of the Japanese menus I know!

"I don't like onions," the violinist confides. "So, when I use them in a recipe, I chop them up really fine so I don't have to see them when I eat. But if you like them, you don't have to do the same thing."

Of course, it's not written that you must be German to make a good Bavarian cream or a goat to make good cheese. By the same token, it's not necessary to be Czech to play Dvořák. So Midori has joined with the New York Philharmonic and Zubin Mehta for a performance of the Dvořák Violin Concerto (Sony Classical MK-44923). And the recording of her triumphant Carnegie Hall recital debut of October 1990 has enough variety to take us around the world several times (Sony Classical SK 46742).

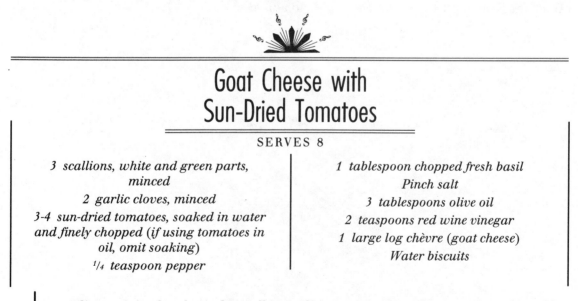

Goat Cheese with Sun-Dried Tomatoes

SERVES 8

3 scallions, white and green parts, minced

2 garlic cloves, minced

3-4 sun-dried tomatoes, soaked in water and finely chopped (if using tomatoes in oil, omit soaking)

¼ teaspoon pepper

1 tablespoon chopped fresh basil

Pinch salt

3 tablespoons olive oil

2 teaspoons red wine vinegar

1 large log chèvre (goat cheese)

Water biscuits

In a medium mixing bowl, combine all ingredients except goat cheese and crackers. Mix well. Place chèvre on a serving dish and pour mixture over. Serve with water biscuits.

Orin O'Brien

Orin O'Brien was the first woman to join the ranks of the New York Philharmonic, in 1966, and she did it with an instrument that's just about as tall as she is, the double bass. "Actually, there was a harpist named Christine Stavrache who played with the orchestra for about three years in the fifties," Orin says. "But I guess you could say I was the first to become a regular member of a section." That was after her graduation from Juilliard and about ten years of free-lancing in New York from the pit of the New York City Ballet to the stage of the American Symphony Orchestra with Leopold Stokowski.

Two of her three teachers also had important affiliations with the New York Philharmonic. Herman Reinshagen was a member of the orchestra during Mahler's tenure (!) and Fred Zimmerman was with the Philharmonic for some thirty-six years.

That kind of long-time association speaks well of the orchestra and its musicians. And Orin O'Brien, carrying on the tradition, speaks particularly well of her colleagues and her orchestra. "The reason I chose this recipe," she confides, "is the cherished memories I have of the Philharmonic, especially in the first few years, where the kindness of many of my colleagues included the sharing of recipes and dinners.

"This recipe for Pecan Pie Surprise Bars is from David Kates,* a member of the viola section for more than forty years. It is as delicious as any Viennese pastry and very easy to make."

Orin selected the music to accompany this recipe. "While cooking," she suggests, "please listen to Gustav Mahler's Symphony No. 4, recorded by the New York Philharmonic with Leonard Bernstein (3-CBS M3X-31437). In the last movement, angels and saints are preparing food!"

But there's another reason Orin O'Brien suggests this symphony. "I love this music, particularly the slow movement. And I treasure the long history of Mahler with the New York Philharmonic and Leonard Bernstein."

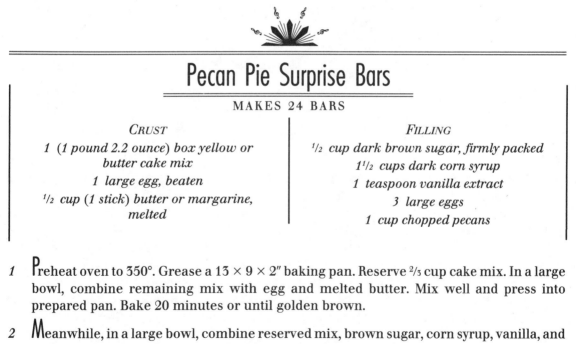

Pecan Pie Surprise Bars

MAKES 24 BARS

CRUST	FILLING
1 (1 pound 2.2 ounce) box yellow or butter cake mix	1/2 cup dark brown sugar, firmly packed
1 large egg, beaten	1 1/2 cups dark corn syrup
1/2 cup (1 stick) butter or margarine, melted	1 teaspoon vanilla extract
	3 large eggs
	1 cup chopped pecans

1 Preheat oven to 350°. Grease a 13 × 9 × 2″ baking pan. Reserve 2/3 cup cake mix. In a large bowl, combine remaining mix with egg and melted butter. Mix well and press into prepared pan. Bake 20 minutes or until golden brown.

2 Meanwhile, in a large bowl, combine reserved mix, brown sugar, corn syrup, vanilla, and eggs. With hand mixer, beat on medium speed 1 to 2 minutes. When crust is golden, pour filling over. Sprinkle with pecans. Bake until set, 30 to 35 minutes. Cool on a rack and cut into 1 1/2 × 2″ bars.

*David Kates is the father of cellist Stephen Kates, (see page 258).

Itzhak Perlman

 tzhak Perlman is probably the only musician who has appeared as both a baritone and a television chef in the course of his career as a violinist. Itzhak's singing debut came, actually, with the New York Philharmonic at a Pension Fund Concert featuring Luciano Pavarotti. The violinist's appearance was a surprise. Suddenly there he was, on stage with the great tenor, singing the part of the Jailer in the last act of Puccini's *Tosca.* It was a debut that was so auspicious and well received that the violinist went on to record a performance with Renata Scotto and Placido Domingo with James Levine conducting (Angel CDCB-49364).

Itzhak Perlman has also established himself as a cook of no small repute, appearing in newspaper articles with recipes, on my radio program, "Kitchen Classics," armed with lots of chicken fat for Passover, and on television with the Frugal Gourmet, crisping up even more fat for fixing unmentionably delicious Jewish dishes.

The outspoken violinist, asked once on "60 Minutes" why so many famous violinists are Jewish, answered without blinking, "Our fingers are circumcised!" In the kitchen, Itzhak is even more outspoken. "I love fat," he proclaims. "You know those crispy little pieces of fat that sort of drip from a nice brown roast chicken?" He's almost drooling now.

"I make a meal on those. Put them on a piece of matzoh with onion," he recommends.

This is not to say that Itzhak eats no lean. He is careful of what he consumes and he loves really good food. But he's particularly partial to good "gribbenes." That's the Yiddish word for those curly, crisp, charred pieces of fat that render themselves so nicely from chicken and roast beef.

Whether it's singing, playing, or cooking, though, everything Itzhak Perlman does is accomplished with zest and cheerfulness. His appearances with the New York Philharmonic always draw enormous audiences. And his goodwill and love of the ensemble imbue the orchestra members with a special excitement that intensifies the musicmaking.

Itzhak's colleague, piano partner, and dear friend is Samuel Sanders. The two of them travel together a great deal and share a passion for food, music, and, perhaps even more, baseball. Among their recordings is a compact disc featuring Smetana's *From My Homeland.* (Angel DS-38134). It's delicious. For pure fun, sample Itzhak Perlman's jazz album *It's a Breeze*, with André Previn (Angel DS-37799). And, for a tribute to Itzhak's life and the way he lives it, listen to *Perpetual Motion* (Angel S-37003).

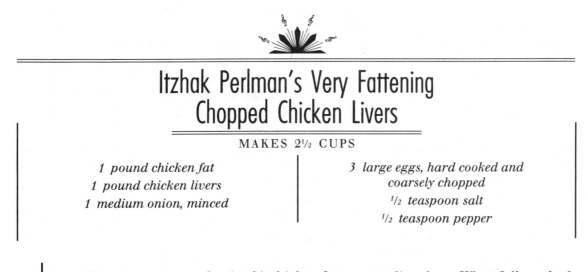

Itzhak Perlman's Very Fattening Chopped Chicken Livers

MAKES 2½ CUPS

1 pound chicken fat	3 large eggs, hard cooked and coarsely chopped
1 pound chicken livers	½ teaspoon salt
1 medium onion, minced	½ teaspoon pepper

1   In a medium saucepot, render (melt) chicken fat over medium heat. When fully melted, turn off heat, add livers and let stew 6 minutes. Add the onion and let sit about 6 minutes longer. Pour livers into a fine colander set over a pot and let fat drain out (don't remove all of it!). In a food processor or by hand, chop the livers and eggs together, along with the salt and pepper. Serve with matzoh or rye bread.

NOTE: *"If you want more tang, add raw chopped onions (that's the way my mother used to make it). Make sure you have plenty of antacids—but it's worth it!" I.P.*

Joseph Polisi

It's somewhat amazing that bassoonist Joseph Polisi's debut didn't make headlines in the *New York Times.* After all, it's not every day that the president of Juilliard performs with the New York Philharmonic on a program that includes such works as *Pervertimento for Bag-pipes, Bicycle and Balloons* and *Last Tango in Bayreuth.*

"It was fun," Joseph remembers. "The program featured works by Peter Schickele (P.D.Q. Bach) and, since Peter is also a bassoonist, whenever he's introduced me at a concert or a function, he's never lost an opportunity to roast me. It's all very good-natured," Joseph assures us. What does Peter Schickele say? "Well, he usually tells people that the only way I could get into Juilliard was by becoming its president."

Joe's history with the Philharmonic goes back many years before his official debut in 1987. "My father was the orchestra's principal bassoonist from 1943 to 1958," he explains. "I remember sitting in a box in Carnegie Hall and listening to my father with such pride.

"The orchestra usually had Friday afternoon concerts in those days. So Friday nights the players were free. That was our family night for a feast. My father would come home from the matinee with that feeling of euphoria you get after a good performance. And we would all sit around the table sharing the food and the good feeling."

What did they eat? "Friday was fish night. My mother did most of the cooking but my father was good with seafood. I've inherited that. My wife does most of our cooking but I love to make fish, especially lobster."

Being the Juilliard School's president has brought a unity into the life of Joseph Polisi. "I came to Juilliard and wound up working with all my father's friends." Unlike cellist Stephen Kates, who grew up calling his father's Philharmonic friends by their first names, Joe looked at his father's colleagues as idols. "When I got to Juilliard it was very hard for me to switch from 'Mr. Baker' to 'Julie.' I felt that all those guys were like the Yankees of the fifties. They were real heros."

The Polisis' Clams Oreganata recipe comes from the kitchen of Joe Polisi's family. Although this is a dish that can be consumed at any time of year, it seems fitting that the music to accompany the food include "Sumer Is Icumen In" performed by Joe's father, bassoonist Joseph Polisi (Crystal S-341). And, since Joe loves to cook and eat shellfish, the perfect song for his passion is Cole Porter's "Tale of the Oyster." Try the funny and touching performance by Sarah Walker and Roger Vignoles (Hyperion CDA 66289).

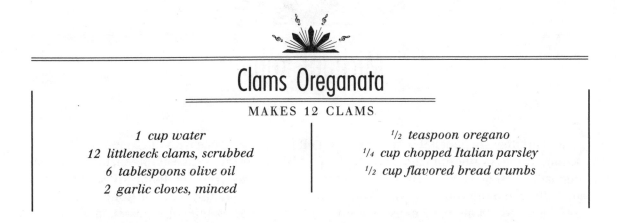

Clams Oreganata

MAKES 12 CLAMS

1 cup water
12 littleneck clams, scrubbed
6 tablespoons olive oil
2 garlic cloves, minced

$^{1}/_{2}$ teaspoon oregano
$^{1}/_{4}$ cup chopped Italian parsley
$^{1}/_{2}$ cup flavored bread crumbs

1 Place water in a medium saucepot over high heat and bring to a boil. Add clams, cover and cook, stirring occasionally until clams open, about 5 minutes. Remove each clam as it opens. Remove clams from shells and chop coarsely. Line a cookie sheet with foil and place 12 half clam shells on sheet.

2 Preheat oven to 350°.

3 Heat $^{1}/_{4}$ cup of the olive oil in a large skillet over medium high heat. Add garlic and cook, stirring, until lightly golden, about 1 minute. Stir in oregano, parsley, and bread crumbs, and mix well. Remove from heat and stir in chopped clams. Fill shells with mixture, dividing evenly. Drizzle with remaining olive oil. Bake 10 minutes until hot. Turn oven to broil. Place clams 2 to 3 inches from source of heat and broil 2 minutes or until lightly browned.

Michael Rabin

Child prodigy Michael Rabin made his first official appearance with the New York Philharmonic under rather unusual circumstances. His debut, at the age of fifteen, took place on the road. It was on October 16, 1951, and the orchestra was in Philadelphia. Mitropoulos was conducting and the young violinist was performing the Paganini D Major Concerto.

There would be many more concerts with the Philharmonic for Michael, in and out of town, but even in 1951 the young violinist was hardly new to the orchestra. After all, his father, George, had already been a fixture in the violin section for years. So the Rabin family was really a Philharmonic family. It was also an eating family.

Michael's mother, Jeanne, a pianist and teacher, was a deft, creative cook. When he wasn't practicing, the young violinist picked up some good, solid kitchen skills. Thanksgiving, for example, was more than a culinary experience. It was an adventure. Eating so much at Thanksgiving that you can't rebuckle your belt is not unusual. Eating at the Rabins' table meant you couldn't get back into your overcoat. Dinner for four included that traditional Thanksgiving staple, matzo ball soup. It was followed by chopped chicken liver, salad, cranberry sauce (whole and jellied), mashed potatoes, yams, string beans, brisket, and turkey with stuffing and gravy. Actually, *two* turkeys with stuffing and gravy. Just in case you were still a little hungry.

Dessert began with pies, continued with cakes, went on to cookies. "Want a little ice cream? Have a nice slice of cheese and take some fruit (it's not fattening)!"

As an adult in his own kitchen, Michael Rabin used those skills to forge a simple, tasteful way of eating that centered around broiled meats, fish, and salads. He knew how to broil a steak. He would first make sure the broiler allowed the meat to rest about two inches from the flame. Then he'd preheat the oven to broil and put about ½ inch of water in the bottom of the broiling pan so the fat from the steak wouldn't catch on fire. He liked his steaks rare, so a good, tender 1½-inch-thick T-bone took about 4 to 5 minutes on each side.

Michael Rabin's career had some bumpy times, but in the last years of his short life (he died of a fall in his home at the age of thirty-six), he was happily playing concerts in cities from New York and Los Angeles to London and Helsinki. He was fascinated with flying and kept a complete log of every air mile he traveled. And he collected musician stories. Like the time the conductor launched into the downbeat and swept his baton into Michael's bow, sending it soaring through the air and into the audience. Michael roared as he remembered the man in the third row catching the bow by the hair and shipping it back to the stage as if it were a wayward kitten, by the scruff of its neck.

When he wasn't traveling, Michael and his close friends got together for evenings of food, stories, and chamber music. That's where he first encountered Adele's Barley Casserole. It wasn't something he would make himself; he preferred broiling and tossing to cutting and baking. But he went for the flavor and texture of this dish in a big way. He even liked it cold, as a nosh from the refrigerator. The Adele of the dish, by the way, is Adele Addison.

Michael Rabin was a quiet man with an enormous sense of humor. He liked his travels but he loved his home. He enjoyed listening to records, mostly other people's. In an interview in the *New York Times* about a year before his untimely death, he told the reporter, "I hope when I die at the age of seventy, they'll reissue my recordings in memoriam." Michael didn't make it to seventy, but Seraphim did put together an album with his performance of works by Saint-Saëns, Sarasate, Dinicu, Kreisler, Massenet, Paganini, and Rimsky-Korsakov. They called it *In Memoriam* (Seraphim 4XG-60199). And EMI Classics has just come out with a six-disc set of CDs featuring almost all of Michael's recorded works (CMS 7 64123 2).

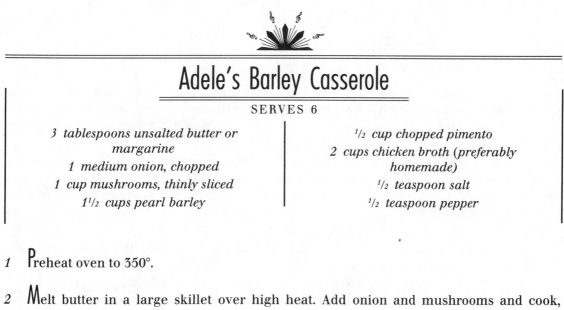

Adele's Barley Casserole

SERVES 6

3 tablespoons unsalted butter or margarine	1/2 cup chopped pimento
1 medium onion, chopped	2 cups chicken broth (preferably homemade)
1 cup mushrooms, thinly sliced	1/2 teaspoon salt
1 1/2 cups pearl barley	1/2 teaspoon pepper

1   Preheat oven to 350°.

2   Melt butter in a large skillet over high heat. Add onion and mushrooms and cook, stirring, until onion is translucent, about 6 to 7 minutes. Add barley and cook, stirring, until barley is toasted and golden in color, about 5 minutes. Scrape mixture into a 2 to 3 quart ovenproof dish. Stir in remaining ingredients and cover. Bake 1 hour, until barley is cooked and all liquid is absorbed.

Jean-Pierre Rampal

"As I never eat before a concert, I am always ravenous at the finish," writes Jean-Pierre Rampal in the introduction to his autobiography (written with Deborah Wise), *Music, My Love.* And, like Arthur Rubinstein in his books, the flutist's narrative is filled with famished descriptions of breakfasts, lunches, and dinners.

Jean-Pierre Rampal joined a small wind ensemble in the mid1940s called the Quintette à Vent Français. But, he writes, "we all had a great fondness for fine cuisine and for the good life—perhaps too great a fondness." So, one of the members of the ensemble dubbed the group the "Quintette à Vin Français." "Not that we were in our cups all the time; we just knew how to enjoy ourselves," the flutist hastens to add.

Jean-Pierre Rampal's recipe for Sangria Blanche almost put me and my friends in our cups while I was preparing this book. As I've mentioned before, Jean Galton tested (and we both tasted) most of the recipes, but the ones that were more alcoholic, I took unto myself. This sangria got tested and tasted (and tasted some more) on the Intracoastal Waterways of Sarasota Bay. My friends Bob and Janet Steele joined me in renting a pontoon boat that, at best, put-putted through the calm waters at a wild fifteen miles an hour. Armed with sandwiches and diet Coke for Bob, our designated pilot who was not to get potted, we set off to spy on some of the finer homes along the bayfront.

The night before, I doused the fruit with the appropriate alcohol, tasting as I went. The next morning, just before leaving the house to pick up the boat at Mr. CB's Rental, I poured the remaining champagne and Cointreau into the drunken fruit and took another taste. Perfect! With thanks to Jean-Pierre, we took off. We waited at least ten minutes before dipping into the Sangria Blanche and found that it was gentle, thirst-quenching, and didn't get you drunk so you'd know it.

I told a couple of musical friends about the sangria and everyone of them said the same thing, "Isn't that just like Jean-Pierre!"

There are certain composers whose music matches this punch perfectly. Ibert was wonderful at making "giggle" music, music that makes you want to laugh from your belly. Jean-Pierre Rampal's recording of Ibert's Flute Concerto would be perfect heard wafting over the nonexistent waves of the Florida waterways (RCA AGL1-3658). For a nighttime cruise, a candlelight party at the pool, or a picnic with punch, Schumann's Three Romances played by Rampal on a recording with the wonderful pianist Robert Veyron-Lacroix sets the right mood, along with the suitable *Undine* by Carl Reinecke (RCA AGL1-4141).

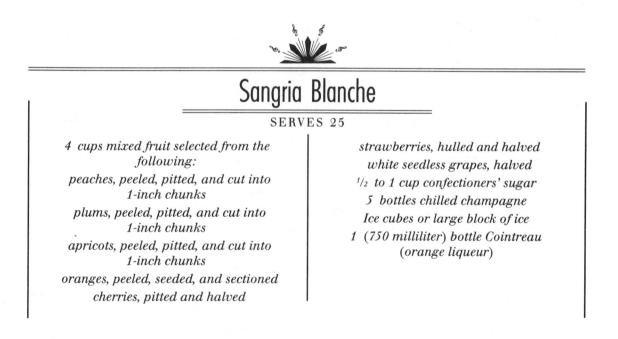

Sangria Blanche

SERVES 25

4 cups mixed fruit selected from the
following:
peaches, peeled, pitted, and cut into
1-inch chunks
plums, peeled, pitted, and cut into
1-inch chunks
apricots, peeled, pitted, and cut into
1-inch chunks
oranges, peeled, seeded, and sectioned
cherries, pitted and halved

strawberries, hulled and halved
white seedless grapes, halved
$1/2$ to 1 cup confectioners' sugar
5 bottles chilled champagne
Ice cubes or large block of ice
1 (750 milliliter) bottle Cointreau
(orange liqueur)

1 Place fruit in a large glass or stainless steel mixing bowl. Add sugar (the amount depends on how sweet your fruit is), and one bottle champagne. Mix well, cover, and refrigerate 8 hours or overnight. Place fruit in a large punch bowl. Add ice cubes or block, Cointreau, and remaining champagne.

Charles and Elizabeth Rex

Charles Gordon Rex, Jr., is the associate concertmaster of the New York Philharmonic. He joined the orchestra in 1980 and made his first solo appearance the following year when he found himself stepping in for Shlomo Mintz at the last moment.

As associate concertmaster, Charles also sits in for the regular concertmaster, Glenn Dicterow, for a number of performances each year.

His wife, Elizabeth, tells us, "For health considerations, Charles is a strict vegetarian and does not eat any meat, dairy products such as milk, eggs, or cheese, stays away from fish, and doesn't use any oil."

Acknowledging the difficulty of this kind of diet, Elizabeth adds, "While cooking for him has been a challenge, it has not really been that difficult since many recipes are easily adapted."

Apparently Elizabeth's mother has a recipe for meat loaf that is really outstanding. So, when Elizabeth makes her vegetarian meat loaf for Charles, she makes the other one for herself, and "I cook them both together for an hour. We both love our version of 'faux' fries and they're great with either meat loaf."

The "faux" fries are very simple: Just preheat your oven to broil, wash and scrub (but don't peel) 2 medium baking potatoes. Slice potatoes lengthwise in half, then in quarters, and then in eighths. Either salt them at this point or leave them plain. Then place the slices skin side down in a microwave-safe plate and zap them on high for 12 minutes, turning once after six minutes.

At this point the potatoes should be well cooked and soft, not hard to the touch, and slightly wrinkled. Then line a cookie sheet with aluminum foil and place slices on it skin side down. Broil about 2 to 3 minutes until brown and crispy. Serve hot.

Think of it . . . no fat at all! And Elizabeth tells us that the Vegetarian Meat Loaf she and Charles created has absolutely no cholesterol or added fat, not even in the bread crumbs that are used. "You can sculpt this into a turkey for Thanksgiving," Elizabeth suggests. "Just let your imagination soar."

Elizabeth and Charles let their imaginations go with the music for their meat loaf. They suggested something by Copland, since meat loaf—vegetarian or not—has become such an

American classic. Elizabeth recommends Copland's *Quiet City*, with the New York Philharmonic and Leonard Bernstein (DG 419170-1 GH). Since this is a recipe that won't easily spoil on a picnic and could be used for sandwiches on an outing, we'll stay with Copland and suggest his *Outdoor Overture* performed by the Cincinnati Pops (Telarc CD-80117).

Vegetarian Meat Loaf

SERVES 6 TO 8

1 (16 ounce) can pinto beans, drained and rinsed

1 (16 ounce) can red kidney beans, drained and rinsed

1 medium onion, chopped (about 1 cup)

2 stalks celery, chopped (about 1 cup)

2 garlic cloves, minced

1 tablespoon teriyaki or soy sauce

1 cup cooked brown rice

1 (8 ounce) can tomato sauce

1 cup fresh whole wheat bread crumbs (made from 2 small pitas)

1 tablespoon dried parsley or $^{1}/_{4}$ cup chopped fresh

1 teaspoon salt

1 teaspoon dried basil

1 teaspoon savory

$^{1}/_{4}$ teaspoon cumin

$^{1}/_{2}$ teaspoon pepper

1   Preheat oven to 350°.

2   Place beans in a food processor and pulse until coarsely mashed (this works best in $^{1}/_{2}$-cup batches). Place in a large mixing bowl.

3   In a large skillet combine onion, celery, garlic, and teriyaki sauce. Cook over medium high heat, stirring, about 5 minutes or until sauce has evaporated and vegetables are soft. Add to beans and mix in remaining ingredients. Mix very well, place in a 9 × 2″ loaf pan, and cut a crosshatch on top with knife. Bake one hour, or until heated through and slightly browned on top.

Fred Sherry

What do Tashi, the Chamber Music Society of Lincoln Center, and Caveman Stew have in common? Fred Sherry. Let's take one at a time.

Tashi, a contemporary chamber ensemble featuring Fred, Peter Serkin, Ida Kavafian, and Richard Stoltzman, first appeared with the New York Philharmonic at Avery Fisher Hall in 1975. Pierre Boulez was the conductor and the program ranged from a Mendelssohn String Symphony to an Ensemble for Strings by Henry Cowell.

More than ten years later, cellist Fred Sherry added a desk and file cabinet to his cello and bow and became the artistic director of the Chamber Music Society of Lincoln Center, a position he held until mid-1992. Fred was a performing director, as was his predecessor, Charles Wadsworth.

Caveman Stew combines the Fred Sherry of Tashi and the Fred Sherry of the Lincoln Center chamber ensemble to give us a contemporary version of lamb stew. On a huge scale. When Fred first gave me this recipe, he described the lamb shanks that he used as being more like half a leg of lamb. I could see him, sitting in his cave, gnawing on the bone between movements of the Mendelssohn Octet. Or, better yet, adding the sound of teeth gnashing against bone to a chamber work by Cage.

We've pared down the basic ingredients a bit, but the flavor is still there and that's pure Sherry! (Although he suggests a rich Bordeaux.)

Fred enjoys cooking. But his style has changed considerably since he got married. Another one of his favorite dishes, prewedding, was Bachelor Bar-B-Q Chicken. There was lots of garlic and all sorts of spices. But times have changed.

If you choose to make Fred's Caveman Stew in huge portions, play his recording of Crumb's *Voice of the Whale* (New World NW-357-1).

Caveman Stew

MAKES 4 SERVINGS

4 lamb shanks (about 1 pound each)
Salt
Pepper
2 tablespoons olive oil
4 medium onions, chopped
(about 4 cups)
4 garlic cloves, peeled and crushed
1/2 teaspoon thyme
1/2 teaspoon rosemary
1/4 teaspoon basil

1/4 teaspoon oregano
1/8 teaspoon ground red pepper
1 bay leaf
1 3/4 teaspoons salt
1 (14 ounce) can whole tomatoes,
with their liquid
1 cup red wine
4 carrots, cut into 1/2-inch slices
3 ribs celery, cut into 1/2-inch slices

1 Sprinkle the lamb with salt and pepper. Heat 1 tablespoon of oil in a large saucepot or Dutch oven over high heat. Add shanks and brown on all sides, about 10 minutes. Remove lamb to plate and drain off fat. Reduce heat to medium high and add remaining oil to pot. Add onions, cover, and cook 15 minutes, stirring occasionally, until onions are translucent. Stir in garlic, thyme, rosemary, basil, oregano, red pepper, bay leaf, and salt. Cook 1 minute. Stir in tomatoes and wine. Return lamb to pot; bring to a boil. Reduce heat to a simmer, cover, and cook 1 hour. Stir in carrots and celery, cover, and cook 1 hour 15 minutes longer, or until lamb is very tender.

Richard and Fiona Simon

If music be the food of love, the New York Philharmonic may be the place for inspiring musicians to fall in love. Married couples are not uncommon to the ranks of the orchestra. But Dick and Fiona Simon, both violinists, come from different sides of the Atlantic (he was born in New York, she in London). Since their marriage in 1980 they've taken up residence on the Upper West Side of Manhattan.

Dick is the chef of the family. His travels with the New York Philharmonic have taken him through Europe and the Far East and, over the years, have whetted his appetite for food from far-flung regions. But Dick is as much a stickler for detail in the kitchen as he is in the concert hall. He loves to read recipes and, the first time around, he follows what's written exactly. That's the rehearsal. The performances are filled with masterful improvisations, added spices, sensible substitutions, and, fortunately for us, helpful hints that make the process easier.

With his mother's cooking, Richard Simon is truly at home. Here an improvisation on a theme is not only logical, it's inherited. And variations on the theme are de rigueur. We suggest you try your own variation. Take the meat of the brisket from Dick Simon's mother's recipe and create an original piece of your own. Begin the musical accompaniment with Milhaud's *Le Boeuf sur le toit* conducted by Leonard Bernstein with L'Orchestre National de France (Angel CDC-47845), and then listen to all the delicious songs sung by Luciano Pavarotti in his recording *Mamma*, with Henry Mancini (London 411959-1).

Mother's Brisket

MAKES 8 SERVINGS

1 first-cut brisket, trimmed of all fat
(about 4 pounds)
2 teaspoons salt
1 teaspoon freshly ground pepper
2 tablespoons plus 2 teaspoons olive oil
4 large onions, sliced

2 tablespoons tomato purée
2 tablespoons ketchup
1 (750 milliliter) bottle red wine
1 pound carrots, sliced
½ pound mushrooms, thinly sliced

1   Sprinkle about ½ teaspoon each salt and pepper over brisket. Heat 1 tablespoon oil in a large Dutch oven over high heat. Brown the brisket on all sides, about 10 minutes. Transfer beef to plate; drain fat. Reduce heat to medium high and add one more tablespoon oil to pot. Add onions, cover, and cook 10 minutes, stirring occasionally, until translucent. Stir in tomato purée, ketchup, 1¾ teaspoons salt, and ¾ teaspoon pepper. Stir in wine and return brisket to pot; bring to a boil. Reduce heat to a simmer, cover, and cook 1 hour.

2   Transfer brisket to a cutting board. Cut against the grain into ¼-inch-thick slices. Return slices to pot with carrots. Cover and simmer 1½ hours longer or until beef is very tender.

3   Meanwhile, heat remaining 2 teaspoons oil in large skillet over medium high heat. Add mushrooms, sprinkle with remaining salt and pepper, and cook 4 minutes, stirring. Add to brisket and stir well.

Thomas Stacy

New York is supposed to be the cultural capital of the world. It is supposed to offer everything there is to offer in the arts, new and old, bad and good, humble and exalted. Yet it took until 1976 for New York City to hear its first English horn recital. And it wasn't until 1977, 135 years after the birth of the New York Philharmonic, that the orchestra presented its first oboe d'amore soloist. In both cases, the person plying the reeds was Thomas Stacy.

But far be it from New York and its Philharmonic to engage an average English hornist. In Thomas Stacy the city and orchestra caught a man of many talents. For Thomas Stacy plays not only the English horn and the oboe d'amore and all related instruments, he also tends a terrific bar. In fact, when he was hired by the Santa Fe Opera, his contract read: "English horn and bartender" (when the company didn't need his services in the pit).

Jean Galton was so overworked testing most of the recipes for this book that I took pity on her and tested Tom's Negroni recipe myself. I did this while visiting Sarasota, Florida. It was hard work, but somebody had to do it. And my conclusion, if I can remember, is that it was terrific.

I'm partial to crushed ice and I was fortunate to be staying in a condo on Siesta Key overlooking the Gulf of Mexico that had one of those miracle freezers with an ice maker in the door. At the touch of a button, these things give you ice, either cubed or crushed. So I filled our glasses with the crushed version, put them in the freezer while I whipped up the drink, tossed out most of the ice, but left some clinging to the frosted glasses, and served the frosted drinks to my guests on the terrace as we watched the sun set over the Gulf.

The music we chose for this occasion began with Tom's recording of Sydney Hodkinson's *Edge of the Olde One* (Grenadilla GSC-1054). Then, as the sun sank in the west, we listened to his performance of Calvin Hampton's *"Variations on Amazing Grace"* (Spectrum 178).

Negroni

SERVES 1

1 ounce gin (2 tablespoons)
1 ounce Campari (2 tablespoons)
1 ounce sweet vermouth (2 tablespoons)

Dash bitters (optional)
Ice
Orange twist for garnish

Combine the first 3 or 4 ingredients and shake over ice. Serve "up" or on the rocks, garnished with an orange twist.

Janos Starker

Janos Starker was performing somewhere in Japan when his manager called to inform him he'd been booked to play with the New York Philharmonic. Concert bookings being the business they are, it wasn't until two years later that the cellist finally walked onto the Lincoln Center stage for his debut with the orchestra. "My primary concern," he confides, "was that I perform as well as I could.

"I thought I did well and the results were gratifying. But about ninety percent of the comments centered on the improved but highly controversial acoustical qualities of the recently renovated hall." Janos Starker is talking about Philharmonic Hall and the first of its several adjustments, from the removal of the acoustical "clouds" that first floated under the ceiling to the later renovation that tore apart the inside of the hall and began from scratch.

"Some found the low notes perfect but not so the highs," the cellist remembers. "With their debates droning in my eardrums, I flew off to Sweetwater, Texas, to play a recital in a high school auditorium. The acoustics of the place were amazingly good so I asked the president of the local music society who had built their hall. He stumbled around and had to ask his assistant the name of some 'local contractor.'

"The next time I appeared with the New York Philharmonic, Avery Fisher Hall had been rebuilt—without the help of that local Texas contractor—and I was glad to hear that all was well. I can't help thinking it's no wonder every young and old artist waits for the phone to ring with a call to appear with the New York Philharmonic."

When Janos Starker isn't thinking about acoustics and calls, he has his mind on food. "Next to the joy of appearing with the New York Philharmonic is the joy of living in the country in the summer and being able to pick from the garden my Hungarian banana peppers," Mr. Starker says with passion. "Every sandwich that enters my mouth invokes childhood memories because of just a few slices of these delicious vegetables.

"I dream of the summer markets that sell the freshly harvested tomatoes, peppers, and onions. When they're mixed with country sausages and bacon, they are transformed into my favorite dish, Lecsó. My all-American bride's reluctance to eat this food evaporated after her first taste. Now she prides herself, justifiably, as an expert Lecsó chef." Janos Starker tells us that this recipe is his wife's version of the dish.

The cellist's obvious love for Lecsó can be heard in his rich description of its contents. Without it, his would be a "Voice in the Wilderness," with or without help from Ernest Bloch (Lon. 6661). And, since there's no doubt that the cellist and his wife will be back for second helpings of this delicacy, the music to accompany their return to the plate should be Janos Starker's *Encore Album* with music by Bach, Saint-Saëns, and Schumann (Denon C37-7302).

Lecsó

SERVES 6

3 tablespoons lard

3 ounces bacon (*about 8 thin slices*), cut into $1/2$-inch dice

3 fresh Hungarian banana peppers,* cut into $1/4$-inch dice

2 pounds Italian frying peppers, cut into $1/4$-inch julienne

1 large onion, halved and thinly sliced

2 pounds tomatoes (*about 4 large*), chopped

2 tablespoons hot Hungarian paprika

1 teaspoon salt

1 tablespoon sugar

$1/2$ pound kielbasa or any other tasty smoked sausage, cut into $1/2$-inch slices

In a 6-quart saucepot, heat lard over medium high heat until melted. Add bacon and cook, stirring, until starting to brown, about 4 minutes. Add peppers and onion and cook, stirring occasionally until soft, about 10 minutes. Add tomatoes, paprika, salt, and sugar and cook another 10 minutes, stirring from time to time. Add sausage and cook until heated through, about 5 minutes.

Serve with crusty caraway rye or potato white bread.

NOTE: *If you desire a lecsó with less heat, substitute sweet Hungarian paprika for the hot.*

---

* These are sweet peppers, 5 to 6 inches in length, and can be purchased at specialty produce markets or ethnic food stores.

Isaac Stern

"The man has changed," Martha Fougères tells us of Isaac Stern. "Now he eats only broiled chicken and lean meat. No fat." Martha, or Mart as she's called in the Stern household, has cooked for Isaac Stern and his family for more than twenty-eight years. "I came when his last son was born and I helped to bring up all three children. Now that son is grown up and married. That shows how long I've been here."

Mart, who is very French, acknowledges that Isaac Stern adores Chinese food. Does she cook it for him? "I try to make it the best I can, but," she says with a meaningful Gallic shrug, "it is best to eat good Chinese food in a good Chinese restaurant, non?"

When the treasured violinist has a performance, "he eats around four o'clock, something very light, oh, maybe a small broiled chicken breast, very plain, you know, with just salt and pepper seasoning. And a salad," Mart adds. "After? I don't know. He usually goes out."

Parties at the Sterns' have also changed over the years. "He used to have big parties.

Sometimes I would cook but if they were very large they were catered. Now the most at dinner are maybe three couples. He likes to sit down with friends and have good wine, cheese, and bread."

As to the borsch recipe, Mart tells us it's one of his favorite meals. "He is from Russian background, you know, and he loves his borsch. His mother used to make this for him and she is the one who gave me this recipe. She made the best borsch of all and it's very nourishing. It's really wonderful on a cold day in the winter with some good, fresh bread."

The man who saved Carnegie Hall and who has given us so much joy in music takes great joy in his food, at home and away. But, with Mart to handle the recipes, we almost have to wonder why anyone would leave home. For Martha Fougères, the beautiful Fauré "Berceuse," played by Mr. Stern with Daniel Barenboim and L'Orchestre de Paris (CBS M-34550). And, for the Borsch, two Russian works: Tchaikovsky's *Meditation* with the National Symphony led by Rostropovich (CBS M-35126) and the Prokofiev Violin Concerto No. 2 with the New York Philharmonic and Zubin Mehta (CBS IM-37802).

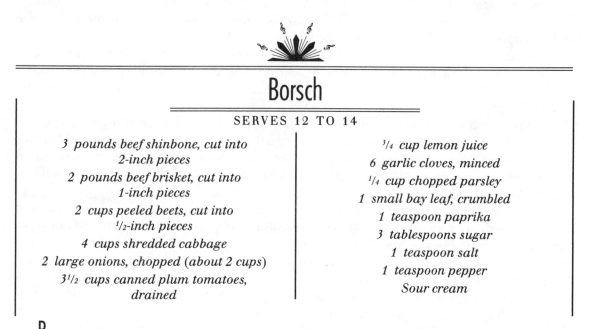

Borsch

SERVES 12 TO 14

3 pounds beef shinbone, cut into
2-inch pieces
2 pounds beef brisket, cut into
1-inch pieces
2 cups peeled beets, cut into
1/2-inch pieces
4 cups shredded cabbage
2 large onions, chopped (about 2 cups)
3 1/2 cups canned plum tomatoes,
drained

3/4 cup lemon juice
6 garlic cloves, minced
1/4 cup chopped parsley
1 small bay leaf, crumbled
1 teaspoon paprika
3 tablespoons sugar
1 teaspoon salt
1 teaspoon pepper
Sour cream

Place meat in an 8- to 10-quart saucepot. Add 2 quarts water and bring to a boil. Cover, reduce heat to a simmer, and cook 1 hour. Uncover, add remaining ingredients except for sour cream, and cook uncovered 2 hours. Remove meat from shinbones, and return to pot. Warm through and serve with sour cream.

Richard Stoltzman

If anyone ever does a study of the link between musicians and food, they'd better start with Richard Stoltzman. This is one performer who goes beyond eating and beyond cooking to the fine art of creating.

Some might call this clarinetist a crossover artist since he has performed traditional classical music as well as jazz and so-called popular songs. *We* call him crossover because he is as comfortable in the kitchen as he is on the concert stage.

Mozart seems to play a part in both sides of Richard Stoltzman. It was the Mozart Clarinet Concerto that introduced him to Philharmonic audiences in December 1979. And it was the Mozart Clarinet Quintet that introduced his recipe for Hazelnut Success to the Amadeus Quartet.

"When I was first invited to join the Amadeus for the Mozart, these four gentlemen had already been making music together for more than three decades," Richard explains. "As we began working more frequently, on the Mozart and later on other repertoire, they confessed that one of their passions was an intimate supper party after concerts where they could sit down and enjoy a special meal prepared especially to their tastes.

"I discovered that they had quite an appreciation of fine wines, good food, and elegant desserts. So when I found out that we would be performing the Brahms Clarinet Quintet in New York, I decided to do something special."

Those special plans included the help of Richard Stoltzman's favorite hosts, John and Anne Straus. Anne, of course, is well known to New York Philharmonic friends, and Richard tells us, "John is crazy enough about chamber music to let me turn their living room into a rehearsal hall from morning till night."

The plans proceeded and "Anne devised a tasty supper, John selected fine libations and I presented my friends in the Amadeus with 'Le Success,' which I had prepared the day before." The concert was played, the supper table was laid, and Richard enjoyed watching the expressions on his friends' faces as he presented them with his Success.

"They couldn't believe that I, dessert in hand, was the same person who'd held a clarinet just a few hours before. But," Richard assures us, "by the last slice, both our Brahms and my dessert were deemed a Success."

Richard Stoltzman's recipe, an improvisation on Julia Child's suggestions for Le Progrès, is both sweet and beautiful. Our suggestions for matching music are Richard's jazz album *Begin Sweet World* (RCA AML1-7124), and his recording, with the Cleveland Quartet, of the Brahms Clarinet Quintet (RCA ARK1-1993).

Hazelnut Success

MAKES 12 SERVINGS

7 ounces blanched slivered almonds
(1³/₄ cups)
3 ounces hazelnuts (³/₄ cup)
1 cup plus 3 tablespoons sugar
1 tablespoon plus 1¹/₂ teaspoons
cornstarch
6 large egg whites, at room temperature
¹/₄ teaspoon cream of tartar
¹/₈ teaspoon salt
1¹/₂ teaspoons vanilla extract
¹/₈ teaspoon almond extract

FILLING
2 sticks (¹/₂ pound) unsalted butter,
softened
1 cup sugar
6 tablespoons orange liqueur
¹/₄ teaspoon almond extract
Pinch salt
2 ounces (2 squares) unsweetened
chocolate, melted and cooled
1 cup heavy cream, beaten until stiff
¹/₂ pint raspberries or 1 cup sliced
strawberries

1   Preheat oven to 350°. Place nuts on separate baking sheets and toast hazelnuts and almonds 15 minutes. Remove hazelnuts to a clean kitchen towel and rub together to remove skins. Cool. Process hazelnuts and ³/₄ cup of the almonds with 1 cup of the sugar and the cornstarch in a food processor until finely ground. Set aside and lower oven temperature to 250°. Butter and flour 2 cookie sheets; trace three 9-inch circles on the sheets.

2   In a large mixing bowl or the bowl of a heavy-duty mixer, beat the egg whites, cream of tartar, and salt at medium speed until soft peaks form. Gradually beat in remaining 3 tablespoons of sugar. Increase speed to high and beat to stiff peaks. Fold in vanilla and almond extracts. Carefully fold in nut mixture, 1 cup at a time, until just combined. Divide nut meringue evenly among the three 9-inch circles and spread to form 3 discs. Bake 1¹/₂ to 2 hours until dry. Turn oven off and allow meringues to cool in oven 1 hour more. Transfer to wire racks to cool completely.

3   To make the filling, process remaining 1 cup almonds until finely ground. In a large mixing bowl, cream butter with electric mixer on medium high speed. Gradually beat in sugar, 1 tablespoon at a time, until light and fluffy, scraping bowl occasionally with rubber spatula, about 4 minutes. Gradually beat in liqueur, 1 tablespoon at a time, until smooth. Beat in almond extract and salt. Fold $2/3$ cup of filling with the melted cooled chocolate in a small bowl. Fold almonds into remaining filling to blend, then fold in whipped cream.

4   To assemble, place one meringue disc on a serving plate. Spread with 3 cups of the almond filling and a third of the raspberries. Top with another meringue disc, remaining almond filling and another third of the fruit. Top with remaining meringue disc, the chocolate filling, and the remaining fruit. Refrigerate at least 4 hours before serving.

Sherry Sylar

"These days I paint food more than I cook it," Sherry Sylar concedes, "although I do like to cook." The New York Philharmonic associate principal oboist is colorful, in her painting, playing, cooking, and character. "As you may know, with my inclusion in the orchestra in 1984, the oboe section's Southerners outnumbered Yankees three to one. But in the spirit of collegial goodwill, we've made Jerry Roth an honorary 'good ole boy' and, in return, he's teaching us Yiddish."

Like Harold Gomberg, longtime principal oboist of the New York Philharmonic and an idol of every reed player, Sherry is trying her hand at oil painting. "But I couldn't possibly fill Harold's shoes in that regard." She is having fun with it, though. "And I have four cats I love dearly," she adds with emphasis.

Sherry also loves this recipe for her grandmother's Glop. "I don't know why it's called Glop," she admits, "but I'll say it *is* a Great Ladle of Punch!

"Tom Stacy makes a terrific barbecue and, when we were talking recipes one day, I thought of Grandma's Glop, a liquid ambrosia which, in keeping with our Southern tradition, would really wash down some spicy ribs or chicken! This recipe is not involved or exotic, but it sure does lend the ambience of a family cookout down South. Sitting on the front porch in a rocking chair, listening to the crickets and suppin' iced tea. Mmmmm," she hums. "Makes me homesick!"

While suppin' this Southern iced tea punch, settle down on your nearest rocker to hear Dawn Upshaw and the Orchestra of St. Luke's in Samuel Barber's evocative *Knoxville, Summer of 1915* (Elektra/Nonesuch 79187-1). Then go on to selections from *Porgy and Bess* conducted by André Kostelanetz with his orchestra (Odyssey MBK 46270).

Grandma's Glop

MAKES ABOUT 9 CUPS

8 tea bags
12 fresh mint leaves (peppermint,
spearmint, or whatever grows in your
backyard)
1 cup sugar
1 quart (4 cups) boiling water

1 cup freshly squeezed orange juice
(about 3 oranges)
1/2 cup fresh lemon juice
Ice
Garnish of fresh mint leaves

Place tea bags, mint, and sugar in a large bowl or pitcher and pour boiling water over. Stir and let steep 6 minutes. Remove tea bags and mint and discard. Stir to fully dissolve sugar and add orange juice, lemon juice, and 4 cups of cold water. Serve over ice with mint leaves for garnish.

Keyboard Artists

Agustin and Carol Anievas

Although Agustin Anievas first appeared with the New York Philharmonic at a Young People's Concert in Carnegie Hall on February 20, 1954, the pianist discounts this debut and moves the date to the late sixties when he appeared with André Kostelanetz for a Promenade Concert in Philharmonic Hall. How can he so blithely brush away such a historic first performance? After all, it did feature conductor Wilfred Pelletier and mezzo-soprano Blanche Thebom, hardly personalities to slip anyone's mind. But, like most performers whose musical roots are planted young, Agustin Anievas doesn't count this debut as the real thing. It happened. It was exciting. But he wasn't a grown-up pianist yet.

The adult Agustin Anievas reappeared with the Philharmonic for an elegant evening at the Proms featuring a gala performance of Gershwin's *Rhapsody in Blue.* Even better than the concert, Gus remembers the rehearsals. "We had some run-throughs without the orchestra at Kostelanetz's penthouse apartment overlooking the East River and the George Washington Bridge and the Statue of Liberty. You could see everything from that living room."

From the elegance and splendor of Carnegie Hall, a penthouse apartment, and Promenade Concerts at Lincoln Center, Agustin Anievas and his wife, Carol, have found themselves traveling to a variety of festivals for the food as well as the music. "Recently I was playing at a festival outside Hamburg," he recalls. "The entire province was involved. I played in a barn; they let the cows out and the musicians in. All the performers who played in the area donated their time to come and play from ten in the morning until ten at night."

What about that elegance we were talking about? "You can eat outside and drink and have a wonderful time. Since I was playing, we didn't take advantage of the food that day. But the next day we went back as spectators and we ate venison that the prince himself had caught in the hunting season." You want elegance? The pianist adds, "We stayed at the prince's estate."

For an elegant evening of food and music, accompany Carol's Malfatti di Ricotta with Gus's recording of Chopin waltzes (Seraphim 4XG-60447). Or for an affair of fantasies, play Liszt's paraphrase of Verdi's Quartet from *Ricotta-letto* with Earl Wild at the keyboard (ETC-2011).

Malfatti di Ricotta

SERVES 6

*2 cups cooked chopped spinach (made
from 2 pounds fresh) or 3 (10 ounce)
packages chopped spinach, thawed and
squeezed dry*
2 cups grated Parmesan cheese
¹/₂ cup unbleached flour
*1 cup (8 ounces) ricotta cheese,
preferably fresh*

2 large eggs, lightly beaten
1 teaspoon salt
³/₄ teaspoon pepper
Pinch nutmeg, preferably freshly grated
3 tablespoons unsalted butter, melted
*Béchamel sauce, recipe follows
(optional)*

1   In a large mixing bowl, combine the spinach, 1 cup Parmesan cheese, ¹/₄ cup flour, the ricotta, eggs, salt, pepper, and nutmeg. Mix well and, using a spoon, shape into ovals the size of walnuts.

2   Bring a large pot of salted water to a boil over high heat. Roll the malfatti in the remaining flour and throw 5 or 6 at a time into the boiling water. Cook until they float to the surface, about 2 minutes. Remove with a slotted spoon to a shallow baking dish. Repeat until all are cooked.

3   Preheat broiler. Pour melted butter over the malfatti and sprinkle with remaining Parmesan. Broil 4 to 5 inches from source of heat about 3 to 4 minutes or until lightly browned. Serve with béchamel sauce if desired.

Béchamel Sauce

2 tablespoons unsalted butter
2 tablespoons all-purpose flour
1¹/₄ cups milk

¹/₄ teaspoon salt
¹/₂ teaspoon pepper

1   Melt butter in a small saucepan over medium high heat. Whisk in flour and cook, whisking constantly for 1 to 2 minutes. Gradually whisk in milk and cook, stirring occasionally, about 6 to 8 minutes or until mixture thickens. Stir in salt and pepper and serve with Malfatti.

Edward Brewer

"It's interesting to see how musicians who play in large orchestras, and have to blow their brains out, adapt to chamber music," says harpsichordist Edward Brewer. "I think they cherish the opportunity to have some finesse."

Ed Brewer made his debut with the New York Philharmonic at one of the orchestra's small ensemble chamber concerts at the Merkin Concert Hall in 1987 with a work of great finesse and style, a Telemann Quartet, from *Tafelmusik* (1733, Book 2, No. 2, if you're counting).

"My whole life is chamber music and I don't have to jump to the whim of whoever is on podium," the harpsichordist adds with a little glee in his voice. He notes that the important thing is listening to one another, something all good musicians do, whether they're blowing their brains out or not.

Edward Brewer is another of those musicians who looks for finesse in his food as well as his performances. "I was playing with the Madeira Bach Festival, which is affiliated with another festival in the South of Portugal. A guidebook I read suggested this restaurant run by a Swiss couple, not exactly what you'd expect to find in the South of Portugal. The place sat about thirty, with two seatings a night. The book said this was the best restaurant in southern Portugal, but it turned out to be the best in my life up until then and one of the best since."

Edward Brewer's voice gets softer as he remembers. "You sit in a garden while you have appetizers and drinks. We were treated beautifully. The food is continental with a Portuguese touch. That means fish, but being Swiss they knew everything about preparing it. And they really knew their Portuguese wines." The name of this find? "La Réserve."

When he's not traveling, the harpsichordist does the cooking at home. "My wife used to take care of it, but I took over a few years ago when we went on a special health diet. I told her that this is the way I want to eat. She said, 'Fine. You cook it.'"

While you brew up Edward Brewer's Gazpacho, taste his recording of Telemann's Bassoon Sonata in F minor (Arthur Weisberg) and his Flute Sonata in C minor (Samuel Baron) (Elektra/Nonesuch 71352). And, after many, many bottles of a rich wine from Portugal, you'll consider yourself *très international* for playing Ravel's *"Gazpacho" de la nuit* (Gaspard will pardon us) in the performance by pianist Martha Argerich (DG 419062-2).

Gazpacho

SERVES 6

2 large tomatoes, cored and roughly
chopped (about 3 cups)

1 peeled cucumber, cut into 1-inch
chunks (about 2 cups)

1 large green or red pepper, cut into
1-inch chunks (about 1 cup)

1 large garlic clove, minced

9 leaves of basil, roughly chopped

2 tablespoons chopped parsley

2-3 teaspoons dark miso paste

$^1/_2$ teaspoon herb salt

$^1/_2$ teaspoon pepper

$^1/_4$ cup olive oil

2 teaspoon rice vinegar (optional)

Throw all ingredients into food processor or blender. Pulse until ingredients are well chopped and combined. Chill until serving time, at least 30 minutes.

Yefim Bronfman

Born in Tashkent in the former Soviet Union, pianist Yefim Bronfman didn't take long to become an active pianist and an international celebrity. Of course, he had a few role models along the way. His father and older sister are violinists, and his mother began teaching him to play the piano when he was seven.

Eight years after his first lesson, he and his family moved to Israel and, within the year, Yefim had played for Eugene Istomin and Zubin Mehta. That brings us to 1973. The following year the young pianist won a scholarship from the American Israel Cultural Foundation and came to the attention of Isaac Stern. The rest, as they say, is history: an international debut with the Montreal Symphony and Zubin Mehta in 1975, a tour of the United States with the Israel Philharmonic with Mr. Mehta and Leonard Bernstein in 1976, and his New York Philharmonic debut in May 1978.

But the pianist is interested in more than solo work. Yefim Bronfman is a devoted chamber musician and he's performed with the best of them, from the Guarneri and Juilliard Quartets to recitals with violinist Cho-Liang Lin and cellist Gary Hoffman.

With a background that's taken the pianist from Tashkent to New York, with an important stop in Israel, it's only logical that Yefim Bronfman's recipe would be something like Blinchiki. This particular version is especially light and delicate. The filling Yefim suggests works well, but you could fill these crêpes with anything from crabmeat to caviar. And, if you use his filling, accompany it with the exquisite plum jam from Ellen Bodow on page 217. They go together perfectly!

The ideal musical accompaniment for Yefim Bronfman's Blinchiki is the pianist's recording of three scenes from Stravinsky's *Petrouchka* (Sony Classical 46481).

Blinchiki

MAKES 8

¹/₂ cup sifted unbleached flour
¹/₂ teaspoon salt
1 large egg, lightly beaten
²/₃ cup milk
1 tablespoon unsalted butter, melted

FILLING
8 ounces dry-curd cottage cheese
1 large egg yolk, beaten
2 teaspoons unsalted butter, melted
1 teaspoon sugar
Unsalted butter for frying pancakes

1   In a large bowl, combine flour and salt and mix well. In a small bowl, combine egg, milk, and butter. Pour into flour and mix well.

2   In a small bowl, combine all filling ingredients and mix well. Set aside.

3   Heat a small skillet over high heat. Melt butter to coat skillet (about 1 tablespoon). Pour in about 2 to 3 tablespoons of batter and rotate pan to coat evenly. Cook about 2 minutes and add 1 tablespoon of filling. Fold in the 4 sides of the pancake to form a packet. Turn and cook 1 to 2 minutes longer or until well browned. Keep warm and repeat with remaining batter and filling.

Serve with sour cream or fruit sauce.

Kenneth Cooper

The Cooper household is a mixed affair of harpsichord and singer, American and Italian, and pure passion—for food, music, and the joy of life.

When Kenneth Cooper sits down at the harpsichord to play Bach, Vivaldi, or Scarlatti, the result is an impassioned outpouring of notes that come from the performer as well as the composer. "I play what I think the composer wrote, based on what I know of the style and the period." Notes seem to fly from the keyboard and there's an electricity and spontaneity that probably would have sent the Baroque composers back to their own instruments to see if they could match Kenneth's virtuosity.

It's this kind of passion and joy in music that the New York Philharmonic's Young People's Concerts have tried to bring to new generations over the years, so it's fitting that Kenneth Cooper made his Philharmonic debut in 1983 at one of these performances. "The important thing is to bring the music to life vividly," Ken tells us. "It's just the way I want my food to be. I love Italian food, not necessarily for the spices, but I'll certainly go for pasta in any shape, size, or form. And as frequently as possible."

How does the harpsichordist eat before a concert? "How? All ways. Before, after, and, if possible, during. I love to eat. As with music, it's not necessary to consume enormous quantities. It's the quality and the liveliness of it. And the people you do it with. It's nice when the good company goes along with the good food. It's much more fun doing good music with wonderful people. It improves the music. And good food can even improve the company . . . just like music."

Kenneth Cooper has participated in the Spoleto Festival in Charleston, South Carolina, for more than a dozen years. He and his wife, soprano Josephine Mongiardo, go for the food as well as the music. And, in some cases, the restaurants in Charleston offer both.

"In Celia's Porta Via, Celia specializes in terrific Italian food. But she's also a passionate music lover and during the festival she makes special things for the musicians who come in after a performance. She has a piano in the restaurant and, after the food has had its effect and the wine has worked, we sit down and play chamber music."

The fun doesn't stop there. Kenneth and Josephine also recommend Robert's of Charleston. "You have to reserve months in advance but it's a real gourmet experience." On top of the food, it seems that Robert is "a beautiful baritone" and he introduces each course with a song. "Sometimes he starts with 'Food, Glorious Food' (from *Oliver*) when he brings the appetizer. There are at least six courses, so you can imagine what the evening is like."

Josephine Mongiardo, born in America of Calabrian heritage, is a soprano of passion with an Italian insight into food as well as music. Her Fiore Cucuzze Pancakes (squash flower pancakes) are very delicate and would go well as an appetizer with a dab of sour cream and some golden caviar, or as a side dish with meat such as roast lamb.

The music we recommend to accompany this unusual pancake is an unusual assortment of well-known Pre-Revolutionary American songs that Kenneth Cooper has arranged in what he feels is close to their original sound. The disc, *Should Auld Acquaintance Be Forgot*, includes some food songs—"Hot Cross Buns," "Make a Cake," originally by James Hook—and, for cleaning up afterward, "Three Blinde Mice," by Thomas Ravenscroft. Kenneth plays on the recording and Josephine is one of the singers (MHS 512415X).

Fiore Cucuzze Pancakes

MAKES 8 PANCAKES

16 squash flowers, stems trimmed,
cut into quarters
1 cup flour
1 teaspoon baking powder

¼ teaspoon salt
2 large eggs
½ cup milk
1 tablespoon olive oil

1   Over high heat, bring large saucepot of water to a boil. Blanch squash flowers for 30 seconds. Drain and cool briefly in cold water to stop cooking. Dry on paper towels.

2   In a small bowl, combine flour, baking powder, and salt. Stir to mix well. In a small bowl, beat together eggs and milk. Stir into flour mixture, mixing until batter is smooth. Stir in squash flowers.

3   Heat olive oil on griddle or in a large skillet over medium high heat. Ladle batter onto griddle, using about 2 tablespoons per pancake. Cook about 2 minutes on each side or until golden brown.

Serve as a side dish or first course with a good hunk of caciocavallo or ricotta salata cheese.

Misha Dichter

Misha Dichter remembers the date of his debut with the New York Philharmonic, January 13, 1968. "Lenny conducted and I played the Tchaikovsky B-flat minor Concerto." But he almost dismisses the event because "I was getting married later that same week and, by comparison, the debut was not exactly uppermost in my mind."

Pianists Misha and Cipa Dichter were married just a few days later, slightly to the north of Carnegie Hall. "The wedding was at the Hampshire House on Central Park South. Itzhak [Perlman] was my best man and Sol Hurok was there." What was served? "I don't remember." Was there any music at this most musical marriage? "We had a string quartet." There's a pause here. To remember. "I *think* we had a string quartet. It was a long time ago."

Since then, the couple has gone on to great artistic success, individually and together. And there have been many more parties and concerts, many of them memorable, even to Misha.

"For our twentieth anniversary we had a special reception with a lot of our friends. I was playing a program in Carnegie Hall that same week" (déjà vu all over again?) "and William Greenberg made a special cake. For our wedding he'd decorated a cake with the opening measures of the Tchaikovsky piano concerto I was playing. For the twentieth anniversary, he used the opening of the slow movement and added the words, "Stick around for the finale.""

Do the Dichters cook for their guests? "Cipa's the great cook. I'm not even allowed in the kitchen. And we have very different tastes in eating." Misha is a cigar smoker and he feels that this has somewhat "stunted" his taste buds. "Cipa loves delicate foods, white fishes with mild sauces that I can't even taste. I love sushi, she won't eat it. And I'm crazy about Chinese food."

"When I travel to the West Coast, I can't wait to go to Chinois on Main in Santa Monica. It's one of Wolfgang Puck's restaurants and it really goes beyond Columbus Avenue Chinese."

"Actually," the pianist admits, "I'm always in search of the perfect sushi bar. The only ones that come anywhere near what I've had in Tokyo are Hatsuhana in New York, a couple of good restaurants in L.A., and maybe the best of them all can be found in Vancouver."

Does Misha Dichter eat the "real" Japanese sushi? Raw shrimp, still wriggling and screaming as they're delicately dropped into an educated mouth? Misha's mouth curves into a smile as he declares, "I'm into traif."

There seems to be an overabundance of music to accompany Misha and Cipa Dichter's musical and culinary lives. We could suggest the old song "Shrimp Boats Are a'Coming," for the "traif" and "The Dance of the Hours" for Cipa's 24-Hour Omelet. But we won't. We'll stick to the more serious side, beginning with Misha's performance of the Tchaikovsky Piano Concerto No. 1 in B-flat minor with the Boston Symphony and Erich Leinsdorf (RCA 6 526-2-RG). And, for the wedding and anniversary celebrations, Saint-Saëns's Caprice-Valse, Op. 76 ("Wedding Cake"), with the City of Birmingham Symphony (Angel CDM-69386).

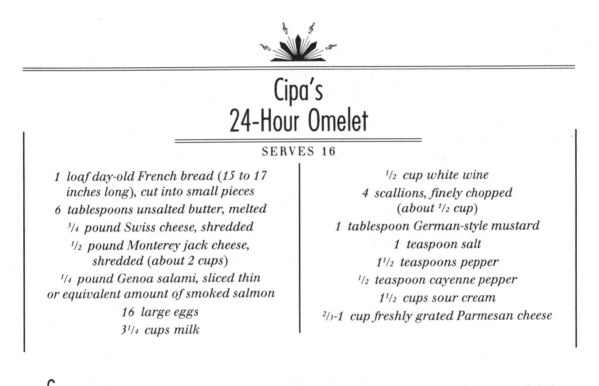

Cipa's
24-Hour Omelet

SERVES 16

1 loaf day-old French bread (15 to 17 inches long), cut into small pieces

6 tablespoons unsalted butter, melted

³/₄ pound Swiss cheese, shredded

¹/₂ pound Monterey jack cheese, shredded (about 2 cups)

¹/₄ pound Genoa salami, sliced thin or equivalent amount of smoked salmon

16 large eggs

3¹/₄ cups milk

¹/₂ cup white wine

4 scallions, finely chopped (about ¹/₂ cup)

1 tablespoon German-style mustard

1 teaspoon salt

1¹/₂ teaspoons pepper

¹/₂ teaspoon cayenne pepper

1¹/₂ cups sour cream

²/₃-1 cup freshly grated Parmesan cheese

1   Grease two 13 × 9 × 2″ (4 quart) baking dishes. Spread bread over bottoms of dishes, dividing evenly. Drizzle each with half the butter. Sprinkle each pan with half the grated cheeses and meat. In a medium bowl combine all remaining ingredients except sour cream and Parmesan. Mix well and pour half of mixture over each pan. Cover pans with aluminum foil and refrigerate overnight.

2   Next day, remove pans 30 minutes before baking. Preheat oven to 325°. Bake covered 1 hour. Uncover and spread with sour cream and Parmesan. Bake 12 to 15 minutes longer or until lightly browned. Cool briefly and serve.

Vladimir Feltsman

Vladimir Feltsman's life has been a series of trials and triumphs, from his public debut at the age of twelve with the Moscow Philharmonic, to the eight years of suffering the pianist endured while he waited for permission to leave the Soviet Union to emigrate to Israel.

Life was filled with glory in the early years. Born in 1952, Vladimir Feltsman was just fifteen when he won first prize at the Concertina International Competition in Prague. After that, it was the coveted crown in the Marguerite Long Competition in Paris. Those were the years the pianist was able to travel and perform with all the major Soviet orchestras and ensembles in Eastern Europe, France, Italy, Belgium, and Japan.

But when, in 1979, Mr. Feltsman announced that he wanted to leave the Soviet Union to go to Israel, life quickly took a different turn. For eight years, the pianist's musical activities were severely curtailed and it wasn't until August, 1987, that he was granted permission to leave. He came to the United States and has since established not only a major performing career, but also a deep commitment to teaching and training young musicians. In fact, Mr. Feltsman is planning to establish a special American music school for gifted children.

Gifted though the pianist may be in both teaching and playing, his real triumph has proved to be at the grill. The recipe he's given us for boned and butterflied marinated leg of lamb is one of the most spectacular dishes I've ever tasted. Jean Galton did the initial testing to be sure the amounts of all the ingredients were correct. I tasted the results and promptly went to the nearest meat market to buy a leg of lamb of my own. It has since become a company favorite, with or without a grill. And it's as good cold for lunch the day after (if you have any left) as it is hot for dinner.

For this delicious dish, we join Benjamin Britten to *Rejoice in the Lamb* with Philip Ledger and the King's College Choir (Angel CDC-47709) and we rejoice with Vladimir Feltsman in his great triumphs with a recording of his *American Live Debut at Carnegie Hall* (CBS2-M2K-44589).

Marinated Leg of Lamb

SERVES 8 TO 10

¹/₃ cup balsamic vinegar
¹/₃ cup extra virgin olive oil
3 tablespoons soy sauce
1 tablespoon dark sesame oil
2 tablespoons lemon juice
3 garlic cloves, minced
(about 1 tablespoon)

1 medium onion, chopped (about 1 cup)
1 teaspoon sugar
¹/₂ teaspoon freshly ground pepper
1 leg of lamb (about 4 pounds),
trimmed and butterflied

1 In a large stainless steel or ceramic pan combine all ingredients except lamb. Stir well and place lamb in marinade, turning to coat well. Cover and refrigerate 24 hours. (Alternatively, place all ingredients in a Ziploc bag, seal, and refrigerate as above.)

2 Preheat grill or broiler. Dry off lamb with paper towels. When coals are white and heat is medium high, grill lamb about 5 to 6 minutes on each side for medium rare. (Alternatively, broil 3 inches from heat source about 4 minutes on each side.) Let sit 10 minutes before carving.

Serve with green salad and Bordeaux. The marinade is very strong when warm and freshly cooked. The next day the taste of lamb is much stronger.

Rudolf Firkusny

Rudolf Firkusny has a twinkle in his eyes, the flawless complexion of his Eastern European ancestry, the gentle demeanor of an old-world gentleman, and the keyboard presence of a master pianist. That's why it was such a shock to see him in a television commercial for sneakers with basketball star David Robinson. It was out of character, but then again, Rudolf Firkusny is full of surprises. "I like to eat, but my life isn't dependent on a gourmet meal," he confesses. "I am not very good in cooking so I must leave it to the others."

On the other hand, this seemingly quiet, unassuming star of keyboard and TV screen enjoys a good party. "I like going to receptions after a concert. Not so much for the food. In fact, I'm not hungry after I play. But I like the company. I don't want to return to my hotel room and contemplate what I did right and what I did wrong on the stage. Also, the people who go to receptions usually have something to do with the orchestra or the presentation and I feel I should be there to give them proper credit for their work."

Let's back up a moment. A musician who's not hungry after a concert? Unheard of! "Actually, I don't even eat before a performance. I have a light lunch and then a big, hearty breakfast . . . the next day!"

When he's traveling, Rudolf Firkusny is happiest when he's in Italy. "I do love Italian food and if I can go to dinner with an Italian, someone who really knows how to order, then it's a different story." The pianist is at home with Czech food but finds it a little too heavy for everyday fare. And he doesn't like anything that's spicy or hot like Mexican. "But I can eat more or less anything in moderation," he concedes.

He needn't concede anything when it comes to performing with the New York Philharmonic. The maestro made his debut with the orchestra in the early 1940s with Artur Rodzinski conducting. "It was during the war and the Philharmonic was putting together programs with soloists from the allied nations," he recalls. "But I've had the good fortune to perform many, many times over the years with the Philharmonic. I've played with Bruno Walter, Bernstein, Mitropoulos, Krips, Steinberg, and the young Guido Cantelli. I've been fortunate," he says in his gentle, seemingly self-effacing way. "Then there was Kubelik, my Czech countryman, and George Szell, whom I admired so greatly.

"I've never toured with the orchestra but I have had occasion to play for some special occasions like their luncheons at the Waldorf. And I've done some chamber music with individual members of the Philharmonic. I love that!"

Rudolf Firkusny may not have toured with the New York Philharmonic, but he's certainly done his share of musical traveling. In fact, he sent this recipe for Red Cabbage on stationery from the Hotel Splügenschloss in Zurich so I wouldn't have to wait until he returned to New York. "It comes from my wife Tatiana," he tells us. "Actually, it was her mother's recipe."

From his commercials for sneakers to his many performances at the piano, Rudolf Firkusny's quiet humor is never far off. That's why our musical menu begins with his recording of Dvořák's Humoresques and Mazurkas (Can. 31070). And, for Tatiana Firkusny: the Letter Aria from Tchaikovsky's "Eugene Onegin" sung by Galina Vishnevskaya with the Bolshoi Theatre Orchestra (Monitor MCS-2072E).

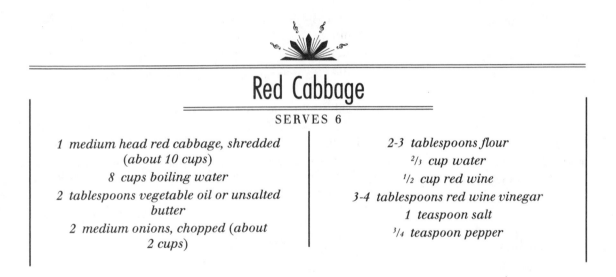

Red Cabbage

SERVES 6

1 medium head red cabbage, shredded (*about 10 cups*)	2-3 tablespoons flour
8 cups boiling water	²/₃ cup water
2 tablespoons vegetable oil or unsalted butter	¹/₂ cup red wine
2 medium onions, chopped (*about 2 cups*)	3-4 tablespoons red wine vinegar
	1 teaspoon salt
	³/₄ teaspoon pepper

1 Place cabbage in colander set in sink. Pour boiling water over and let drain. Meanwhile, in a 5- to 6-quart saucepot heat oil over medium high heat. Add onions and cook, stirring, until soft, about 6 to 7 minutes. Add cabbage, stir, and cook 5 minutes. Stir in flour, ²/₃ cup water, and reduce heat to low. Cook about 20 minutes, stirring frequently, until cabbage is quite tender (add more water if it starts to stick). Stir in wine, vinegar, salt, and pepper. Cook 5 minutes longer.

Serve with roast duck, goose, pork, or game. It can be made a day ahead and the flavor actually improves.

Claude Frank, Lilian Kallir, and Pamela Frank

Lilian Kallir and Claude Frank are pianists. They are also husband and wife. Sometimes they play concerts together but, for the most part, they have separate careers. Lilian made her debut with the New York Philharmonic and Mitropoulos playing Mozart in 1957. Claude made his first appearance with the orchestra two years later, performing Beethoven with Bernstein.

"We were married a few months before Claude's debut," Lilian tells us. "The wedding took place up in Marlboro, Vermont, at the very end of the summer music festival. There were only about fifteen of us. It was just family, the Serkins, and our best man was Eugene Istomin." Like pianist Misha Dichter, whose Philharmonic debut also took place around the time of his marriage, Lilian hasn't the foggiest notion what they ate at their wedding celebration. "We weren't thinking about food that day."

Add to the Claude Frank–Lilian Kallir music family a daughter, Pamela. "Our daughter started studying the violin when she was just five and a half years old. She wasn't drawn to the piano but she loved the violin from the start," Lilian remembers. "She must have known it was right for her."

Pamela Frank obviously made the right choice. She's grown up to be an Avery Fisher Award winner, she played in Carnegie Hall when she was fifteen with Alexander Schneider and the New York String Orchestra, and she's recently made her debuts with the Philadelphia, Cleveland, and Vienna orchestras. The entire family has appeared together at the Metropolitan Museum in New York and conductor George Cleve brought them all out to California for a program on which they each played a Mozart concerto.

So here we have a family of three major musical careers. Together and apart. That adds up to a lot of memories. And, being musicians, many of those memories have to do with eating.

For instance, Lilian remembers sharing a meal with Dmitri Mitropoulos the week before her debut with the Philharmonic. "We ate at La Scala on Fifty-fourth Street. I thought the food was great but he wasn't terribly interested in eating." What? A musician who doesn't care about food?

"Mitropoulos was an ascetic. He was somehow otherworldly, very shy and a deeply religious man. I once saw his two rooms at the Great Northern Hotel. He had only the barest furnishings and he just wasn't interested in material things.

"Not like me," Lilian confesses. "I like good food no matter where it comes from. I've had wonderful meals in Morocco, for example. I even ate with my hands. You know, when in Rome . . ."

Does this fascination for food run in the family? "I should say so! Claude loves to eat. Pamela is an absolutely magnificent cook, very creative. And I like recipes I can cook while I'm practicing."

How does that work? Lilian Kallir has the perfect method. "I put it in the oven, set the timer, go to the piano, and work until the bell goes off. Then I take a break to stir it, set the timer again, and go back to work. Dinner is ready at the end of the sonata."

We'll let Canadian Brass serenade this musical family with a medley of apropos songs by Gershwin: "Clap Yo' Hands" for all three of them; "Someone to Watch Over Me," sings Claude to Lilian; "Nice Work if You Can Get It," sings Lilian about her cooking method; and, from Pamela and Lilian to Claude, "The Man I Love" (RCA 6490-2-RC).

Claude's Muerbe Teig

MAKES 16 WEDGES

1 cup flour
2 tablespoons sugar
Pinch salt
1 stick unsalted butter, chilled and cut into pieces

1 egg yolk
1 teaspoon grated lemon zest

1   Grease an 8- or 9-inch pie plate. Set aside.

2   In a medium bowl, stir together flour, sugar, and salt. With a fork or pastry cutter, stir in butter until it forms small crumbs. Stir in egg yolk and lemon zest just until mixed and dough holds together. Pat into prepared pie plate and score into 16 wedges. With a fork, prick each wedge several times. Chill at least 30 minutes.

3   Preheat oven to 350°. Bake muerbe teig 30 to 35 minutes or until lightly golden. Cool in pan, then remove, cut in wedges, and serve like shortbread.

This can also be used as a pie dough with the addition of $1/2$ cup more flour.

Lilian's Beef Goulash
with Sausage

SERVES 8

2 tablespoons unsalted butter

2 large onions, chopped (about 2 cups)

2 pounds round steak, cut into
1½-inch cubes

1 cup boiling water

1 cup red wine or 1 cup ketchup

1 teaspoon salt

½ teaspoon pepper

1 tablespoon Hungarian paprika

1 pound knockwurst or weisswurst
(3 or 4), cut into ½-inch slices

1 cup sour cream (optional)

1   In a large saucepot, heat butter over medium high heat. Add onions and cook, stirring, until translucent, about 5 minutes. Push onions to side of pot and add beef. Brown beef on all sides about 6 to 7 minutes, and add 1 cup boiling water, the red wine or ketchup, salt, pepper, and paprika. Lower heat to a simmer, cover, and cook 1½ hours or until meat is tender. Check occasionally to make sure there is enough liquid and add a little water if necessary. Add knockwurst and cook 15 minutes longer or until knockwurst is heated through. If desired, turn off heat and stir in sour cream.

Serve with buttered noodles and Senfgurken (recipe follows).

Senfgurken

MAKES 6 CUPS

3 cucumbers, peeled, cut in half, and cut lengthwise into ¹/₂-inch wedges
1 bunch dill
1 teaspoon salt
¹/₂ teaspoon pepper
3 tablespoons sugar

³/₄ cup water
1 cup distilled white vinegar
10 allspice berries
5 whole cloves
2 bay leaves

1   Place cucumbers and dill in a 1-quart jar. In a medium saucepan, combine remaining ingredients and bring to a boil. Simmer 2 to 3 minutes and pour over cucumbers. Cover and refrigerate 24 hours.

"Erich Leinsdorf flipped over these," says Lilian.

Pamela's Chocolate-Covered
Kahlua/Coconut Macaroons

MAKES 18

¹/₃ cup unbleached flour
2¹/₂ cups shredded sweetened coconut
¹/₈ teaspoon salt
²/₃ cup sweetened condensed milk

1 teaspoon vanilla extract
¹/₂ cup Kahlua
6 ounces semisweet chocolate chips

1 Preheat oven to 350°. Grease a large cookie sheet.

2 In a large mixing bowl, combine flour, coconut, and salt, and mix well. Add condensed milk, vanilla, and Kahlua, and stir until thoroughly combined. Drop the batter by heaping tablespoonfuls onto cookie sheet, leaving about an inch between cookies. Bake 18 to 20 minutes or until golden brown. Remove from sheet with a spatula to a rack and cool completely.

3 Meanwhile, melt chocolate in top of a double boiler or in a microwave (1 to 2 minutes in a microwavable bowl on high power, stirring twice). Dip the tops of the macaroons in the chocolate and let cool until chocolate has set.

Gary Graffman

While it's no secret that most musicians share a passion for both music and food, few of them have shared careers as pianists and professional food critics. That puts Gary Graffman in a very special class. "I was a food critic for the *Village Voice* for about three or four weeks in 1986," the pianist confesses. "The regular critic had to take off for a month and the editor asked Bud Trillin if he knew someone who might be good in the job," Gary Graffman explains, referring to the writer Calvin Trillin, who once said that musicians are "undoubtedly the most devout searchers-out of quality restaurants."

Now the director of the famous Curtis Institute in Philadelphia, Gary Graffman was only teaching there at the time. "I found a message at Curtis to call the *Village Voice* and, when I did, they asked me if I could take over as food critic for a little while. They didn't want me to write just straight reviews. They told me to do something different. I was told I could visit each restaurant twice and I could take a few people with me so we could taste a variety of the food. When they got around to discussing the salary, I stared at them and said, 'You mean I'm going to be paid?'

"I grew up in Manhattan on West Ninety-seventh Street. There was an Irish bar on the corner that reeked of stale beer. And, in those days, there was only one Chinese restaurant in the neighborhood, Gung Ho. These days there's a Chinese restaurant on every corner. So, for one of my first reviews, we visited every Chinese restaurant in that neighborhood and compared them. Then I went to work on Indonesian restaurants in New York. (There were only five of them.) I even went out to those crazy Russian restaurants in Brighton Beach. It was like being in old Russia. And, finally, I went back to two of my old favorite restaurants, the Carnegie Deli and Trader Vic's, to see how they'd changed after twenty-five years."

Gary Graffman sighs a bit at the recent demise of Trader's. "I took Skitch Henderson there," he adds.

Waxing nostalgic, the pianist tells us, "When I was a kid we always went to the Russian Tea Room. It wasn't that expensive in those days. In my late teens I went to five or six concerts a week and after every performance, we'd settle in at either the Carnegie Deli or the Russian Tea Room."

Where did he go after his own debut with the New York Philharmonic in 1950? "Well, I remember the program. Leonard Bernstein conducted and I played the Brahms D minor." So much for that.

The Russian Tea Room apparently had its influence, though. "I was making my own flavored vodkas long before all those professional companies started bottling and selling them. And mine are different from theirs. I have *two* kind of pepper flavors, for example. I use peppercorns and chili peppers. And I get my peppercorns from Hédiard in Paris. They specialize in exotic spices and they send me a special mixture of peppercorns."

With great pride, the pianist–conservatory director–food critic informs us, "I have three supplies of vodka now, one in my New York apartment, one in my Philadelphia home, and one in my office at Curtis. When Slava Rostropovich comes to visit, I have to replenish the supply."

For a Russian taste with any flavor vodka, we suggest Gary Graffman's recording of Rachmaninoff's Piano Concerto No. 2 with the New York Philharmonic and Leonard Bernstein (CBS MT-31813). After an evening of tasting every flavor vodka you can manage, get out the Philharmonic's recording of *The Classic Silly Symphony* (CBS MGT-44588). And don't forget Gershwin's classic song "Vodka."

Flavored Vodka

MAKES ½ GALLON

½ gallon vodka (inexpensive brand)
Zest of 4 limes, tangerines, or lemons, cut in strips, or

1 to 3 tablespoons ground pepper or mixed peppercorns

1 Mix the zest or pepper with the vodka. (Start with 1 tablespoon of the pepper to test potency—you can add more if you would like it hotter.) Let the citrus vodka sit at room temperature for 3 days before using, and let the pepper vodka sit for two days. Shake once or twice a day. Serve over ice or frozen.

Leonid Hambro

"Y ou can divide musicians into lots of categories," pianist Leonid Hambro says philosophically. "There are jazz musicians and Baroque musicians, for example. The thread between them is improvisation.

"Similarly, there are different kinds of cooks. There are cooks who use a recipe and there are those who cook by intuition. But they all love food."

Leonid Hambro spent many years as the New York Philharmonic's official pianist. He played orchestral works that had small piano parts and he played ensemble pieces that put the piano in the spotlight. He and Jasha Zaydee made a world-famous piano duo for many years. And Leonid toured and teased with Victor Borge for several seasons.

But this versatile pianist is also a world-class raconteur, spouting stories of classical musicians and performances that amuse and enlighten his audiences.

"When the New York Philharmonic celebrated its 125th anniversary," the story-telling pianist begins, "they put together a humungously long program. It ended with a piece by Kolliwode. Leonard Bernstein was conducting and he felt that it was only proper on that auspicious occasion for the orchestra and the orchestra alone to be on stage to take the bows at the end of the performance. So he gave the downbeat to start the music and walked into the wings.

"Well," Leonid Hambro remembers, "the audience was just astonished. They cheered the players at the end. Many came backstage to congratulate them on how well they'd played. It was clearly the best part of the program."

Leonid, who was part of the Philharmonic at the time, had been listening to the performance. Later, many of his colleagues came up to him to see if he thought they'd really played so well. " 'Is it true?' they asked me. 'Were we really that good? How come we played so well without the conductor?'

"I told them it wasn't about Bernstein. It was just a phenomenon you could chalk up to one word: hostility. And it would have been that way with any conductor. How can an orchestra get back at the one who's always telling them what to do? Play better without him!"

Does Leonid Hambro feel the need to get back at the people who write recipes? "I love to cook. But I'm one of those who 'plays it by ear,' " or, in this case, by taste. "My first cooking adventure was inspired by omelets. I hated them. No one could make an omelet or scrambled eggs that I liked. So I used my analytical musical mind and decided to take my taste apart. For example, I realized that I didn't like anything I had to work at. I hate bones and shells and things I have to struggle with. I like casseroles."

Leonid Hambro and his wife, Barbara, haven't had much spare time since the pianist began touring with his Hambro Quartet of Pianos. We, on the other hand, are in the fortunate position of being able to cook, eat, and listen to the Hambro Quartet as they perform Debussy's *Fêtes*, a fitting piece for Leonid Hambro's sparkling playing and conversation, and Dukas's "*Sorcerer's Apprentice*," which may well describe the pianist when he's in the kitchen (XTV-408888).

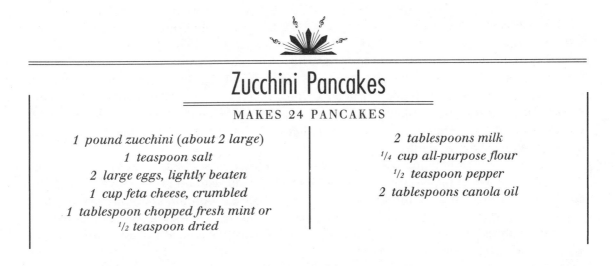

Zucchini Pancakes

MAKES 24 PANCAKES

1 pound zucchini (*about 2 large*)
1 teaspoon salt
2 large eggs, lightly beaten
1 cup feta cheese, crumbled
1 tablespoon chopped fresh mint or
$1/_2$ teaspoon dried

2 tablespoons milk
$1/_4$ cup all-purpose flour
$1/_2$ teaspoon pepper
2 tablespoons canola oil

1 Shred zucchini on large holes of a hand grater and place in a medium-size bowl. Toss with salt. Place in a colander, weight down, and place colander in the sink or a large bowl. Let drain at least 30 minutes.

2 Meanwhile, combine all remaining ingredients except oil in a medium-size mixing bowl. Squeeze excess moisture from zucchini and add to egg mixture. Stir well.

3 Heat oil in a large skillet over medium high heat and drop in pancakes by the tablespoonful. Cook until well browned, about 3 to 4 minutes on each side. Serve at once.

These would be great with lamb for dinner, or with warm glazed orange slices for brunch.

Grant Johannesen

Grant Johannesen remembers the first of his many performances with the New York Philharmonic. "It was in 1949 and I played the Chopin Piano Concerto No. 2 with Szell." After that, the pianist played regularly with the orchestra at home and on tour.

"Mitropoulos conducted a major trip with the orchestra to the western part of the United States and Europe. I was playing the Beethoven Third. I performed with Ozawa and Szell and, of course, Kostelanetz. In fact, I think there were three concerts I did at the Promenades and they were all very happy occasions because I'd grown up with Kostelanetz. He was a wonderful conductor. I remember Alice Tully telling me, 'You'll have a great time with that man.' She was right."

But of all the conductors Grant Johannesen remembers, George Szell stands out as being extraordinary. "He was a real gourmet. In fact he was brilliant in so many fields—food, music, art, science. He was upset that they hadn't asked his opinion about the acoustics in Philharmonic Hall because he knew so much that could have helped. I asked him what he thought the third time they redid it. He said, 'Before it was like a beautiful girl with warts all over her face. So far, they've removed three.' "

The pianist recalls a tour he played with the Cleveland Orchestra and George Szell. "Actually, I did three trips to the Soviet Union and on each of them I came away without much impression of their food. But the last time with Szell and Cleveland, the National Hotel came through because they were still serving great caviar from the Caspian. But on all three trips the only place that impressed me was the Europeskaya in Leningrad."

The pianist laughs at the memory. "One night they brought a pineapple to my table. It was like something out of a dream. They brought the whole fruit and a knife and I thought, now that's communism at its best. I devoured it out of sheer hunger."

Moving on to other journeys, Grant Johannesen remembers a wonderful restaurant in the Continental Hotel in Oslo. And, at home, "I love Chanterelle in New York. It's a beautiful but simple restaurant. Those are qualities I cherish. When I travel I like to be rather pure about food, no sauces, and I've learned to be professional that way so my performance is a happy one for myself and others. Food becomes a very big issue."

The pianist says that receptions can be difficult for him. "They always serve lots of sweets at those parties for some reason, and that's not for me. I prefer just to sit and talk, have a drink and tell jokes. My job at a reception is to shake hands."

Perhaps if they were to serve Grant Johannesen's Norwegian Waffles (his mother's recipe, by the way), the pianist would shake hands with his fork. To celebrate this special Norwegian dish, we suggest some special Norwegian music: Grieg's Piano Concerto with Grant Johannesen as the soloist (Vox/Turnabout CT-2121).

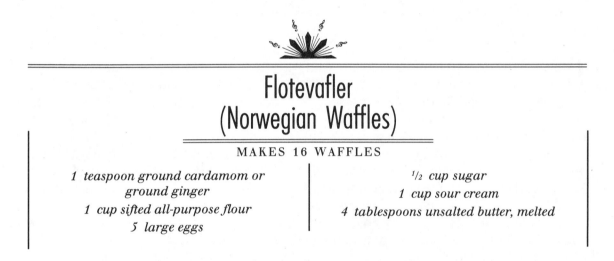

Flotevafler
(Norwegian Waffles)

MAKES 16 WAFFLES

1 teaspoon ground cardamom or
   ground ginger
1 cup sifted all-purpose flour
5 large eggs

½ cup sugar
1 cup sour cream
4 tablespoons unsalted butter, melted

1   In a medium-size bowl mix cardamom and flour together. Set aside. In another medium-size bowl, combine eggs and sugar. Beat with an electric mixer 2 to 3 minutes on high or until light-colored and thick. With a wooden spoon or spatula, mix in half the flour and then half the sour cream. Repeat and stir in the melted butter. Let batter rest 10 minutes.

2   Heat waffle iron—either a traditional Norwegian one or an American electric. Pour ½ to ¾ cup of batter onto the iron. Bake until golden brown (about 4 to 5 minutes) and serve with lingonberry conserve or other tart jam.

Igor Kipnis

Although Igor Kipnis made his official debut with the New York Philharmonic at a series of four subscription concerts in January 1975, playing the Bach Brandenburg Concerto No. 5 and the Falla Harpsichord Concerto, it's the performance of the Bach that he did six months later that he remembers most vividly. "It was one of those Rug Concerts with Boulez. You remember—they used to put the orchestra in the area that would normally be the first few rows of seats for the audience. And they put part of the audience up on the stage where the orchestra would normally sit. So it was something like theater in the round. Some of the listeners actually sat on the floor, and that made for a somewhat younger audience. Younger and more enthusiastic," the harpsichordist adds.

"About a third of the first movement of the Bach is a cadenza. Now, you know that at the end of a cadenza the audience is not supposed to applaud. Audiences worth their salt aren't supposed to make a sound until the very end of the piece. But this group treated my cadenza like a jazz riff. They went wild." Did this lack of decorum upset Igor Kipnis? "I found it tremendously stimulating."

The reception after the official debut was memorable too. He remembers that John Coveney, the head of EMI-Angel records, "wined and dined anyone who was supposed to be wined and dined." But Igor noticed something about this urbane gentleman. "John had his martini watered down with Perrier. That's how I got the idea for my vodka martini.

"John explained that he had to take people out to dinner very often and he said, 'I love martinis but if I have them every night I can't function too well the next day.' From that time on we started to make martini spritzers. He was right. It helps."

Like pianist Gary Graffman, who also makes flavored vodkas, Igor Kipnis spices his supply with a variety of ingredients. "The composer David Fox suggested adding fresh hot peppers like jalapeños. I cut two or three of them in half lengthwise, leave in the seeds, and let them sit in the vodka for at least two or three days before drinking."

Igor suggests that you serve the vodka ice cold (keep it in the freezer after it's brewed), "and you have an iced 'hot' vodka." Water it down? "Only if you have to function the next day."

COLE PORTER, THE VODKA SONGMAN

This vodka-making goes way back in the Kipnis family. The harpsichordist's famous father, bass Alexander Kipnis, actually made his *own* vodka. "My father used one quart of grain or other alcohol, such as potato or sugar, one quart of distilled water, and one half teaspoon of glycerin." After just sipping this Russian moonshine, Igor suggests if you can find this rare recording, you listen to his father's performance of "The Song of the 'Vodka' Boatmen" with the RCA Victor Chorus and Orchestra conducted by Jay Blackton.

Judy Kipnis's recipe for Bisque La Varenne is a reconstruction of a dish served in the mid-1600s. Judy tells us, "Varenne was a very innovative cook in seventeenth-century France. I reconstructed this recipe the way someone might reconstruct a harpsichord. You have the basic structure, try to stay as close to the original ingredients as possible, and update only when necessary for today's tastes."

She assures us that cockscombs can be found even today. But she generally serves her bisque with sweetbreads.

Igor slips into the kitchen one last time to suggest the music for his wife's Bisque La Verenne. "What else," he asks, "but Bach's '*Bisque* du bei mir' " performed by soprano Judith Blegen with Igor himself at the clavichord (Nonesuch 79020-2).

Bisque La Varenne

SERVES 4

STOCK

5 pounds mixed bones (veal neck, lamb neck, chicken backs, and beef marrow)

2 Spanish onions, quartered

4 parsnips, quartered

4 carrots, quartered

2 ribs celery, quartered

2 leeks, cleaned well, white and green parts, quartered

5 bay leaves

1/2 teaspoon white peppercorns

1/2 teaspoon black peppercorns

5 garlic cloves, whole, unpeeled

SQUAB

4 squab (about 1 pound each)

4 slices bacon

1/2 teaspoon salt

1/2 teaspoon pepper

1 tablespoon lard (butter can be substituted)

1/2 cup dry vermouth or white wine

4 cups meat stock

4 whole cloves

1 large sprig rosemary or 1/4 teaspoon dried

2 tablespoons unsalted butter, softened

4 slices day-old white or whole wheat bread, cut in 3/4-inch-thick slices

1 teaspoon lemon juice (optional)

GARNISH

2 tablespoons unsalted butter

1/4 pound mushrooms, thinly sliced (about 1 1/2 cups)

1 (9 ounce) package frozen artichoke hearts, thawed

2 tablespoons pistachios, shelled

1 tablespoon lemon juice

1/4 teaspoon salt

1/4 teaspoon pepper

1   In a 10-quart stockpot, combine all ingredients for stock. Add water to cover and bring to a boil over high heat. Skim off any scum that rises to the surface and lower heat to a simmer. Cook 4 hours. Strain. Degrease 4 cups of the stock to use and refrigerate or freeze remainder (the remainder can also be boiled down to make demiglace, which will last a very long time).

2   Wrap each squab with a strip of bacon, fasten with a toothpick and sprinkle with salt and pepper. In a large heavy saucepot or Dutch oven, melt lard over high heat. Add squab and brown on all sides, about 10 minutes. Remove from pot and pour off fat. Add vermouth and stir up brown particles from bottom of pan. Cook 1 minute and add 2 cups of the

stock. Add cloves and rosemary and return birds to pot. Lower heat to a simmer, cover, and cook 45 minutes or until birds are tender.

3 While birds are cooking, heat the remaining 2 cups of stock in a large skillet. Spread the butter on the bread slices and add them, butter side down, to the heated stock. Cook, simmering, until stock is reduced and thick, about 45 minutes. Add lemon if using, and remove bread to a serving platter. When squab is ready, place a bird on each slice and pour bread stock over. Keep warm while preparing garnish.

4 In a large skillet over high heat, melt butter. Add mushrooms and cook, stirring, until lightly browned. Add artichokes and cook, stirring, 2 minutes. Add pistachios, lemon juice, salt, and pepper, and stir until heated through, about 2 minutes longer. Serve as a side dish.

Traditionally, the garnish included sweetbreads and cockscombs as well.

Ruth Laredo

Ruth Laredo was brought up on simple food and hard work. The food was served by her mother, who stuck pretty much to the basics. The hard work was dished out by the young pianist at her keyboard. It wasn't until Ruth went away to study at Curtis in Philadelphia that she began cooking for herself.

"I didn't eat very well until I left home," Ruth tells us. And now, all these wonderful Korean markets we have in New York have really taught me a lot about vegetables."

One of the highlights of her musical career came on December 12, 1974, when Ruth Laredo made her debut with the New York Philharmonic. Pierre Boulez was on the podium for the Ravel G Major Piano Concerto and they got a standing ovation for the performance.

"I was coming downstairs from the dressing room, headed for the stage, and I was sort of clutching my purse," Ruth remembers. "Boulez looked at the purse and then at me and said, 'What have you got in there, the ashes of Ravel?'"

After the concert, a group of friends took Ruth across the street to a brand new restaurant, Fiorello's. "I remember it had just opened," Ruth adds. "Jennifer O'Neil, the actress, was with us. She was the date of one of my friends. There I was with this famous star and people were coming up to *me* and speaking to *me*. I guess it was because I'd just played across the street."

Like most peripatetic pianists, Ruth Laredo has traveled to many parts of the world on her concert tours. But when it comes to food, two countries stand out. "I'll never forget the Shabu-Shabu in Japan. It was a real theatrical presentation." The other country that remains in Ruth's culinary mind is the former Soviet Union. That was surprising because Soviet restaurants had been roundly booed by most members of the New York Philharmonic after more than one of their tours.

But it wasn't the restaurants that got Ruth's raves. "My interpreter, Irina, took some rubles and bribed people to bring me food before my concerts. The hotel restaurants were just impossible," she agreed. "You needed reservations, their resources were limited, they were only open at certain times, and their schedules didn't fit my needs. So every night my dear Irina would take the rubles and soon someone would knock on my door and bring me a tray with good, hot, nourishing soup, some kind of meat, fresh, homey dark bread, and a Pepsi. That they had!"

If you serve Ruth's Rice Parmesan, you might want it as an accompaniment to a crisp goose. The music to be served at the same time is, of course, Ravel's *Ma Mère l'Oye* (Mother Goose) in a performance by Ruth Laredo (Denon CD7907). Or, if you're keeping the meal strictly Italian, try the opera overtures by Rossini and Verdi performed by the New York Philharmonic under the direction of Guido Cantelli (AS-516).

Rice Parmesan

SERVES 4

2 tablespoons vegetable oil
2 tablespoons chopped onion
1 cup long-grain rice
2 cups chicken stock or broth
$^{1}/_{3}$ cup dry white wine

1 cup fresh mushrooms, sliced
2 tablespoons unsalted butter
$^{1}/_{2}$-$^{3}/_{4}$ cup freshly grated Parmesan cheese

Heat oil in a medium saucepot over medium high heat. Add onion and cook until transparent, about 4 to 5 minutes. Add rice and cook, stirring, until rice just starts to brown, about 3 minutes. Add stock, wine, and mushrooms. Cover, lower heat to a simmer, and cook about 12 to 15 minutes or until liquid is absorbed. Add butter and Parmesan to taste and mix well.

Cecile Licad

Pianist Cecile Licad was practically born playing the piano. It took her only seven years from her birth to make her orchestral debut and she wasted very little time after that in establishing an international career. Unlike tiny violinists and cellists, small pianists have no quarter-size pianos on which to learn. Seven-year-old hands haven't grown an octave's span but seven-year-old Cecile managed quite well, thank you.

Five years after her debut at the age of seven, Cecile Licad came to the United States from her home in Manila to study with the heavyweights: Mieczyslaw Horszowski, Seymour Lipkin, and Rudolf Serkin at the Curtis Institute of Music in Philadelphia. That brings us to 1973.

Seven years later, at the age of nineteen, Ms. Licad became the first musician in a decade to receive the prestigious Leventritt Gold Medal. Since then, she's performed as a soloist with just about every major orchestra in the world. But one of her passions is chamber music, and it was as a collaborator in the Bach Triple Concerto that she first appeared with the New York Philharmonic. Cecile performed with pianists Stephanie Brown and Lydia Artymiw, with the orchestra under the direction of Alexander Schneider at a special concert on a Sunday evening in May 1979.

In this spirit of chamber cooperation, she's appeared on television with Mstislav Rostropovich and teamed with the Guarneri Quartet, and the Chamber Music Society of Lincoln Center. She's given recitals with violinist Jaime Laredo, pianists Murray Perahia and Peter Serkin, violinist Nadia Salerno-Sonnenberg, and cellist Antonio Meneses. She also happens to be married to Mr. Meneses. And they and their young son have homes in New York and Switzerland.

Perhaps it's this international influence that prompts Cecile to proffer her pizza. Or it may be the presence of a toddler in the house. Whatever the reason for its invention, Pizza Cecile is a hit. So is the pianist's recording, with violinist Nadia Salerno-Sonnenberg, of the Brahms A Major Sonata (Angel CDC-49410). And for a bit of an international flavor, sample Cecile Licad's performance of the Chopin Piano Concerto No. 2 in F minor with the London Philharmonic and André Previn (CBS MK-39153). It won the Grand Prix du Disque Frédéric Chopin.

Pizza Cecile

MAKES SIX 8-INCH PIZZAS

DOUGH
4 (¹/₄ ounce) packets active dry yeast
¹/₂ teaspoon sugar
1¹/₃ cups warm water
(about 100 degrees)
1 teaspoon salt
¹/₄ cup olive oil
4 cups all-purpose flour
1 tablespoon cornmeal

SAUCE
1 tablespoon olive oil
1 small onion chopped (about ¹/₂ cup)
1 garlic clove, minced

1 (28 ounce) can tomato purée
¹/₂ teaspoon dried oregano
¹/₂ teaspoon basil
¹/₂ teaspoon salt
¹/₄ teaspoon pepper
2 teaspoons freshly grated
Parmesan cheese
1¹/₂ pounds coarsely shredded cheese—
a mixture of equal parts mozzarella
and Monterey Jack, with a dash of
provolone, or cheddar (about 12 cups)

1 In a large mixing bowl or the bowl of a heavy-duty electric mixer, combine yeast and sugar with ²/₃ cup of the water. Let sit 5 minutes or until yeast bubbles. Stir in remaining water, the salt, oil, and flour and mix well. If very sticky, add a bit more flour. Knead by hand or with the mixer's dough hook for about 5 minutes. Place in an oiled bowl, cover, and let rise in a warm place for about 1 hour or until doubled in size. Punch it down. Sprinkle the cornmeal on counter and roll out dough to form six 8-inch or two 14-inch pizzas.

2 Meanwhile, make sauce. In a large saucepot heat olive oil over medium high heat. Add onion and cook, stirring, about 5 minutes or until soft. Add garlic and cook 1 minute longer. Add remaining ingredients except cheese and stir. Bring to a boil, lower heat to a simmer and, cook 30 minutes. Stir in Parmesan cheese.

3 Place pizzas on cookie sheets and spread about ¹/₂ cup sauce on each. Sprinkle each with about ¹/₂ cup of the mixed grated cheeses, and place on the bottom of a cold oven. Turn oven to 500° and bake 15 to 20 minutes or until crust is browned and cheese melted. (Alternatively, bake in preheated 500° oven for about 15 minutes.)

Nadia Reisenberg and Robert Sherman

Nadia Reisenberg made quite an auspicious debut with the New York Philharmonic back in 1941. It was a Sunday afternoon and Sir John Barbirolli was on the podium in Carnegie Hall. The pianist wasn't there to play just one concerto. She performed the premiere of a concerto by Mischa Portnoff on the first half and, after intermission, returned to play the Liszt A Major.

"I think her Philharmonic debut came about because of the Mozart series she did the season before," remembers her son, Robert Sherman, executive producer of WQXR. "In the 1939–1940 season she played all the Mozart piano concertos, one a week, with Alfred Wallenstein on WOR in New York. It was a landmark event."

Then there was the time Nadia Reisenberg premiered the Kabalevsky Piano Concerto No. 2, again with Barbirolli and the Philharmonic. "Mother practiced it all the time so I really got to know it and, to this day," Bob says, "I'm still highly annoyed that nobody plays it. It's sort of a poor man's Rachmaninoff." Becoming more incensed, Bob insists, "They must be crazy!"

While the Kabalevsky didn't become a tradition, the Reisenberg-Sherman family quickly established some traditions of its own. "After a concert we always went to the Russian Tea Room because in those days everything in the Tea Room was Russian, the waiters, the food, everything. During the war we went there and tried to order in Russian, and the guy had to confess that because of the war they couldn't find any Russians and they'd had to hire him. He was from the Bronx." Bob grins. "My favorite was their seven-layer cake. I guess that wasn't Russian, either."

The family was certainly Russian. And certainly musical. Nadia's sister, Clara Rockmore, became one of the world's rare—and greatest—theremin artists. So it was left to their third sister, Newta, to become the solo "food maven" in the family. "She's a wonderful cook," Bob reports, "but her 'precise' instructions run along the lines of 'keep tasting it and add a little lemon or salt or whatever else it needs.' We had a cook when I was a child because

Mother and Clara were so deeply involved with their careers they didn't have time." But they all had the time to eat. And to eat well.

Nadia Reisenberg continued playing, mostly chamber music and recital programs in her later years. And she had a tremendous following as a teacher, at home and at both Mannes and Juilliard. Ask any student about "Madame" Reisenberg and, along with memories of musicmaking, they'll talk about being fed cookies both coming in and going out. The pianist may not have cooked, but she knew the fine art of feeding, musically and emotionally.

For our own musical and emotional nurturing while preparing Newta's Piroshki, we recommend Clara Rockmore's recording—with pianist Nadia Reisenberg—of the music of Rachmaninoff, Saint-Saëns, Falla, Stravinsky, Ravel, and Tchaikovsky, played on the theremin (Delos DCD-1014). For something a bit less esoteric, choose from any of at least five recordings of music by Chopin performed by pianist Nadia Reisenberg on the InSync label.

Newta's Piroshki

SERVES 8 TO 10

PASTRY

2 sticks (¹/₂ pound) unsalted butter, softened

1 (8 ounce) package cream cheese, softened

2 cups unbleached flour

¹/₄ teaspoon salt

FILLING

2 tablespoons unsalted butter

3 large onions, chopped (about 3 cups)

1³/₄ pounds mushrooms, finely chopped

1 pound ground beef

¹/₂ bunch fresh dill, chopped (about ¹/₄ cup)

4 large eggs, hard cooked, peeled, and chopped

¹/₂ cup cooked rice

2 teaspoons salt

¹/₂ teaspoon black pepper

1 egg yolk for glaze

1 In a large mixing bowl or the bowl of a heavy-duty mixer, beat butter and cream cheese with an electric mixer until very creamy. Stir in flour and salt until well blended and chill at least 30 minutes.

2 Make filling: In a large skillet over high heat, melt butter. Add onions and cook until softened, about 7 minutes. Add mushrooms, and cook until moisture has evaporated, about 7 to 8 minutes. Pour mixture into a large bowl. Add beef to skillet and cook, stirring, until browned. Drain off fat and add beef to onion mixture. Stir in dill, eggs, rice, salt, and pepper, and mix until well combined. Set aside to cool.

3 Preheat oven to 350°.

4 Divide dough in half. Roll out one half to fit into a 9 × 13″ baking pan, covering the bottom and sides. Fill with meat mixture. Roll out remaining dough to fit over meat and place on top. Seal edges together by pressing with the tines of a fork. Brush the top with the egg yolk and bake 40 to 45 minutes or until golden brown. Slice and serve hot.

Arthur Rubinstein

I f there were a king of culinary commitment in the arts, Arthur Rubinstein would surely have worn the crown. The legendary pianist traveled the world in search of the perfect meal and, most often, he found it. Over and over he writes in his autobiographies, *My Young Years* and *My Many Years*, more of menus than music. In Russia, a waiter announces to Rubinstein that his fish is ready to be served. "We returned to our table and ate it with delight. The same procedure took place with the next course, the meat. We chose a chunk of raw beef to be cooked. . . . The preparation of an elaborate dessert allowed us to play two long games of piquet. We washed down the whole meal with a fine French Burgundy. This luncheon," the gastric gourmet tells us, "lasted until nine in the evening."

A friend invites him to supper after a concert. "He took me to a large room at the hotel where I was staying," Rubinstein writes. "There, a huge table was set for about thirty people, and it was laden with an enormous hollow block of ice, completely filled with unsalted, fresh caviar. It was the most delicious caviar I had ever tasted. Before I knew it I had gulped down two or three vodkas."

With a flourish, Rubinstein lets us know that they ate the caviar "with large soup spoons" and goes on to write, "The supper was endless: fish, Caucasian shashliks flambés with rice, followed by an array of sweets, Turkish halvah, rahat loukhoum,* and cakes; ice cream; fruits of all kinds, dates and nuts filling large silver containers. It must have been four or five in the morning when I saw that everybody was drunk but myself." Unfortunately, the pianist proceeds to get deathly ill at that point but we'll omit that description, this being a cookbook and all. However, he was up, chipper, healthy, and hungry again the next morning.

"A regal breakfast was served, beginning with a new display of caviar accompanied by the unavoidable vodka, followed by eggs, cold meats, sausages, cheeses and finally by some hot coffee with a vast variety of rolls, breads and cakes, honey and jams. All this lasted until noon, when I barely had the time to pack and catch my train." He doesn't mention what the dining car served for lunch.

Arthur Rubinstein does write about music, too. Here's his description of an evening with Jacques Thibaud, Lionel Tertis, and Albert Sammons: "The hungry lot of us rushed into the dining room and actually devoured the succulent delicacies from the Savoy Grill. When the happy noise around the supper table subsided, Thibaud gave the signal: 'Come on, boys, let us play a little quartet.' "

There are decadent descriptions of picnics in Spain and a plethora of parties in Paris. And then there was the concert to be played in the London home of one Colonel Clayton and his family. "The whole house had been turned upside down," Rubinstein writes, with "large pieces of furniture removed . . . and the main drawing room transformed into a concert hall. We lunched in town so as not to disturb the preparations for dinner," which was to coincide with that concert by Rubinstein, don't forget. So, here we are on the day of a performance. Does the pianist practice, relax, contemplate? Well, yes. He contemplates lunch. " 'Let us have some lobsters at Scott's,' said Colonel Clayton. Scott's," Rubinstein explains, "was the name of a famous restaurant on Piccadilly Circus, the only place where you could find fresh lobsters with claws larger than tails."

Dinner time comes and, after a meal described by the maestro as excellent—"our hostess was French!"—they all go to the big room for his concert. How does it go? "I have forgotten the program I played, but I do remember the last two pieces: 'Isolde's Love-Death' from Wagner's *Tristan*, arranged by Liszt, and the famous 'Ride of the Valkyries' in my own arrangement."

Some people walk off a big meal. Rubinstein invented the *play*-offs.

Not to be outdone and, we think, in order to keep up, the pianist's wife, Nela, published a cookbook. She says in the introduction that Arthur, "being a famous 'gourmet' . . . knew the best restaurants all over the world. Then I discovered that I had an odd but very useful talent:

See Nimet Habachy, page 89.

much as one might have a musical ear, I had the ability to decipher and identify the ingredients in even fairly elaborate dishes—and made a sort of game (and challenge!) of reproducing them at home without asking for recipes." And so a cookbook was born.

From our readings of Arthur Rubinstein, the two delicacies the pianist enjoyed more than any others were fresh caviar and shellfish. Particularly lobster. On a trip to visit Picasso, he describes one of his favorites. "It was getting on toward midnight when [Picasso] asked us with an innocent expression on his face, 'Are you hungry?' and without waiting for an answer, he took us on a longish walk to his restaurant and said, 'It is a good place. I have ordered our dinner.'

"The dinner Pablo had ordered arrived after quite a long wait; it was a huge bouillabaisse! That did it," the pianist writes with a whoop of joy. "This was a great red-letter day of three bouillabaisses in twelve hours!"

Since so many of Arthur Rubinstein's concerts took place before and after (and sometimes during) dinners (or breakfasts or lunches), it is only reasonable that this bouillabaisse recipe, made especially for our cookbook by Jean Galton, have equally delicious music to accompany it. Ravel seems fitting: his Trio, with Rubinstein's friends Jascha Heifetz and Gregor Piatigorsky (RCA 7871-1), followed by Ravel's *Valses nobles et sentimentales* (RCA 5665-2) so we can dance off the feast.

Bouillabaisse
for Arthur Rubinstein

SERVES 6

¹/₄ cup extra virgin olive oil

1 large Spanish onion, chopped

3 leeks, white part only, cleaned and thinly sliced

2 bulbs fennel, chopped (about 2 cups)

4 garlic cloves, minced

1 (14 ounce) can peeled Italian tomatoes, drained, seeded, and chopped

2 cups fish stock or 2 (8 ounce) bottles clam juice

¹/₂ cup dry white wine

Large pinch saffron threads or ¹/₈ teaspoon powdered saffron

1 bay leaf

1 1¹/₂-pound lobster, cut into 4 pieces

1 pound monkfish, skinned and cut into 1-inch chunks

12 small mussels, scrubbed and debearded

1 pound sea bass fillet, skinned, bones removed, and cut into 1-inch chunks

2 tablespoons chopped parsley

QUICK AIOLI

4 garlic cloves

1 cup prepared mayonnaise

1   In large saucepot, heat oil over medium high heat. Add onion, leeks, and fennel, and cook, stirring, about 7 to 8 minutes or until vegetables are quite soft. Add garlic and cook 1 minute longer. Stir in tomatoes, fish stock, white wine, saffron, bay leaf, and bring to a boil. Simmer 5 to 6 minutes and add lobster chunks. Cover and simmer 8 to 9 minutes. Add monkfish, cover, and cook 3 minutes. Stir in mussels and sea bass and cook 3 minutes longer. Stir in parsley and serve with aioli.

2   For the Quick Aioli, use a mortar and pestle or a knife to smash or mince the garlic until it becomes a paste. Stir into mayonnaise. Makes 1 cup.

Rudolf Serkin

Rudolf Serkin's name is synonymous with so many memories of music: recitals, concerts, family performances, and Marlboro. The pianist first appeared with the New York Philharmonic on February 20, 1936, in Carnegie Hall. Arturo Toscanini was the conductor of the four-concert series and the pianist appeared on both parts of the program, playing the Beethoven Fourth Concerto on the first half, and returning for the Mozart K.595 after intermission. There were many more happy returns to the Philharmonic over the years. That was the Serkin of the City.

The Serkin of the Country finds its spirit everywhere at Marlboro, the summer festival in Vermont. It emanates from the intense practice sessions from the woods to the porches, in the romances of the pianists and violinists and cellists, in the din of the dining hall where wet napkins are hurled through the air in good-natured explosions. Rudolf Serkin will always be there.

Richard Caplin, the manager and head chef of the eating facilities at Marlboro, remembers the pianist. "We had this huge buffet after the final concert one season. Mr. Serkin was so happy with what I'd made that he tried to lift me up on his shoulders and carry me around the dining room." Did the frail-looking pianistic giant do it? "Yes. With a little help from his friends."

Richard is at Marlboro all year. "I cook for the college in the winter and the festival in the summer. And I'm working on a Marlboro College Cookbook."

One of Richard's fondest memories of Rudolf Serkin is a special concert he planned for the kitchen staff one year. "He arranged all the music and wrote the lyrics. It was all about food and music and he gathered everyone in the dining room and they played and sang it for us.

"I guess one of his favorite dishes was sauerbraten," Richard adds, getting back to basics. "He really loved that. And he also loved this lemon cake."

Rudolf Serkin had excellent taste, in food as well as music. This recipe is one of Maida Heatter's most delectable, and we're proud to reproduce it as part of our tribute to Rudolf Serkin and the New York Philharmonic.

To bring everything together, we suggest two pieces of music to accompany this fantasy from the festival at Marlboro: Beethoven's Fantasia in C minor for Piano, Chorus, and Orchestra with Rudolf Serkin and the New York Philharmonic (MYK-38526), and the Mozart Piano Concerto No. 12, performed by Mr. Serkin with the Marlboro Ensemble (Sony Classical 46255).

62nd Street Lemon Cake

SERVES 10

Fine, dry bread crumbs for pan
3 cups sifted all-purpose flour
2 teaspoons baking powder
$^1/_2$ teaspoon salt
2 sticks ($^1/_2$ pound) unsalted butter,
softened
2 cups sugar

4 large eggs, at room temperature
1 cup milk, at room temperature
Finely grated zest of 2 lemons

GLAZE
$^1/_3$ cup lemon juice
$^3/_4$ cup sugar

1 Preheat oven to 350°. Grease a 9 × 3$^1/_2$″ tube pan and dust it with bread crumbs.

2 Sift together flour, baking powder, and salt, and set aside. In a large mixing bowl or the bowl of a heavy-duty mixer, cream butter. Add sugar and beat 2 to 3 minutes. Beat in eggs, one at a time, beating after each addition. On low speed, add dry ingredients in 3 additions, alternating with milk in two additions. Scrape the bowl with a rubber spatula to keep mixture smooth and stir in lemon zest. Pour into prepared pan and bake 1 hour and 10 to 15 minutes or until a cake tester comes out dry. Let cake rest in pan about 3 minutes, then cover with a rack and invert. Place rack over a large piece of foil or wax paper and prepare glaze.

3 Stir together lemon juice and sugar and brush it all over the hot cake until it is all absorbed. Let cool completely and place on serving plate. Let sit several hours and cut.

Ilana Vered

Ilana Vered is more than a pianist. She's the Sol Hurok of the music festival syndicate. This internationally established musician has managed to establish herself as both director and soloist of major music festivals in the Northeast. And she's made them so attractive to other artists that she's drawn superstars like pianist André Watts to perform in her series.

Ilana thinks and talks as fast as her fingers fly over the keyboard. Ideas explode from her ever moving mind and programs take on a life of their own as they blossom into such musical tributes as Women Pianists of the Nineteenth century, Beethoven and his Friends, and clever twists on simple themes that other impresarios wish they'd thought to present.

Then there is the family side of Ilana Vered. Naturally, everyone cooks, husband and even mother-in-law. And with a rich ethnic background that takes us from Romania to Israel, they're bound to produce some fascinating food that's equal to Ilana's concert creations.

Ilana's debut with the New York Philharmonic took place on a program as varied as her background and career. Morton Gould was the conductor that Saturday night in March 1980. The evening opened with two works by Samuel Barber and continued to Rachmaninoff's C minor Piano Concerto with Ilana at the keyboard. Then it was time for excerpts from Prokofiev's *Romeo and Juliet.* The evening ended with two encores, one by Tchaikovsky and one by Prokofiev. Clever? Almost the kind of program that Ilana herself would put together!

After all this talk about the pianist, we must have her play something for us while we whip up her meringue. We've chosen the Mozart Piano Concerto No. 21 with Ilana Vered and the London Symphony (Lon. STS-15568). And, since one of the first festivals Ilana founded was based at Rutgers University, we'll hear from the New York Philharmonic and Leonard Bernstein in Brahms's *Academic Festival Overture* (CBS MLK-39451).

Meringue Walnuts

MAKES ABOUT 100

2 jumbo egg whites, at room temperature
1 cup sugar
1 tablespoon lemon juice

2¹/₃ cups walnut pieces (buy 2 pounds and shell them yourself—preshelled are never fresh enough)

1   Preheat oven to 350°. Grease 2 large cookie sheets.

2   Place egg whites in a large mixing bowl or the bowl of a heavy-duty mixer. With electric mixer, beat on high power to stiff peaks. Gradually add sugar and lemon juice, beating constantly until stiff peaks form again. Stir in the walnuts and drop by teaspoonfuls onto cookie sheets, about ¹/₄ inch apart. Bake 10 to 12 minutes or until slightly golden. Turn off oven and leave 4 to 5 minuts longer. Remove from sheets while still warm and transfer to a cooling rack.

NOTE: These keep fresh for weeks stored in a tin or in a plastic bag.

Index of Names

Index of Recipes